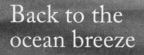

Back to the
ocean breeze

D0168150

Back to **Spain** soon

ESPAÑA

Balearic
Islands

www.spain.info

GRANTA

12 Addison Avenue, London W11 4QR | email: editorial@granta.com
To subscribe go to granta.com, or call 020 8955 7011 in the United Kingdom,
845-267-3031 (toll-free 866-438-6150) in the United States

ISSUE 155: SPRING 2021

CONTENTS

CONTENTS

Introduction

When two iconoclastic young editors took over Cambridge University's then nearly century-old student magazine in 1979, their purpose was to open avenues in the Old World for New World writing. The British weren't reading the new American writing. This idea – the construction of a transatlantic literary bridge – is part of what spurred us to create a Spanish-language edition of the magazine in 2003. When *Granta*'s new publisher and now editor, Sigrid Rausing, took over the magazine in 2005, she encouraged Spanish *Granta*, fostering the magazine's increasingly internationalized spirit. In Spain, the fact that *Granta en español* was being run by a pair of outsiders was bad enough – one of whom, myself, wasn't even a native speaker. But our point was that fiction from the Americas – 'challenging, diversified and adventurous', to quote Bill Buford and Pete de Bolla in their first edition of *Granta* – was not as well known as it should have been in Spain. Editors here were slow to pick up South American gems. But the opposite was also true – there was a dearth of Spanish writing in the Americas.

'If a good part of contemporary Spanish literature seems eccentric to Europe,' Aurelio Major, co-founder of Spanish *Granta*, wrote in the introduction to the first Spanish-language selection in 2010, 'Latin America has always been the literary Far West.' That Far West is composed of nineteen countries and territories where Spanish is the main language, and it has given the world six Nobel prizes in literature: Gabriela Mistral, Miguel Ángel Asturias, Pablo Neruda, Gabriel García Márquez, Octavio Paz and Mario Vargas Llosa. But writing from that eccentric country on the outskirts of Europe, from which come five Nobels in literature and the first modern novel in any language, *Don Quixote*, wasn't being given the attention it deserved either. The curiosity of foreign editors had been satiated, there was already a go-to group of sellable writers, so no need to strike out into the stormy waters of new writing. Out of those slackened sails came Roberto Bolaño, but he wasn't the only one. The Spanish *Granta* project was launched to remedy this: to open the transatlantic conversation, New World and Old, and to encourage translation into and out of the two languages.

Now, a little under twenty years later, we are publishing our second selection of the best young Spanish-language novelists. At its inception in 1983, let's be honest, the whole notion of a list of twenty writers under forty was no more than a gimmick, a marketing ploy originally whipped up to throw a lifebuoy to the (yes, beleaguered) British literary novel, and tempt more readers into buying them. Heroic. *Granta*'s publication of that inaugural 'Best of Young British Novelists' issue came at a time when writers were still private creatures who largely shunned the spotlight, preferring to let the work speak for itself. The campaign's greatest value was, as then-editor Bill Buford wrote later, that 'it became, despite itself, a serious statement about British literary culture'.

Sift a little time onto something, and you raise a tradition. We launched the call for candidates for the issue you are holding now in March 2020, just as the reality of the pandemic was moving like a shadow across the globe. Thanks to the generosity of Ángel L. Fernández Recuero of *Jot Down*, who helped us quickly transition to a digital process, and to Cristóbal Pera, with an early swan dive into the project as our first Spanish-language partner in Vintage Español, we could go ahead. We chose a jury of six. The judges, novelists Horacio Castellanos Moya, Rodrigo Fresán and Chloe Aridjis; poet and co-founder of Spanish *Granta*, Aurelio Major; Gaby Wood, the Literary Director of the Booker Foundation, and me, Valerie Miles, were all in some sense or other outsiders. We wanted to avoid the local friendships, rivalries, jealousies, or resentments that might cloud our judgment. We had our differences, luckily, but relished the challenge, the art of persuasion, which made our discussions particularly memorable, substantial and great fun.

The call was for candidates born on or after 1 January 1985 (thirty-five or younger), with at least one novel or story collection published or under contract. Initially, we decided to reduce the list to twenty (in 2010 we had featured twenty-two writers), understanding our task not as verification – these are the writers of this generation – but of selection: these are the 'best' writers of this generation, a much more delicate and difficult exercise. Any preconceptions we may have had regarding the slim pickings of a digital generation with addled brains and non-existent attention spans turned out to be dead wrong: twenty was not enough. We found our ideal number at twenty-five, each member of the jury sacrificing favorite writers to the pyre of consensus. Every selection is a compromise. Being on a jury is like playing the Ouija board. A sort of force field builds while discussing readings and idiosyncrasies of taste: 'I love', 'I hate', 'over my dead body'; it's like a collective swinging forward, backward, side to side, then the dime drops, and the planchette comes to rest at the 'yes' spot, the X on the map. And that's what happened to this jury when we decided on this group. A different jury, or the same jury on a different day, would no doubt have led to a different list.

We received over 200 entries, and began an internal process of reading during those scary days of the early lockdowns. Leticia Vila-Sanjuán's knowledge and discriminating reading helped us whittle down to a longlist of sixty-eight. Sadly, we had to drop a few writers who would have likely made the list, but for a 'wafer-thin' span of time: Daniel Saldaña París (Mexico) and Lina Tono (Colombia) were born a few months too soon to be eligible. Juan Gómez Bárcena (Spain) was born a few weeks too soon. Inevitably, as happened in 2010, when writers like Valeria Luiselli (Mexico) took their first steps in fiction moments after we had closed the list, we've now read *ex post* the work of writers like Lorena Salazar Masso (Colombia), and wish we could have considered them. We know we will have missed others. The shortlist featured twenty-nine women and thirty-nine men, and the final selection, eleven women and fourteen men. There are thirteen countries and territories represented: six writers from Spain, four from Mexico, three from Argentina, three from Cuba, two from Chile, one writer each from Colombia, Ecuador, Equatorial Guinea, Nicaragua, Peru and Uruguay, and one who is from both Costa Rica and Puerto Rico.

The significant differences in our final list from the first selection in 2010 is the change from one Mexican writer to four, and the irruption of a fine group of writers from Cuba: Eudris Planche Savón, who lives on the island; Carlos Manuel Álvarez, who lives between New York, Mexico City and Havana; and Dainerys Machado Vento, who is studying for a PhD at the University of Miami, the first Cuban ever to be given a student visa to attend a US institution. And, for the first time, we are featuring an Equatorial Guinean writer, Estanislao Medina Huesca, adding a new African voice to the mix.

What stands out about this selection of young Spanish-language novelists is the fact that the writers' work grows out of a single language that is expressed in twenty-three different nationalities and the discrete infinity of ever more local permutations – regions, towns, villages; a single language with endless bifurcations of tradition, history, amalgams of races and religions and geographies, spanning four continents: Europe, North and South America, and Africa. Most Spanish-speaking countries share space with other languages, co-official or not, which feed into and influence this magma of constantly evolving registers and variations in syntax and lexes: Catalan, Euskera and Galician in Spain; French, Portuguese and Fang in Equatorial Guinea (among six other autochthonous languages); Aymara and Quechua in Peru and Ecuador; Bolivia is the country with the most co-official languages in the world, thirty-seven. Guarani in Argentina and Paraguay, Nahuatl in Mexico, Mapuche in Chile – the list goes on. So many of the original vocabularies of the Americas have also seeped into English: cacao, tomato, potato, toboggan, coyote, hurricane, cannibal, hammock and yes, even caucus. It is a rich linguistic palimpsest, and it's vibrantly on display in this issue.

The word for green beans is a good case in point. In Spain they are *judías verdes*, in Mexico, *ejotes*, in Argentina *chauchas*, in Chile *porotos verdes*, in Peru *vainitas,* in Colombia *habichuelas.* Nabokov liked to equate Russian vowels with oranges and English vowels with lemons, and I wonder if Spanish vowels wouldn't be more like the clusters of red arils in a pomegranate. Spanish is the world's second-speediest language, after Japanese, by syllables spoken per second, which should come as no surprise to Almodóvar fans. The longest word in the language is '*hipopotomonstrosesquipedaliofobia*', meaning, appropriately, the fear of long words. How not to adore a language capable of something like that? One that has beautiful words like *nefelibata,* from the ancient Greek *nephélē,* meaning 'cloud', and *bátēs,* 'walker', coined by the Nicaraguan poet Rubén Darío and echoed by Spanish poet Antonio Machado: 'Arise, arise, though watch out, Nefelibata, your foot can get caught in the clouds, too.'

In fact, perhaps one clear difference between this 2021 selection and the 2010 list, is how many of these young writers seem to be turning a very sharp ear toward written language's sonant quality. We talk about writers as *voices*, often as mere cliché, or use it as a synonym compositionally to avoid repeating the word 'writer' too often in a text. But here there seems to be a particular preoccupation with using *sound* to capture subtle tones of location. On the 2010 list, if you reset the stories geographically and removed specific markers, it would have been difficult to distinguish the nationality of the writer. But not here. And not because of dialogue, but because of light gradations in voice clear in even the third-person narrators. These writers forgo the idea of a more 'neutral' Spanish – urbanized, peripatetic – to capture the exuberance of myriad cadences and melodies, timbres and tonalities, but not in a baroque or affected way. It's impossible to read the pieces by Eudris Planche Savón and Dainerys Machado Vento and not find yourself suddenly taking on a Cuban accent in your mind's ear, even as Eudris's characters ventriloquize British or French accents. Or José Ardila and that melodic coastal Colombian, or Andrea Abreu's Canary Island pizzicato, or Mónica Ojeda's choice of words, where you can hear the clacking, convulsing Inti Raymi dancing at the Incan Festival of the Sun. Then there's Estanislao Medina Huesca and the strangeness of a nimble and expeditious, even old-fashioned Spanish, from a country linguistically isolated on the west coast of Central Africa. Or Miluska Benavides's impeccably ordered syllables from the southern coast of Peru, and whose story is quite extraordinarily organized around a mysterious sound. You can hear the Mexican *bisbiseo* in Aniela Rodríguez's incorporeal narrator in the second person. Or the sounds of Chilean slang in Paulina Flores, whose narrator is always cleverly entering and exiting the story so that the reader is never at a loss for meaning.

These linguistic peculiarities can be heard even in translation, which is due, in no small part, to the exceptional prowess and enthusiasm of the translators we assembled, and carefully paired, for the English version of this issue. The painstaking creative work of the writers relies on the painstaking creative work, the talent and skill, of these translators. In celebration and acknowledgment of their brilliant work and their co-starring role at the center of this project, the translators' names and bylines have all been made visible in a section of the Spanish edition too.

The back-cover text of the first American selection of 1996 opens: 'Who are the best young novelists in the United States of America? A bad question. Writing can't be measured like millionaires, athletes and buildings – the richest, the fastest, the tallest.' And in the introduction, Tobias Wolff, one of the judges, writes: 'The idea of choosing twenty writers to represent a generation . . . [is] a process [that] mainly exposes the biases of the judges . . . Which isn't to say that our list is not a fine one . . . on it you will find many writers of eccentric and even visionary gifts.' Twenty-five years later, those words are still true. Virginia Woolf says that any reader, by judging with great sympathy and yet with great severity, helps writers improve the quality of their work, because by reading and judging we raise the bar on what is expected; 'Are they not criminals, books that have wasted our time and sympathy, are they not the most insidious enemies of our society, corrupters, defilers, the writers of false books . . .' The standards we raise and the judgments we pass have an effect on the atmosphere where writing is taking place, on the influence of scope. And the only way to judge is to compare. Is the reason so many writers on this list have particular *voices* and an *ear* for language because we, as a jury, preferred this kind of writing? Or is it a trend? It's hard to say.

One of the trickier problems, as *Granta* editor Ian Jack found in putting together the third Best of Young British list in 2003, is weighing the one-book author against those more established. Do you take the gamble on naming someone early in a career? It's safer to choose writers whose age is closer to the cut-off date, or who started earlier and are on a second or third novel, perhaps even translated. It's safer to choose writers whose books have been published in the larger, more established imprints. But a writer's second or third book may not hold up to the brilliance of the first. And there is a vibrant, ever-vigilant indie publishing scene that has developed throughout Spain and Latin America, whose editors are clever and on the stick with young literary talent. This list reflects and celebrates their work, specifically. There are five writers born in the 90s on the list – Irene Reyes-Noguerol, the youngest, was born in 1997. The oldest writers, born in 1985, have had twelve more years to read, write and publish (and just to put that in perspective, it's half of Irene's life). As a jury, we decided to challenge ourselves, step out of the box a little, take risks and follow our hunches, even if later we may be proved wrong.

We were all curious to see if the changes in attitude brought about by #MeToo and the women's movements, all the glass-shattering of this past decade, was truly unleashing some heretofore untapped female talent, and if so, in what way: quantity, quality or both? What we found is that women are now participating much more than before in the realm of Spanish-language literature, and their contribution is both quantitative and qualitative. In 2010 we received 228 nominations, 163 by men, 65 by women. This time around we received 194 eligible nominations, 112 by men and 82 by women. Though there are fewer women than men on this 2021 list, eleven to fourteen, of the five writers born in the 90s, four are women. And this is the telling detail overall; the majority of the nominees we received who were born in the 90s, even the 2000s, were female. Clearly, there is a coming generation of female writers. In fact, we received more nominations for women than men in Spain and Argentina, and an equal number in Chile.

What we've read, and what you will read in these pages, is fine evidence that women are the ones now pushing form to new places. The female writers in this issue are ambitious, they are experimenting, their writing is untamed and unleashed, there's an anger, a passion, their storytelling has drive and power. There are many more examples of this in writers we admired but who sadly didn't make it onto the list, such as Karen Villeda, Elisa Levy and Olivia Gallo; or Raquel Abend van Dalen, Alba Ballesta, Jessica Natalia Farfán Ospina, Aixa de la Cruz and Natalia García Freire. You can feel it particularly in the opening and closing pieces here, Mónica Ojeda's fierce Andean cosmography and Cristina Morales' Pindaric ode – a tour de force – on female contact sports. Boys in the bordello stories, or violence for the sake of violence, now seem passé, outmoded and grating.

Curiously, one of the most-cited writers in the applications – aside from the ever-looming monster who is Bolaño, 'grand hooded phantom, like a snow hill in the air' – was Sylvia Plath. Can it be that Plath's Esther Greenwood may be taking the pole position of teenage angst away from Holden Caulfield? Plath, she of 'Lady Lazarus': 'Out of the ash / I rise with my red hair / And I eat men like air.' Beware!

We wanted work of the imagination. Fiction. Consciousness captured on the page. Storytelling. No essay, no memoir, no reportage. No selfies with a bit of Photoshop to pass it off as fiction. Story that is peeled from the merely testimonial, from the very tiresome use and abuse of the first person. Originality. Attitude. Yeah, attitude. Writers writing like their lives depended on it. Writers writing about things I had no idea I was interested in. Writers channeling the worlds of the inarticulate, who have not spoken for themselves or whom we cannot hear. Things that are familiar made strange or re-enchanted. Writers like the ones who came before. The ones who didn't know about Instagram. Writers who are not readers, but rereaders. Who you think may, at some point in the future, put sentences together that will cause your spine to tingle and the hair on the nape of your neck to stand on end. Who can do it now. Writers who dare, whose ambition may have gotten the best of them, but tried anyway. That's a tough order for a young writer, but that was our bar, and we were willing to read with an eye to the future.

There were several extremely talented writers who didn't make the list either because they worked in genres not eligible for this selection, or whose work we felt hadn't *yet* met with an equally strong métier in narrative. For example, the brilliant poet Elena Medel, or Jazmina Barrera, whose non-fiction book, *On Lighthouses*, we enjoyed immensely. Santiago Wills has written largely reportage to date. Juliana Delgado Lopera's clever and engaging fiction is written in English, making her ineligible. We enjoyed Antonio J. Rodríguez, Bruno Lloret, Pablo Herrán de Viu, Vanessa Londoño, Giancarlo Poma Linares, Luis Othoniel Rosa. Gabriel Mamani Magne brought us news from an unexplored place, the Bolivian migrants living in São Paulo. And a shout-out to Fabricio Callapa Ramírez, whose stories come from someplace strange and compelling.

What will you find in these pages? Juror Chloe Aridjis writes: 'Ruminative narratives and more boisterous ones; some raw and instinctive, others crafted and scholarly; narratives that interweave highbrow and popular culture, others that possess a poetic stillness or otherworldly aura; works in which the author creates an elaborate alternative reality, and those in which the author is the construct him or herself. The Spanish language is being put to use in new and thrilling ways.' And Rodrigo Fresán: 'The adjective "interesting" is an ambiguous one. The expression, "May you live an interesting life" – apocryphally attributed to China by Westerners for many years – has been seen as either a curse or a blessing, but always as something worthy of attention. Beyond the obvious blessings, the quality of the writing, it seems to me that the additional forward-looking appeal of this selection is an eloquent sampling of how one can write in the proper direction/intention for a generation, yes, *cursed* by the excesses of life online and the easy and base temptations of the so-called *literatura del yo* – which young people think is a new trend, but is in fact very, very far from that – the compulsion for testimonial, fictions of the self that inevitably crash because they're going too fast, or going too slow. I like to believe that here you'll find a resistance to an era's passing fad, and find instead the commitment to what is timeless and destined to continue engaging what has always nourished and given rise to good fiction: telling the story of a unique world, finding the form and style necessary to explore it, and make it known. In short: welcome to the work of decidedly *interesting* writers.'

We found significantly more humor, satire and irony in this generation, and they are on display here in the writing of Michel Nieva, Cristina Morales, Eudris Planche Savón, Dainerys Machado Vento, Estanislao Medina Huesca, Mateo García Elizondo, Paulina Flores and our dirty realist, Andrea Abreu. They all use humor in varying degrees of tongue-in-cheek. It's a trend that sits well alongside the linguistic panache of this generation, perhaps something the jury was particularly drawn to in these times of pandemic. We agreed that the Cuban writing came in like a breath of fresh air. Machado Vento's cantankerous protagonist is a subtle and masterful exercise in character, and Planche Savón uses Hemingwayesque dialogues and interior monologues to appropriate and satirize, from a Havanan perspective, British and French culture in works like Katherine Mansfield's 'The Garden Party' and Luis Buñuel's *Belle de Jour*. Michel Nieva's story uses elements of manga and Philip K. Dick to satirize (politically) a future Argentina where mosquitoes are more than what they seem. And Mateo García Elizondo suspends our disbelief to bring a criminal and his pet plant into mystical communion with the cosmos. Bolaño wrote that 'sarcasm is a virtue, it's a posture that resists seriousness and boredom: seasonings that allow you to open unexpected windows to the strangest of places. Humor is what allows us to see the back of reality, its hidden face.' We welcome it. We need it!

A few stories here allow us to glimpse a more Indigenous mythopoesis, one of the truly valuable contributions of Latin American literature. In the Nicaraguan writer José Adiak Montoya's story, the narrator gives an Indigenous version of the birth of Christ and the slaughter of the innocents. A Judeo-Christian myth is absorbed by the continent's powerful original undercurrents, refashioned and retold. This is a register we also hear in Mónica Ojeda, and in Aniela Rodríguez's Rulfian tale of a man who kills his child out of neglect. Or Miluska Benavides and her generational story set around the mining town of San Juan de Marcona. Tangentially, we could include the breathtaking piece by José Ardila on the innocent cruelty of children and the powerful figure of an Afro-Colombian grandmother as a Madonna della Misericordia.

Other writers have a theatrical, more than cinematographic, touch to them, and you can imagine their work being adapted for the stage; like the fairy-tale nightmare told in incantatory, poetic prose by Irene Reyes-Noguerol, or Camila Fabbri's story of family dysfunction, or Gonzalo Baz's piece whose sparse prose and simplicity hide a very complex mechanism, circular, ticking, that seems to expand as you read it, as if each section were a drop of water on a dry sponge. Aura García-Junco is one of the writers clearly pushing form in her allusive, fragmentary story of correspondences, and Alejandro Morellón, who in just a few pages brings us into a glassy, visionary world of Nabokovian symmetries. There are pieces with more traditional storytelling structures, which stand on the strength of their engagement with reality, subtly political, honest and clear-eyed, like those of Carlos Manuel Álvarez, David Aliaga and Diego Zúñiga, who spin a mean yarn. Aliaga brings in work on the Jewish experience, linking Spain with European tradition. There are also deep meditations on literature and art in the work of Carlos Fonseca and Martín Felipe Castagnet, and on being, more philosophical, existential, in Munir Hachemi's story, which jibes with Estanislao Medina Huesca's tale of corruption and abuses of power not from on high, but all around us. You will find recurring motifs in these stories, which happened by chance: the figure of the grandmother as savior (another sign of coronavirus? Or have we finally realized how silly it was to think that because digital culture was *en arrivant*, older people were somehow rendered useless?), and the figure of the lost or dispossessed child. There is also what I call a 'statues suite'. See if you can find the three movements, and ask yourself: why statues? Why now? And with Andrea Chapela's story of apocalypse and polyamory, 'Borromean Rings', we tie a final knot. Fluidity. Or 'flow' as Paulina Flores's Buda Flaite would call it, her delightful young character who uses they/them pronouns. Spanish-language writers are reconsidering gender and love, deeply, compellingly, resoundingly full-voiced. This is what is in our collective unconscious, transformed, and being writ anew.

Art lives upon discussion, Henry James said, upon experiment, upon variety of attempt, upon the exchange of views and comparison of standpoints. This is what allows us to transcend mere cultural milieu and touch on the universal. Those of us who dedicate our lives to the arts, and particularly to literature, know this is the reason we do such a thing: for the geometry of transformation, the correspondences, the connections, the existential bridges to the realm of the other, myriad, endless adventures of human experience. So, here's to the ten years to come. And as to the state of letters in the Spanish language, to quote our beloved *Don Quixote*: 'Thou hast seen nothing yet.' ∎

Valerie Miles

MÓNICA OJEDA

1988

Mónica Ojeda was born in Guayaquil, Ecuador. She is the author of the novels *La desfiguración Silva*, *Nefando* and *Mandíbula*, as well as the poetry collections *El ciclo de las piedras* and *Historia de la leche*.

INTI RAYMI

Mónica Ojeda

TRANSLATED BY SARAH BOOKER

They told of trills, they told of masks. They told of feathers, hills and neighing trees. They told of embers. The wind swept the fire westward, and their footsteps could be heard over the dry, uncultivated earth. It was seven against one. Seven heads of bear fur and tiger teeth. The children crossed the valley of ringing rocks, of bird bones, of fox feet. Their hair was pulled back into ponytails, and tagua necklaces hung around their necks. Their faces were painted, their nails black, their bodies excited by the solstice dance. Behind them the festivities glimmered, a pool of light in the middle of a mountain range where the adults, inebriated, were dancing Sanjuanitos. The sky was the turbid color of blood, and the kicked-up dust rose to their eyebrows, but the children ran, jumped, bellowed, panted, following the trail of the four-eyed elephant, the white rhinoceros, the blind hippopotamus: Huguito the snitch, Huguito the traitor.

'We'll hunt you down, you stupid walrus!'

'Tralalá, tralalá.'

'We'll eat you up, you ugly mammoth!'

Daniel and Alan sang out their threats while Ingrid, Mene and Max pounded their chests like gorillas. Every time she climbed to the top of a rock Gala let out a howl. And beside her, Belén pawed the dirt with her left foot like a bull. The fire at the heart of the festivities was nearly imperceptible from a distance; insects crawled from the rocks, and birds flew in the opposite direction of their steps. Had he been there, the shaman would have warned them that this was a bad thing, an omen of danger still to come. 'Birds sing of the future,' he had told them earlier, holding the yellowing skull of a condor in his hands. 'The light of the sun and the stars show them the way.' The children knew nothing about ornithomancy, but they were nine, eleven, thirteen years old and feverish from the sun. The future was that scorching glow burning their innards, that Andean sunset gleaming over the frailejón plants, and that image of a white rhinoceros crossing the paramo, making its way to the river.

'Run, asthmatic whale, run!'

From very early in the morning they had been witness to the unflagging dancing of the Diabluma, his two-faced mask, his delirious, planetary eyes hiding behind the smoke of the bonfires. 'Jump, children, jump!' yelled Ingrid's mother and Mene's mother, disheveled and sweaty with veins drawing promontories across their foreheads. 'Diablo Huma brings chaos to the Pachamama!' Max's father sang, stomping the blackness of the earth. 'He brings chaos to the universe!' Once a year, the adults brought the children with them to the valley where they braided each other's hair, dressed in colorful clothes, drank San Pedro and turned into strange people. It has always been this way during Inti Raymi: the songs, the dancing, the concoctions that make their eyes roll, the crowd of plump, flaccid bodies twisting to the rhythm of the drums, quenas and guitars. But last year was different. Something had happened to them amid all the celebrations, far from the central square and beyond the thick-trunked trees that looked like a herd of frenzied horses. They couldn't explain to their parents the nature of this difference, nor did they try, but they recognized it in the way that mountain animals are capable of perceiving even the faintest flutter. This was the first time they had ever sworn a pact of secrecy, the first time they had the feeling of something intimate being put in jeopardy by that cowardly tapir, that wild piggy, that blonde boar.

'Fat traitor!' Ingrid sang, hopping around.

'We're coming for you, butterball!' Belén shouted.

They had sworn an oath to keep the secret despite the cattle tongue clenched in their jaws, the black frog squatting on their chests. They had joined their hands, blackened with volcanic ash, and buried their baby teeth beside the stream. Together they said: 'Any tattletale gets thrown into the crater.' 'Tattletales into the magma.' Only fear could forge a secret. They were nine, eleven, thirteen years old, but they already knew about power, about the night and about fervor. About limits, the great expanse and destruction. They were, as the shaman told them, descendants of the serpent, children of the macaw, creatures of mud and feathers. They had suspected Hugo right from the start, especially the eldest ones, Daniel and Alan, who could smell the fear on him, its stench of weakness. They all knew their friend: he trembled in the wind, bled with the moon. He would cry when someone dropped to the ground, exhausted from dancing, or when his parents' bodies convulsed before Aya Huma's floating feet, his eternal dance. Even the youngest of them understood that it took courage to keep your mouth shut, it took the heart of a surviving animal, and survival meant knowing how to make a secret of fear.

'What's a secret?' Gala once asked her mother, and she responded: 'Something that good little girls don't have.'

At the festival they amused themselves with the smoke, the laughter, the colors, the food, the fire. They let the music outside of them grow inward toward their hearts. They galloped around on all fours, imitating the power animals the shaman had assigned to them. They spat chicha at each other. They sang words they didn't understand until they discovered that shouting was also a song that moved through their bones and made their bodies vibrate. Their parents never watched them during Inti Raymi, and maybe that's why they realized too late that Hugo was missing. They searched for him among the violet legs, the orange and earth-splattered legs, among the jubilation, the frenetic stomping of feet, the saliva. They caught sight of him crying, his face red like a slab of raw meat, pulling on his mother's dress and pointing at the submerged spirit, at the Diabluma, who kept jumping and jumping with the energy of water, streaming torrents of sweat, letting groans of pain and exhaustion escape from beneath his mask. 'The little piggy's gonna tattle!' Belén shouted, tugging at Alan's sleeve. 'He's gonna tattle, he's gonna tattle!' But Hugo's mother's eyes were black as coal, a panther's eyes, deep and sinister, and with her elbow she pushed her son's chubby body away. 'Bad piggy!' Ingrid shouted. 'Oink, oink!'

Their vengeful glares threatened him. Hugo was confronted by Daniel's angry brow, Alan's clenched fists, Mene's bright white teeth, and he ran. He fled the people telling stories of a boneless god, an oculate god who created the first men and turned them into monkeys, foxes and lizards. He fled the people telling of ancient times, when the mountains were gods floating in the fragrant waters of the newly birthed world, of trees that had horses locked inside their trunks, of condor women who soared in the night with their arms extended, of flowers that bled and sorcerers who could separate their heads from their bodies. All the stories that thrilled everyone but Hugo: his fear had always hovered like a threat.

'He's over there,' Max shouted, pointing toward the volcano.

The stuttering triceratops's footprints inevitably led them to the cave, a deep hole carved from volcanic rock they'd dared to explore the previous year. 'We got him! We got him!' Gala ferociously screamed before howling for what felt like a full minute. 'Auuuuuuu!' The children followed her, quickening the rhythm of their legs as they followed the trail of shoulder blades, pelvises and skulls. There was light enough. They could see fissures, dust, carrion. The wind pushed them toward the mouth of the rock, straight toward the labyrinth of gray stalactites, green scarab beetles and white spiders that descended to the very depths of creation. That's where their secret had begun twelve months earlier, in that place of terror and wonder. But there was nowhere else to hide in the whole valley. Like his friends, Hugo knew the magnitude of darkness, the heaviness of blood. 'Fear makes a refuge of fear,' the shaman sang at daybreak with his arms spread wide. The children alone understood his words, that's why they threw themselves into the cave with leaden breath, frightened, convinced that if they concealed their fear it would all go away.

They shrieked, snorted, hissed, roared.

They got down on all fours like a pack of animals, hungry and electrified by hatred. 'We're gonna get you, you albino tapir!' Belén shouted just to hear the wild reverberation of her voice levitating toward the center of the earth. The first fifteen meters were difficult. They grabbed onto the rocks, used their toes to find stable places to step. It was steep, but they already knew the way: the natural formation of solid rock alongside the brittle, slippery, sharp material. When they reached the tunnel, they allowed their rage to intensify, a gesture of rebellion against the waning light. A purple ray illuminating the basalt was all they had now, and beyond that lay the blackness of the labyrinth. 'The witching hour,' the shaman had told them, 'announces the setting of the sun and the end of the party, my little ones.' It was a dangerous hour. Outside, the afternoon shadows would be in retreat, making way for the longest night of the year.

'We have to find the fatso,' Daniel anxiously said, before the echo of a bovine moan brought a smile to his face.

Snot-nosed whimpers could be heard a few meters ahead, not too far from where they were, at the first fork that led down a short, narrow passageway. It surprised them that Hugo would have made a mistake like that: hiding at the surface of fear and not deep inside its entrails. The cave's solid blackness, unexplored territory, eternal like the throat of some mythological animal, had been enough to keep him from venturing beyond the more exposed area of the cavern. He was in their vicinity now, moaning beneath a grooved rock, and his breathing drew them to him like an ancient invocation.

'We've got you now, asshole!' Alan shouted.

Mene was the first to pounce after their prey. He barked, he growled, and the rest followed him, dragging their fingertips across the live crust of the walls. His strength compelled them on, even when the ceiling of solidified lava caressed their hair. They dropped to their knees and crawled, slithered and stood up again because they were descendants of the serpent, children of the macaw: they weren't afraid of the depths of the rock, only of the depths of time. Time is what burned the chuquiraguas, made the paramo grow old and nourished the condors. What made transparent bodies mysterious like tree water, what hardened the magma and oriented the flights of birds. Time created the darkness, protected the wild. They intuited what could happen to them should they turn their backs on the relentless duration of things.

'We found you, we found you!'

'Tralalá, tralalá.'

'You'll see!'

At the end of the passageway stood Hugo, more terrified by the scarcity of light than by the presence of his pursuers. His knees were bloody, his arms scratched up, and he was sweating heavy drops that slid from his skin to the ground. He was crying, just like last year when he found himself surrounded by fur and tongues, but this time he was on his own and it was a different horror: one that anticipated commotion and trauma. The true time of bones.

'What did you tell your mommy, you stupid manatee?' Ingrid shouted at him, her voice deformed by the tunnel's depths.

Belén charged at him before he could respond, and Hugo fell to the ground. Max and Mene started jumping around him like orangutans.

'You were gonna tell,' Alan told him. 'You know you can't.'

'There's nothing to tell,' Daniel added, and Gala tugged at her braids: 'Fat snitch! Traitor!'

There were scorpions, bats, cockroaches and snakes in the cave, but most of them shrank from the light and human presence. The children sensed the world was full of crawling things, of blind, venomous creatures; and their young minds were a refuge for their own abyssal creatures. 'A mind can nourish unfathomable beasts,' the shaman had said to show them the unpleasant nature of things never illuminated by the sun, how shadows give birth to twisted things, how the landscape that was a llama by day turned jaguar by night. How the jaguar holds dominion over the llama, but never the other way around.

Last year they learned the true size of their shadows. They played with them on the scorching paramo, they skipped across the stream, across the rocks that sounded like musical instruments, and were startled by the sight of the Diabluma at the entrance of the cave.

'What's he doing there?'

'Wasn't he just at the festival?'

'Creepy!'

A man who was not a man but a god with two faces, motionless, with tattered clothes and dirt-stained hands. Not the Aya Huma of Inti Raymi, but another being, barefoot and wearing a mask that was singed around the edges. He plunged into the cavern like the sordid inverse of the submerged spirit. The children ran in after him. 'A scorched Diabluma!' Gala shouted. 'An evil Diabluma!' They slipped on the igneous rocks and looked up to take in the deep, sunken black space, with reliefs and textures that seemed to come from another planet. 'We're on Uranus!' Ingrid shouted. 'We're on Pluto!' The rock had veins, hands, mouths, joints. Human and animal figures appeared and disappeared as they strode into the belly of time, because the subterranean cathedrals, the sculptures forged from the blood of volcanoes, were forged from pure time.

'Where'd he go?' asked Max.

And there he was, the man who was a god receiving a ray of red light from out of the penumbra, clacking his teeth like castanets, dancing vigorously, his movements feverish. They would have run back outside had it not been for a brownish bird flying above the Diabluma; it was the size of a pigeon, and its squawks sounded like the song of the women of the paramo. Its presence forced them to stay put. It was the first time they'd ever seen a bird penetrate the vast underground expanse, and also the first time they'd ever heard an animal's song swell and amplify until it occupied every last corner of their minds.

'Let's get out of here!' Hugo had begged, on the edge of tears.

They wanted to leave, but something held them fast to the danger, and out of their fear grew both curiosity and desire.

The god with the singed mask was dancing with his bare feet and dirty hands. His dance was strange and unfamiliar, a dance of brusque movements, contortions and irrational spasms. In no way did he resemble the Diabluma of the village festival, though none of the children could have explained why. 'The first dance takes place in the mother's womb,' the shaman sang that morning, walking as if under a river. 'Bodies hold inside themselves the pulse of the universe: the beating heart of the sun.' It surprised them to find a bird that would fly below the earth, that the Diabluma's bones lit up and went out with every jump, and that their fear was full of desire. 'All dance is obscure because it comes from somewhere remote.'

'All dance is rebirth.'

The false Diabluma began breathing with the strength of the mountain. Bound by gravity, swelling and shrinking, his body compelled Gala to drop down on all fours and roar. 'What are you doing?' Ingrid asked, but she kept acting like a wild animal. Before long Menc, Max and Belén were imitating her ferocity; it was as if they were trying to overcome the man who was a god, who had been locked in some sort of invisible battle.

'I wanna go! Let's go!' Hugo screamed, covering his shirt with snot.

The children could clearly remember the instant they first heard the shadows of their bodies. They couldn't express it in words because there never were any. They hadn't noticed it at first: they jumped, they snarled, they tried to scare the man with the singed mask, same as he scared them with his choreography of contractions and expansions, of tangles and jerks and jolts. And then they were water, bear, frog. They moved as if playing a game while the Diabluma bent his legs and his arms in a frenetic rhythm. The stone held the memory of that skeletal logic, the sweat and the origin of what was to come.

Beyond, in the depths of the tunnel, a leg lay motionless on the ground. At a distance, nearly swallowed by the shadows, it looked like the fragment of a nightmare. ■

JOSÉ ARDILA

1985

José Ardila was born in Chigorodó, Colombia, and has lived in Medellín for almost twenty years. He is the author of *Divagaciones en el interior de una ballena* and *Libro del tedio*, and he is currently working on his first novel.

JUANCHO, BAILE

José Ardila

TRANSLATED BY LINDSAY GRIFFITHS AND ADRIÁN IZQUIERDO

There lived an idiot on Calle Estrecha.

He'd walk by our house very early in the morning and back again in the evening, most times shouldering a bundle far too heavy for any human to bear.

He was an idiot, and ugly, and big.

And he reacted to his name being called and to a single command, *Juancho, baile*, hips swaying and lips stammering as if with a primal and animal joy:

Baile, baile, baile, he'd respond.

And dance he did.

And when he finished, he'd continue on his way, his face expressionless as usual, as if nothing, as if he had been trapped for a moment in another dimension and had already forgotten about it.

It was always pretty funny.

Íngrid and I would laugh at him from the sidewalk, and sometimes she was the one to yell *Juancho, baile*, and sometimes it was me, and sometimes it was the both of us at once who, like an involuntary chorus, yelled a *Juancho, baile* in dueling and unbridled voices, racing from the living room to the sidewalk, from the bathroom to the sidewalk, from the bedroom to the sidewalk, because all of a sudden we had sensed his arrival or we had picked up the signal of someone else's call in the air – from Julio. From Topo. Or from Yainer. And the call was *Juancho, baile*, and then his response, *baile, baile, baile*, and of course the giggling that came right after, and sometimes during, and even before the dance itself, before the yell itself, before his grotesque silhouette, like an eclipse, appeared in the firmament that was our street corner.

Such was the size of our anticipation for the idiot to arrive.

And such the extent of our boredom, and the weight of those dead hours in the village.

We'd come back from school, change our uniforms, have lunch and stand by the door or the window to watch the day drift by, or better yet, to watch it in retreat hour after hour until our street – that is, the entire world – cooled to a temperature that Mamá judged reasonable. It was the same for all the other kids on the block – for Yainer, of course, dark as she was. And Julio. And Topo. Each one of our heads poking over the threshold of our own worlds, limited by the boundary of an incandescent line.

Crossing that line was not a good idea.

Not so much because of the sun but because of Mamá and her unyielding resolve never to deal with the complications that come with sunburnt kids:

Like taking us to the hospital.

Enduring the doctor's scolding.

Rubbing us with lotions three times a day, two weeks straight.

Breaking our fevers with baths of *matarratón* leaves.

Coming to rescue us from our midnight delirium.

Excusing us from school.

Pushing us not to straggle behind after the missed classes and homework.

There was no way of knowing what kind of punishment was in store if Mamá found us playing under the sun's scorching heat, say, placing bets on who could ride their bike around the block first – with Julio. With Yainer. With Topo. But Topo almost always won, so taking any risk on that bet was totally pointless. Not even Mamá's mood was a reliable clue. She could be perfectly happy and still give us two or three lashes out of nowhere, on our legs, on our backs, on our asses, or she could be very furious or very sad, often both, and only give us the gentlest warning, harmless, almost a caress: Can't you see, mijos, that your sweet little faces are gonna get sunburnt? And we were left feeling, I don't know, a kind of emptiness or maybe heavy-heartedness, so we would go back inside in silence, hurting deep in our flesh, in our bones, in the very marrow of our souls, wishing for those three lashings on any part of us instead of seeing Mamá for the rest of the day in that gray mood, everything *peye*, as if on the edge of the abyss.

Juancho had no one to fuss over his sweet little face, no one to lash out at him with a belt when his skin was getting burnt. He lived with his grandmother and an aunt. The aunt looked after the old woman, and no one looked after Juancho. When you passed by their house you knew Juancho was inside because the voice of his aunt – like so many bright feathers poised mid-air – flitted around inside the walls, always clucking his name: Juancho this, Juancho that, she shouted, get over here, Juancho, you useless *pedazo de atembao*, help me lift Mamá, Juancho, where's the cash, Juancho, you want us to live on shitty bananas alone, you damn retard? Juancho! Juancho! Juancho! If only I could work, you hear me, Juancho? What took you so long, you're so slow, Juancho! Oh, Lord, when are you gonna take him? Juanchooooooo! Are you deaf or am I not making myself clear?

Nobody ever heard the grandma. If you didn't know any better – say, if you hadn't heard the adults talking about how, many years ago, the old woman could make the infertile fertile, dry up the impulses of the unfaithful and destroy rivals on request, by the sheer force of prayers and herbs brought from Chocó – you might've thought she'd been dead her entire life. She was a quiet, unmoving thing. You'd see her in her living room, on the sidewalk, in her backyard, when the door was open. But you never saw her move. She was here or she was there and that was it, no evidence of her ever having stirred. I imagine she was moved about depending on the whims of the aunt: a disheveled and enormous woman, not as enormous as Juancho, but a lot scarier. We – with Topo, with Yainer, with Julio – would tease the aunt, then dodge her like a bull on the nights we were most bored. We would, for instance, throw a ball at her house, which was always like agitating a mad dog. She'd come out armed with broomsticks, with stones, with boiling water and even with fresh shit, and we could feel her chasing after us at a speed that didn't match her weight, which made it all the more fun, a genuine, high-risk game, and her shrill voice, always shrill, so hilarious, breathing right down our necks. Bastards, she'd say, bastards, ha! Go fuck your grandma's pussy, ha ha ha! Scamps, you should all be thrown in jail or sent to hell. Oooh! we yelled back, so says the tough lady of the barrio. And then Juancho's aunt would dig her heels into the ground, slippers and all, and charge with beastly might, but soon enough her fatness, her broken-down-old-hag energy betrayed her, and we'd leave her behind in the dust, safer and safer the farther we ran, our hearts rioting in our chests with the terror and the adrenaline rush of having once again escaped those jaws, those salivating chops, and we would turn back and see her panting, furious, frustrated because she hadn't caught her prey, because she couldn't wring our necks, I'll get you, she said, ha! One of these days I'll get you, you'll see, *pelaos malparidos.*

Too funny.

That's basically all we knew about Juancho's family.

From Monday to Sunday, like the sun in the sky, out went the idiot in the mornings and back he came in the evenings, his skin glistening and vaporous after a hard day's work. Skin blacker than Julio's or Yainer's. Blacker than his aunt's or his grandma's. Blacker than the blackest person we had ever seen. As black as a tree that has burned all night long in a fire.

Sunburnt, probably.

Delirious with fever every night, I imagine.

No hospital.

No doctor's reprimands.

No lotions.

No *matarratón* leaf baths.

Cured, each time, in the long hours of the night, by the sheer force of the scoldings of a sleepless aunt.

He had always been there, Juancho, like many other things in any other village, like the church, like the river, like the biggest tree in the park. When Mamá was our age, she'd run to the door of her house and yell, *Juancho, baile*, and she'd laugh like we did, and Juancho would reply *baile, baile, baile*, and he'd dance and then he'd continue on his way as if nothing had happened.

Always the same.

And so did all ten of Mamá's siblings.

And her cousins.

And the people who had lived forever on Calle Estrecha and on every street where Juancho had any work. Don Jairo, the shopkeeper, did it when he was a boy. And so did Doña Brunilda, the Jehovah's Witness. And Don Wilson, who drove the Coca-Cola truck. And the vendors in the marketplace where Juancho would go to load and unload things a few hours every day. And Julio's parents and Yainer's. But not Topo's parents, of course, because they had moved from the city far too late and they, Topo's parents, believed – and Topo did too, if truth be told – that they were better than all of us. Everything here seemed to them truly barbaric. The dusty streets. The noise. The weather. There were no lashes for Topo if he played under the scorching sun. Instead, standing in the doorway, his mother would call to him – or rather, purr – *mi amor*, come on inside now. My darling, you'll wake up sick tomorrow. Please, my angel, think about what you've done wrong and then we'll talk. How in the world could they understand the beauty of a good old, well-shouted *Juancho, baile*? Or the value of every little thing that came after. The fact that Juancho would stop in his tracks, for instance. His expression utterly dumb and vacant. And the fact that he'd respond with a *baile, baile, baile*. And that he'd dance. And that, afterward, he'd continue on his way. And it had been exactly the same all the way back, four generations roughly counted.

Juancho at forty: *baile.*
Juancho at thirty: *baile.*
Juancho at twenty-five: *baile.*
Juancho at sixteen: *baile.*
Baile, baile, baile.

Probably some village child had already been saying, *Juancho, baile* back when Juancho himself was a kid, but no one knows who said it first. Who activated that hidden mechanism, and under what circumstances. Who realized how it worked and then spread the discovery with others, little by little, passing it down from parent to child, parent to child, parent to child, until it came to us, until it painted this exact scene of Íngrid and me and Yainer and Julio and even Topo positioned on the sidewalk, eyes set on the slow course of the retreating sun.

Our house sat almost at the very beginning of the street, which meant that we could see Juancho coming before anyone else could, before Julio or Yainer or Topo, who said often and to a certain degree rightly, that his eyesight was better than anyone else's, better than Íngrid's, better than Julio's, better than Yainer's, better than mine, better than anyone else's on our block, in our neighborhood, in our entire village, and that he ran faster than everyone too, and jumped higher, that even in Medellín he couldn't be beat, and that one day he'd be stronger than even Juancho, but not to load and unload firewood or bananas or bundles, but to be an Olympic medalist and a famous soccer player.

We believed everything he said, Íngrid and I, except when it came to Juancho, of course.

There was no way anyone could outmatch the strength of the idiot. Every 31 December Juancho was asked to restrain the hog for the big dinner on the block. And he did it all by himself. Him alone against a white pig that had to be 350 pounds, give or take. He'd wrap the beast in the iron clutch of his gigantic arms and wouldn't let go. Not when the animal was unloaded from the truck, and not when they stabbed the hog right through the heart, sending it into violent

contortions, instinctively fighting for its life, and not during its last
spasm, its final squeal. One night I said as much to Topo: That's a
lie, mijo. You're a liar. Don't you remember the December pig? You
go do something like that and then I'll believe you. Got it? Big mouth,
I said. You hotshot. Go on, show some of that famous strength, I
said. C'mon, let's see it. And since Topo kept quiet, and I saw him
poisoned with rage, and everyone, Íngrid, Yainer, Julio, looked about
to burst into laughter, ready to grant me the victory, I went ahead
and threw in that he was a big show-off, period, that he had always
been one, that he showed off with everything, with his house, with
his bike, with his Medellín, with his brand-new professional soccer
ball, with his natural history album, with his new Nintendo, with his
new games, and that all his stuff was no big deal, that he showed off
with his stupid things and his lies, I said. And if life in Medellín was
so good why'd you come here anyways? I said. C'mon, fess up. Or
you think we're dumb, right?

At this point, everyone was dying of laughter, and it took Topo
a minute to answer: At least I don't have a tar face like you, *chilapo*,
and he pushed me and turned to go back to his house and, oof, it was
like a fire had been ignited in me somewhere, who knows where, deep
down, deep in a place I don't understand yet, because even though
Topo had barely turned his back, and even knowing there was
nothing I had to do to save face, and even knowing Topo had been
unquestionably defeated, that tone he used got deep under my skin,
that I'm-better-than-you, I'm-smarter-than-you, I'm whiter-than-you
tone, my-life-is-better-than-yours, and by the way, my-mamá-is-
better-than-yours-too attitude.

And since nobody messes with Mamá, I grabbed a stone
and hurled it right at Topo, and cracked his head open with a
marksmanship I didn't know I had; that is, with total beginner's luck
because, unlike Topo, becoming an athlete, or a soccer player, or
anything too difficult, was not in the cards for me.

And then, of course, came the drama.

The screaming.

Topo screamed with the terror of someone who had never been hurt before.

Yainer and Julio too, and Íngrid, and even I could see myself in their screams, in the sharp reflection of their fear, screaming with the promise of punishment to come. With the freshly acquired duty to pay for a new Topo to give back to his parents.

The blood.

Not as much as in the December slaughtering, but enough to wreak havoc.

His head, red all over, blood-soaked.

The neighbors.

Their shameless hunger for something new.

Doña Brunilda: In the holy name of Jesús, Our Lord.

Topo's mamá: What happened to you, my angel. Take a deep breath. Tell me. What have they done to you?

And my mamá. Her eyes half sad, half furious, glowing in the midst of the small crowd. Silent at the center of all the chaos.

Except for school, we didn't leave the house for almost two weeks.

Nothing was forbidden, really.

But Mamá walked from the bed to the kitchen, and from the kitchen to the sewing machine, and from the machine to the bathroom, and never a single word for us.

Food was on the table.

Always.

Our school uniforms, clean and ironed every dawn.

But Mamá had annulled our presence in the house the way you remove a couple of traitors from your life.

And it was true, in a sense: maybe I had betrayed her.

I.

Betrayed Mamá.

Me alone.

In the suffocating darkness of night, we could hear her cry.

I'd say: Íngrid . . .

And she'd reply: Yes . . .

And there was no need for words. Mamá's heart was broken. And it was our duty to cry with her until morning broke or until she fell asleep. Whichever came first.

Now we saw the world pass by through our door or window, not much in the mood for anything at all. Not even for yelling, *Juancho, baile* at Juancho. Not even laughing when Yainer or Julio yelled it, almost like a reflex, almost as if to keep the custom alive, as if not to break with tradition. And so it was an empty *baile, baile, baile,* bereft. Devoid of any purpose.

Wanna play dodgeball? they'd ask.

And we'd say no.

That we couldn't.

That Mamá wouldn't let us.

But it was a lie, of course. Mamá would be watching her soap opera on TV with the same pained indifference she had shown us over the past few days.

So Íngrid and I spent hours on end watching them – Yainer and Julio – throw and dodge a sorry ball back and forth, in the sorriest execution of a game since this whole sorry world was first created.

Topo was released from the hospital that same night. We were told that he got exactly forty-two stitches in his head. And we respected him a ton because of it, to tell the truth. Tough guy, we said. Credit where credit is due.

Of course, he wasn't allowed out either. I imagine he spent his days in front of his Nintendo, trying out the new games his relatives from Medellín had asked his relatives in the US to send to him. His mamá would walk by our house, her head held high and her gaze decidedly fixed on something in the distance, who knows where, though clearly a place where Íngrid and I and Mamá had ceased to exist, and even Calle Estrecha, and our neighborhood and this filthy village they had to live in after a whole life in the city.

On the thirteenth day of our captivity, though, just after lunch, we caught sight of Topo's timid face emerging from his window.

It was the hottest day of the year. The rays of sun shone down vertically and so intensely that things just a few feet away looked blurry. Íngrid and I leaned out the front door, more desperate to catch a sudden breeze than to see anything, really. I guess that's why Topo was there too, after so many days, and why Yainer and Julio were also leaning out their own doors and windows. And several other neighbors were too, fanning away the afternoon fire under the few covered sidewalks on our block. Melting at the thresholds of our homes, we all sniffed at the street like starving dogs, lethargic, awaiting with resignation the appointed hour of death.

The rest of the day went by just like that.

Dissolving into that boiling fever foreign to our own bodies.

All of us connected by this kind of universal sunstroke.

No lotions.

No doctor's scoldings.

No *matarratón* leaf baths.

No mamá to tend to our delirium.

Near the day's end, Topo and I eyeballed each other for the first time.

It was a simultaneous gesture.

Instinctive.

Animal.

Íngrid, Yainer and Julio took much longer to react.

I stepped out onto the sidewalk.

Topo did too.

And we just stood there.

Like in the cowboy movies.

And that was it.

Just a few seconds later, the idiot rounded the corner. The load he was carrying was so heavy that, despite plodding along resolutely, he took care to measure every step with unusual precaution. I was the first to fire from the hip: *Juancho, baile*, I said. I yelled. I leaped out into the street. And Juancho stopped, as expected, and said, *baile, baile, baile*. And he danced. And then continued on his way. And just when I was starting to feel good about it, Topo picked up the baton:

Juancho, baile, he said. And Juancho stopped again, as expected. And he replied, *baile, baile, baile.* And he danced clumsily, only as allowed by the load he was carrying on his shoulders. With an expression of consummate idiocy fused with a vague gesture of fatigue. *Juancho, baile,* I said. And Juancho danced for us again. And he said, *baile, baile, baile.* And then he continued on his way again. But Íngrid yelled from the sidewalk, *Juancho, baile.* And that's when things started to take a turn. We trailed each of Juancho's strides down the street. *Baile, baile, baile,* he said. And he danced. Sometimes Yainer was the one to say, *Juancho, baile,* and sometimes it was Julio, or Topo, and sometimes it was me, sometimes Íngrid. And it went on like that. And we laughed. And we yelled, feverish with excitement. As if the sun were burning from deep inside, scorching our very souls. We were happy for the first time in thirteen days and we knew it. Juancho danced for us, or better, he danced for all of Calle Estrecha. Because as we walked, as daylight faded away and evening settled in, we heard more of the voices of our neighbors cheering. The gradual blooming of a party. *Baile, baile, baile.* We followed the idiot all along. Our yells trampled each other. We kept saying, *Juancho, baile,* all at the same time, or someone else was already ordering Juancho to dance again before he even finished. And Juancho didn't know what to do with all of those overlapping voices. And he danced, of course, only to start up again right away. Though he no longer said *baile, baile, baile,* but kept dancing on until, I guess, he'd settled the mental debts of each *Juancho, baile* called one after the other, *baile, baile, baile. Baile, baile, baile. Baile, baile, baile* . . . and then he'd try to continue on his way and sometimes he even made it a few inches, but one of us would already be armed with the next *Juancho, baile* to throw at him. We carried on for I don't know how many hours. We shadowed Juancho all the way, from the beginning of the street to his house, and we kept on yelling, *Juancho, baile,* even when he fell, and that was really something to see, because we didn't know that Juancho had been born with the ability to fall down, and we had never suspected weakness. And right there, with Juancho down on his knees, barely holding up the load he'd been carrying, which clung to his shoulders more out of a kind of obstinacy than habit, we said, *Juancho, baile*, and Juancho danced, as expected, and he said, *baile, baile, baile*, with his perpetual expression of being far away, or at least of wanting to be, and when he tried to stand up we asked again that he dance and he obeyed, of course, he obeyed even when lying out flat in the dust of the street, *baile, baile, baile*, looking so much like a stabbed hog, so alike in those last spasms and final squeals. But we didn't stop, even then. We said, *Juancho, baile*. And he muttered, *baile, baile, baile*, and moved as much as his exhaustion would allow. And we wore on saying it even when the raging aunt pushed through, and tried to get him up by scolding. You gonna let them fuck up your life, you dumbass? she yelled. Can't you see you're bigger than them? Get up, Juancho, don't embarrass me in front of people, she cried. Get up, my mamá is waiting for you! And when she saw she wasn't going to get him up, she went straight after us because we hadn't stopped saying, *Juancho, baile* to Juancho, and Juancho hadn't stopped dancing, splayed out there on the ground as he was. He danced with the convulsions of a seizure. All very funny. Very electric. Very fish out of water. And we took turns, Íngrid, Julio, Yainer, Topo and me. We slipped through the arms of the fat aunt, dodged her flying slippers, her walloping broomstick, her stone projectiles, ha! And everyone laughed, Topo, Yainer, Íngrid, Julio, everyone. Ha! Doña Brunilda, the Jehovah's Witness, Don Jairo, the shopkeeper, Don Wilson, the Coca-Cola truck driver, Julio's parents, Yainer's parents, even Topo's parents were standing there, with their constipated giggles, but, hey, it was better than nothing, we thought, and the best thing: Mamá's unexpected smile, faint and still far away, but evidently amused. She had forgiven us. And the joy we felt was pure. Mine. Íngrid's. Because Íngrid and I communicated through the secret wavelength of siblings. And we looked at each other. And we roared with laughter as we fended off Juancho's aunt. And that sun, the one deep inside of us, shone bright, it burned like a supernova. And we danced to the rhythm of a tune made up on the fly with the instructions for Juancho. With the *Juancho, baile* that we kept saying. *Juancho, baile,* we sang. *Baile, baile, baile. Juancho, baile. Baile, baile, baile. Juancho, baile. Baile, Baile, Baile.*

And we would've gone on that way, would've sung and danced and laughed for the rest of the night, and worn out the fat aunt in the process, till she could hardly move from chasing us around, so consumed, so fatigued, so much dancing to our tune, so exposed to the stellar fire our bodies gave off. I mean, nothing would have stopped us if Juancho's grandma hadn't appeared, in the midst of it all, intact in the living flame, same as how she'd just appear in her living room or on the sidewalk or in her yard: without anyone noticing.

We all stopped.

And then we fell silent.

Grandma standing at Juancho's feet.

Unexpectedly tall.

No evidence of illness.

Juancho, lying still. So still. Though mumbling yet a few *baile, baile, bailes.* White from wallowing in the dust of the street. Whiter than Topo and his papá and mamá. Whiter than the whitest person we had ever seen.

And with the entire block in the most absolute silence ever in its history, paralyzed by a fear the adults had thought long forgotten, we heard the wounded voice of the old woman: a frail sob at first that grew little by little into a wailing, like something from the depths of the virgin jungle.

Boundless.

Omnipresent.

Reverberating against every wall.

Every piece of furniture.

Each and every one of our bodies.

Like a lament for all the sweet little faces burned by the sun since the beginning of time.

Then, clinging to the most primitive of instincts, we retraced our steps to the front doors of our houses.

And they remained there.

Them.

Distant.

Alone.

The fat aunt near collapse.

The old woman bent over the idiot, wrapping his entire body in her arms, her long, long arms.

And then we couldn't see them anymore, of course.

Because doors.

Because walls.

Because orders: sleep now and lights out.

But we all heard the old woman until first light the next morning, and I doubt very much that anyone on Calle Estrecha was able to get a good night's sleep, to ignore her, to sleep at all.

No one ever saw Juancho pass by their house again.

Rumor has it that he became terrified of the street.

That the grandma wouldn't survive exposing her boy to that again.

That the idiot went on forever saying, *baile, baile, baile,* that he never settled his debt. ∎

Clare knows only *bad* girls shoot people and start fires, but being a *good* girl won't save her best friend.

"A sharp, compelling novel of love and pain." (*Kirkus Reviews*)

"[Clare] grasps her adult world with both hands and gives it a genre– (and mind–) bending shake... in a class of its own." (Midwest Book Review)

"With elements of modern noir and gothic horror... the novel goes to volatile extremes in a plausible manner... with scenes unfolding like a controlled burn." (*Foreword* Clarion Reviews, 4 stars)

"The action is fast–paced and the ending utterly satisfying." (blueink review)

"Esther kissed me once for free, when we were both just girls." — Clare, before the storm starts everything unraveling

CINNABAR MOTH
PUBLISHING LLC

978-1-953971-02-9 hardcover
978-1-953971-00-5 paperback
978-1-953971-01-2 ebook
978-1-953971-03-6 audio (by Ivy Tara Blair)

PAULINA FLORES

1988

Paulina Flores was born in Santiago, Chile. Her story collection *Humiliation* (*Qué vergüenza*) was published in English in 2019. Her first novel *Isla decepción* will be published in 2021. 'Buda Flaite' is the first chapter of what she hopes will become her next book.

BUDA FLAITE

Paulina Flores

TRANSLATED BY MEGAN MCDOWELL

And there was our protagonist, ambling along through Reyes Park with unhurried steps, but still never losing that *fixa*. In our personage's left hand was a fuchsia fidget-spinner, spinning, and in their right was a burger from which the occasional bite was taken. The Bad Bunny song 'Bendiciones' was playing on a cell phone, and the volume was just right – not loud enough to bother anyone, just loud enough to supply good vibes to anyone around who might need them. 'I'm here,' the music irrevocably affirmed – any music, always – and the weight of another cell – a stolen iPhone – in our hero's pocket only served to second that enthusiasm.

'I don't wanna *choriar*, but I gotta,' our subject had silently repeated before perpetrating the theft, and we who now accompany this adventure believe it. There are still a couple pages to go – not many – before we delve more deeply into our champion's heart and recognize the genuine sincerity there; shortly, as well, we will learn of the difficult circumstances currently at work upon our star. But first, we must clarify a few things. First, the name.

We are talking here about Buda Soto Rojas, known to most as Buda Flaite, and this includes the people who use the name with respect and esteem, as well as those who in the past have sought to wound and offend. Age: Buda just turned fourteen.

As for a gender, we could propose the definition 'non-binary', but the truth is that Buda doesn't give the matter much thought – wanting, perhaps, to indicate that the mere act of classification is too closed or static for their person to brook. They knew that people referred to them as boy or girl according to what those people wanted to see (thus projecting their own personal virtues, defects or shortcomings), and so they didn't take it personally. And if anyone ever felt curiosity – and/or disgust – at their singular appearance and asked a direct, 'What are you?' Buda simply responded: 'I'm me,' adding, 'your favorite *flaite*,' if the situation merited coyness.

As for your humble narrator – who also holds a multiplicity of voices – we will follow Buda Flaite's example and not complicate life: we will flow between various genders – or none at all – as the case seems to call for, and leave it at that.

Okay then, now that we've got those details down, we can turn our eyes back to the scene: Buda Flaite with fuchsia spinner, burger (soy) and stolen cell phone. Some bluish locks floated down to their shoulders, matchless eyes asparkle, and they wore clothes that screamed *fixita*: Nike, Puma and Guess, from shoes to hair. All genuine articles that weren't stolen (at least not by Buda's hand, because they were gifts from their father). It's true that, these being Buda's only clothes, they were clearly short a few washes. But this fact did not diminish our person's fineness or style, and the same could be said of Buda's face and hands, darkened by *piñén*: neither dirt nor the cheapest brand of clothing could rob Buda of their regal aura. And so it is no coincidence that, in this precise instant, they should be walking through Reyes Park – given to Chile by the selfsame Spanish royals in honor of the forebears who had financed Columbus's travels; that is, in honor of the monarchy, and, as such, of themselves. In fact, right there was the España Fountain, which the royal couple had inaugurated on their first visit to the country, though now it was dry and much further removed from the hand of God than it had been back in the nineties. Buda Flaite popped what remained of the burger into their mouth and ran to gaze at the sculptural composition from up close. At one end was the figure of a Chilean *huaso* peasant with a straw hat and reverential mien. At the other, the king and queen themselves were sculpted in metal: Sofia of Greece and Juan Carlos I – today accused of corruption and self-exiled in the United Arab Emirates – greeted the *huaso* with a raised hand.

Buda Flaite gamboled inside the fountain (which reeked of piss), then climbed up the central column and ran in circles again. Before definitively leaping free of the monument, Buda put their brilliant wit on display by slapping the King Emeritus with a *wate*, and sticking an evil rabbit sticker there, on the nape of the kingly neck.

And now that this word *wate* has appeared, I think it opportune to interrupt this tale – even at the risk of running on or coming off as overly discursive – to insert a few idiomatic clarifications.

It is well known that Chile's dialect and colloquial language do not enjoy the massive diffusion or popularity of other nations on the continent, such as Mexico (thanks to rancheras, telenovelas like *María la del Barrio* and the cultural hegemony of *El Chavo del Ocho*); Colombia (telenovelas again, plus Shakira and, for a few years now, Medellín's reggaeton artists); or Argentina (legends of rock and soccer, of modeling, politics, the papacy et cetera, et cetera . . . I was going to make a sarcastic remark about how everything sounds better in the deep, swaggering, indifferent tone of the folks across the Andes, but that passive-aggressive logic strikes me now as overly masculine, so I'll just bare my feelings honestly: Argentina, I love you all!).

As it stands, for a long time (especially in the nineties), the absence of these and other symbolic spaces of power made Chile develop an inferiority complex – a situation that has started to change precisely thanks to personalities like Buda Flaite's. However, that diffidence did not limit the country's linguistic variety and richness – quite the opposite: it was thanks to its scarcity of resources that the Chilean language's great expressive creativity took shape. But the effort to define a couple of terms here is not born of chauvinism, but rather has the goal of – well, I was going to borrow a few theories from the philosophy of language, but since I'm not so good with those concepts I'll just say: of getting to know the spirit and mind of Buda Flaite through their very own words. What's more, these are no longer the days of the standard Spanish used to dub *Dragon Ball* episodes.

So, *choriar* means to rob. *Fixa* or *fixita* is the updated version of 'to have flow' or to be *de pana* (this last phrase imported from the Caribbean to Chile and revamped to mean 'all good') in a way that is generic but also specific with regard to clothing: because to transmit that 'drippin' good feeling and that confidence, we need the mediation of clothes, hair, makeup, etc. But it's not just about wearing pricey brands, but rather having the ability to make one's *pinta* (look) into an expression of one's unique attitude and assuredness. As a comparison, perhaps it's worth adding that *estar fixita* could be considered the friendlier/happier version of *tener pikete*. And *piñén* comes from the Mapudungun language and is translated as 'grime stuck to the skin'. *Doméstico* – which we will see further on – is a person who steals from their own social class, and *pera*, well, that's 'fear'.

The semantic content of *flaite* is more complex, and deserves a couple extra lines. As tends to be the case with all great words, its etymological origin is obscure, but one hypothesis attributes it to Nike Air Flight sneakers: 'This product was in high demand among young people with scarce resources, who began to be referred to as *flaiters*. From thence, their epithet *flaite*,' says the dictionary of Chilean slang.

It's true that at first the term was exclusively used as a classist insult, but in recent years it has begun a process of reappropriation, as the hegemonic narrative is subverted by means of the first-person affirmation. That is, *flaite* people began to feel proud of being *flaite*. An example of this can be seen in the trap song 'Flyte' (2019) by Pablo Chill-E. We won't copy the song's lyrics here (since it's more efficient and aesthetically pleasing for y'all to look it up yourselves on YouTube), but it is important to record here that said video was Buda's first flirtation with lights and fame: at only twelve years old they had a starring role in the clip, which was filmed in Puente Alto and has now accumulated millions of views.

And finally, *wate* is a light tap with the open hand, similar to the movement of a whip, on the nape of the neck or head. That was the friendly gesture Buda Flaite gave Juan Carlos – and, to a certain extent, it calls to mind the king's iconic '*Por qué no te callas*', the day he told Hugo Chávez to shut up – with the tap and bunny sticker serving to cut the king down to size, and, along with him, the genocidal monarchy and the whole colonial capitalist system. Now just try to tell me this is not a charming character!

Now that we've got that all cleared up (y'all can determine for yourselves whether it's necessary to go back and read from the beginning – we for one recommend it), the path is clear for us to turn to Buda Flaite's lineage and its direct relationship to their current circumstances. But given that our heroine – the feminine is intentional – has quite an elevated sense of honor and wouldn't appreciate our justifying any of her behaviors with woeful dramas, we will address the subject in the most succinct and objective way possible, steering clear of the slightest sentimentalism or condescension.

Of Buda's ancestors there is not much record – and what record exists is full of empty spaces, especially in the line of masculine succession – but it's pretty likely that they have been poor forever. Buda's mother, Érika, disappeared shortly after giving birth and recording their name (the reasons for her peculiar choice vanishing along with her, though we suppose she must have achieved enlightenment at merely seeing Buda's eyes open).

Since Buda's father, Chalo, had been recently *encanado* ('deprived of freedom in prison'), Buda was left in the care of some neighbors of Érika's. Said neighbors were known narco-traffickers in the northern sector of the city, which was why Buda's maternal grandmother, María, feared it would be very difficult to ask them to hand the baby over to her. And it was. But after a couple of months, the neighbors, who were very taken with the child (enchanted by Buda's almond-shaped brown eyes and the power of granting the baby a better economic future), acquiesced to the grandmother's pleas.

María and Buda became great chums, and remained so until the lady passed away – it was from her that Buda inherited their taste for tangos, *tragaperras* (gambling machines in neighborhood bodegas) and courtroom shows like *Caso Cerrado* (Case Closed), among other profound personality traits. Buda, then six years old, went to live with their paternal grandmother – Chalo was still in jail. That old lady turned out to be pretty rude – not to say she lacked the most basic sense of compassion – and soon turned Buda over to the National Child Welfare Service (Sename), which in turn sent – sentenced – them to a home called Galvarino del Bosque.

More than thirty children shared the house under the care of a couple of assistants – 'mommies' and 'daddies', as the kids called them. Buda survived – because 'lived' would be an exaggeration – six years there. They ran away the day some of their fellow inmates swallowed ground glass to keep one of the 'daddies' from ever sexually abusing them again. And the truth is that Buda's decision to flee didn't stem so much from the possibility of rape as it did from the the prospect of having to choke down glass too, or something worse.

From the ages of twelve to fourteen, Buda Flaite bounced around between their father's house in Puente Alto (finally, Chalo was free!); the family of their half-sister Camila in Quilicura (sixteen years old and she already had a two-year-old); the various and not very elegant places where their half-brother Mauricio tended to spend the night (one anguished day, high on *pasta base* [a cheap drug made from cocaine paste, similar to crack], Mauricio stole the laptop the government had awarded Buda for good grades); and the comfortable apartment where their maternal aunt Isabel (extremely sensitive to Buda's situation, though not very practical) lived in the city center.

For its part, Sename experienced its own crises and changes. Following reports that 1,670 children in various centers had died over the past decade, and after the subsequent 2019 citizen uprising, the governmental organization came to an end. By 2022, when Buda

Flaite was detained for a trivial theft in a transnational supermarket – shoplifted items included a cheap shampoo, two deodorants and a couple Oreo cookies – the Childhood Protection Service (Sepin) already existed.

Inspired by Finnish centers, these homes did have appropriate personnel and facilities. Buda was left open-mouthed at the sight of the spacious and comfortable room they would share with only *two* other teenagers, a room that offered matching laptops, tablets and LED screens, and was painted a lavender color as warm as it was versatile. They were also surprised by how affectionate and beautiful these new caretakers were – their eyes, Buda thought, really did hold a hint of respect and consideration toward their person – and also by the fact that the psychologist didn't visit him only to prescribe pills. In fact, she didn't prescribe any, and instead proposed EMDR trauma therapy and a variety of lessons (piano, manual ceramics and swimming), all given at the same home.

In sum, all the place needed was a roller coaster and a McDonald's to make it the fantasy of any child on earth. But for some strange reason, Buda couldn't quite get used to this novel prospect. He felt uncomfortable – the masculine is intentional – even more uncomfortable, out of sorts, and repressed than at Galvarino del Bosque. And he wasn't the only one – Jesú, his best friend from their Sename days, felt something similar. And so it was that after much consideration the two of them decided that the only solution was to run away again. Of course, this time it didn't have to be in secret and over the rooftop; Sepin only asked them to fill out a short request form and they could go right out the front door. Though this measure was eminently reasonable, a mysterious and irresistible need for danger led the pair to again flee out the window, with the result that Jesú crashed noisily down and twisted her ankle. Perhaps it was fate that Buda should have to depart without company, and that after *macheteando* (begging) a whole morning without results, they would come up with the idea of stealing (without really wanting to), of breaking a car window (no need to intimidate anyone) and extracting bills from a handbag resting candidly on the passenger seat (after first taking the precaution of heading up to the posh neighborhood so as not to be a *doméstico*), plus the phone, and – though the Royal Academy has Spanishized the term, Chile continues to prefer the French – the ID *carnet*.

Now, with all that out of the way, we can continue – praise heaven! – with the action: at the end of the grounds Buda came to a big skatepark and sat on the grass nearby. Their intention was to examine the stolen iPhone, but the truth is the skatepark kind of intimidated them, kind of a lot, so much that they turned down the volume on the song 'Hablamos Mañana' that was playing from their pocket. Their inhibition was nothing class-related, because, fortunately, skateboarding had long since stopped being a hobby for the rich in Chile (with the resulting improvement in the sport's athletes). No, what unsettled them were the attractive skate clothes on the boys and girls riding boards. Still, it only took a couple minutes for Buda to conclude that after so many pirouettes and falls, they were all equally dirty, sweaty and stinky. They also thought this could be opportune: perhaps the adolescent energy the kids gave off as they practiced would help raise Buda's morale: on seeing them enter, turn and exit the bowl they had the impression the skaters were seeking that feeling of riding a wave, and it seemed so beautiful and natural, so undramatic – as curves always are – that they even got the urge to learn how to slide around on a board too. Plus, since they had nowhere to go, it would be for the best not to feel lonely.

The park was entirely covered in graffiti, and under a scrawled ACAB Buda saw the iconic line from the 2019 insurrection: NO + SENAME – that is, 'Down with Sename'. Maybe it was all the mid-afternoon emotion, but Buda thought the paint still looked fresh.

Buda Flaite had also participated in the protests, but now regretted it . . . No, they didn't regret it – how could they regret closing down the soul-devouring demon?! It was something else, only right now they couldn't quite understand it (Buda said this out loud, as she tended to do when inspiration was near). 'It's something else, I just can't understand it right now,' they repeated, and then their eyes met those of a skater kid who was on the edge of the highest bowl. Judging from his frightened aspect he must have been a beginner, and he was looking at the slope that awaited him as if it were the side of a skyscraper. But he can't do it afraid – that's where Buda's thoughts went, something along the lines of: fear is your worst enemy. What they said to themself out loud was: '*Voh dale: siempre con la fixa y nunca con la pera.*' The attentive reader will recognize a couple words we've already mentioned, but still, this kind of phrase is what the faint-hearted refer to as untranslatable. Even so, we'll take Buda's advice and give it a try: It's something like, 'Go on and get it, always savage, never shook.' Get it?

'Amiga!' Buda shouted to a skater girl as she rode past. 'You got a smoke?'

The girl looked at them in the grass. Buda noticed that her eyebrows were bleached and they trembled almost imperceptibly, just an instant.

'Tobacco,' said the girl.

Buda made a head movement that seemed to say: 'It's all good.'

While she took out the implements, the skater asked their name.

'Buda. What's yours?'

'No way! Sick!' said the skater girl with a smile, and, feeling an instant attraction, she sat down beside Buda. 'My name's Azul.'

'Azul like the sky?' asked Buda mischievously.

'Nope, like the ocean.'

'Yeahhhh!'

They had an awesome time smoking tobacco, plus a little weed that sunk them into a state of balsamic serenity, very much in keeping with the golden rays that paid tribute during those hours to the paltry patches of grass in the decrepit park. Then their conversation turned to subjects of the deepest, most interesting and entertaining sort you could ever imagine. Not about information or data points – Elon Musk this or Pfizer that, or centennials versus millennials, the kinds of things people go around repeating not even to sound smart, but just to have something to say, things that only put on display (as is well known) a disagreeable and unhealthy addiction to processing and accumulating (garbage). No, these two focused on gathering their own information, on taking in precisely what they had in front of them, that delicate human dimension, and they shared genuine emotions – a whirlwind of them – as well as their own life experiences, and it filled their hearts with an immense joy and made them see the world through the one and only truth. They laughed until they were breathless, and it was like eating a bowl of beans, so strong did they feel – the kind of strength that shows itself and shouts at you: 'It's summer!' While they listened to Azul, Buda Flaite pondered synchronicities, and thought that, perhaps, everything that had happened over the course of their fourteen years was taking on its full meaning now, in the meeting and conversation with the skater girl with bleached eyebrows. And it was worth it.

Two hours later the girl skated off, and Buda was left alone again with their reasons.

There was still the matter of the stolen cell phone, which miraculously still had battery, so Buda took out the *carnet* they had also swiped from the purse. The photo showed a young woman: Elisa Alcalde, blond and white, born 31 December, in 1994. 'Capricorn,' Buda deduced, and tried to unlock the iPhone with the digits of the birth year. The first guess was a bust, and they tried the second most common password: month and year. The screen unlocked to display a drawing of a flying pegasus as the background image. 'Interesting,' judged Buda, then immediately snapped a couple selfies, since the phone's camera was much better than theirs.

While they were sharing the photos via Bluetooth, Buda heard a grating noise that stopped their heart from beating. Looking up, they saw the municipal worker gathering the beer and cough syrup bottles that dotted the ground, then throwing them into a large container. That was the source of the harsh sound that made Buda swallow hard, remembering the glass their companions had ground up with rocks before raising it to their mouths. Glass, a material both hard and fragile, transparent, just like the boys and girls from the home. From *my* home, Buda thought. Ground-up bodies, leftovers.

Sorrow pierced Buda's throat and they shivered again from pure fear. But, as it was not in Buda's nature to hide their emotions, they gave seven jumps and blurted out seven curse words, though it came off as more funny than offensive.

After this explosion of rage and vitality, they told themself: 'Not disposable bodies, recyclable ones.' Because they had to remain optimistic, they had to: it was more a responsibility than a simple aspiration. With the same purpose in mind, Buda opened YouTube and pressed play on the first video. It was a performance by a gringo singer. His face was made-up as if he'd been beaten, but he was dancing on a triangular dais on the enormous balcony of a Manhattan skyscraper. A helicopter was circling him, and its vigilant sound, combined with the effect of the lights and the circular drone shots, made Buda dizzy. The man sang about being shown how to love. And when dozens of fireworks started to rise up from the water and explode magnificently in the night sky, Buda Flaite felt like they were about to have a stroke. The hairs on their arms stood up, and they smiled without realizing it.

The singer said he was running out of time, and the line pulled Buda from their trance to remember what was truly important: they still had to *reducir* (fence) the iPhone they were holding.

There was just one more matter to attend to first. Because one thing Buda liked about stealing cell phones – aside from the eco-conscious and redistributive nature of the job – was that they could spend a little time digging through and getting inside the lives of their previous owners. In the photos folder Buda found hundreds of selfies and images of paintings, and, since the same young woman from the *carnet* sometimes appeared with paintbrush in hand, they deduced the artworks were hers: an artist.

The paintings were compositions of cupcakes, flowers and bottles – pink predominated – although on occasion there were also jars of mayonnaise or Nutella, a can of Coca-Cola, or razors that threatened tenderly. Buda liked them. There were more selfies, and screenshots of Japanese cartoons. Selfies and photos of a little blond boy. The boy drawing, reading, and with a cat. The woman and boy hugging. Maybe it's her son, thought Buda, having already formed an idea of who this Capricorn was. And then, they moved on to the really interesting part: the voice memos.

It was incredible and marvelous how much people recorded themselves on their phones: thoughts, dreams, ideas for a business or a movie, in voices that were excited, sleepless, nostalgic, lonely.

In the first memo, the voices of mother and son. They were talking about a domestic problem. No, about a difficulty at school. 'The English teacher hates me, she really gets mad at me,' said the boy.

'Hate, Pablo? That's a very serious accusation,' the woman replied.

Buda Flaite brought the phone to their ear to listen more closely, as if to a secret.

'Yeah, she's always yelling at me and I don't do anything bad. The other day she told Ignacio he shouldn't play with me,' argued Pablo in an overwrought voice.

'But Pablo . . .'

The boy started to cry, and his nasally little voice went on explaining all the ways the English teacher had it out for him.

'But Pablo,' repeated the mother, and from her tone it was clear she was trying to be firm instead of indulgent, and also that she was stifling her laughter and the tenderness her son's woe provoked in her (that must be why she was secretly recording him in the very first place). 'Try to make a little more of an effort. I talked to your teacher and she wants to help you, we all want to help you. But I can't be going to your school every other day.'

The voice memo ended with a promise: the boy was going to behave better, and the mother would have a talk with the teacher to ask for more understanding and patience.

'I know it's because you already speak English and you get bored,' she reassured him. 'I love you so much.'

Buda Flaite put the phone away and sat for a moment listening to the sound of the skateboards sliding over the cement. No, they didn't sound like waves.

'I love you so much,' they repeated to themself, very softly.

Then they stood up.

The traffic is starting to grow dense and the garbage along the Mapocho River is looking uglier – more dangerous, maybe – but there are still some hours of daylight left. Buda Flaite turns around and starts walking, determined and capable: first, sell the iPhone, then look for a place to spend the night.

We'll be right behind them. ∎

MICHEL NIEVA

1988

Michel Nieva was born in Buenos Aires, Argentina. He is the author of the poetry collection *Papelera de reciclaje*, the novels *¿Sueñan los gauchoides con ñandúes eléctricos?* and *Ascenso y apogeo del imperio argentino* and the essay collection *Tecnología y barbarie.*

DENGUE BOY

Michel Nieva

TRANSLATED BY NATASHA WIMMER

Nobody liked Dengue Boy. It might have been his long beak, or the constant annoying buzz of his wings rubbing together, which distracted the rest of the class, but whatever it was, when the kids rushed into the yard at recess to eat sandwiches, talk and joke, poor Dengue Boy sat alone at his desk in the classroom, staring into space, pretending to focus intently on a page of notes to spare himself the embarrassment of going outside and revealing that he didn't have a single friend to talk to.

There were all kinds of rumors about how he got the way he was. Some blamed the pestilential lot where his family lived, full of rusty cans, old tires and festering pools of rainwater. They said a mutant species had bred there, a giant insect, and that it had raped and impregnated his mother after killing her husband in gruesome fashion. Others claimed the giant insect must have raped and infected his father, who upon ejaculating into his mother had sired the misfit creature, only to run off the minute he got a glimpse of the baby, disappearing forever.

People had plenty of other theories about the poor kid, but there's no need to go into them now. Whatever had happened, when his classmates got bored and saw that Dengue Boy had stayed behind in the classroom pretending to work, they were sure to tease him.

ARGENTINA
POLITICAL MAP
2272

SOUTH PACIFIC OCEAN

ARGENTINE SEA

SOUTH ATLANTIC OCEAN

PATAGONIAN ARCHIPIELAGO

N
E · W
S

CANAL

VICTORICA ●

SANTA
ROSA ●

PAMPAS
CARIBBEAN

© Gustavo Guevara

'Hey, Dengue Boy, is it true your mom was raped by a mosquito?'

'Ho, bug boy, what's it like to be born from rotting bug scum?'

'Hey, fly crud, is it true your mom's cunt is a smelly hole full of worms and cockroaches and other bugs and that's why you came out the way you did?'

Immediately Dengue Boy's little antennae would begin to quiver with rage and indignation, and his tormentors would run off laughing, leaving Dengue Boy behind to nurse his sorrows.

Dengue Boy's life wasn't much better at home. His mother considered him a burden – he was sure of it – a freak of nature who had ruined her life forever. Wasn't she a single mother with a kid? Raising children alone is hard, of course, but as the years go by a mother's efforts are more than repaid. Eventually the boy becomes a young man and then an adult, a companion and a source of support for his mother, who in her old age thinks back nostalgically on their beautiful shared past, filled with pride by the accomplishments of her firstborn. But a mutant child, a dengue kid? He's a monster she'll have to feed and care for until she dies. A genetic mistake, a sick cross between human and insect who in the disgusted gaze of acquaintances and strangers will bring only shame, never once granting his mother the slightest achievement or satisfaction.

That's why his mother hated and resented him – he was sure of it.

In fact, she worked from sunrise to sunset to provide for him. Every day, even weekends and holidays, she rode a crowded ferry the wearisome 150 kilometers to Santa Rosa. During the week she worked as a cleaner in the financial district, while on Saturdays and Sundays she was a nanny for wealthy families in Santa Rosa's residential districts. When she got home at night she was too tired to do much, and having endured her bosses' rough treatment all day she had no patience left. Sometimes when she opened the door and saw the mess Dengue Boy had left on the table and the floor (he didn't mean to but he had no hands), she would scream, 'Stupid bug! Look what you've done!'

And she would clean up resignedly, eyeing him with bitter hatred – he was sure of it.

Dengue Boy's mother was still young and pretty, and since she didn't have time to go out and meet anyone, she went on virtual dates in her room when she thought her son was asleep. From his own bed, Dengue Boy could hear her talking animatedly and even laughing.

Laughing!

The sound of wonderful happiness: something he never heard when she was with him. Dengue Boy was so curious that he flitted stealthily from the kitchen to his mother's door (making a great effort to control his buzzing), and put one of the ommatidia of his compound eye to the keyhole. As he suspected, his mother looked happy. She was wearing a beautiful flowered dress, laughing and telling jokes, almost like a stranger or even a new person, since in their everyday lives she was always worried, tired or sad.

As he spied through the keyhole, Dengue Boy grew somber, and thought how much better his mother's life would have been if a mosquito had never invaded her vagina and given her a repulsive mutant child.

The ghastly horror of the bitter truth!

He was a monster, and he had ruined his mother's life forever!

It was then, unable to sleep and in the dawning light, that Dengue Boy went back to his room and looked at himself in the mirror, shrinking in disgust.

Where his mother had surely hoped for sweet little ears, Dengue Boy had big hairy antennae.

Where his mother had surely hoped for a sweet little nose, Dengue Boy had a long beak, black and brittle as a charred stick.

Where his mother had surely hoped for a sweet little mouth, Dengue Boy had misshapen flesh bristling with maxillary palps.

Where his mother had surely hoped for pretty eyes the color of hers, Dengue Boy had two grotesque brown globes composed of hundreds of ommatidia moving constantly and out of sync, to the disgust and loathing of all.

Where his mother had surely hoped for fat little feet with darling baby toes, Dengue Boy had spindly bicolored claws, sharp as four needles.

Where his mother had surely hoped for a cute little tummy, Dengue Boy had a rough abdomen, rigid and translucent, containing a clump of reeking greenish guts.

Where his mother had surely hoped for sweet little arms, his wings sprouted, their ribbing like the varicose veins of a disgusting old man. And where his mother must have hoped for little giggles and enchanting burbles, there was that constant, maddening buzz, grating on the nerves of even the calmest person.

His reflection in the mirror thus confirmed what he had always known: his body was revolting.

Brooding over this awful certainty, Dengue Boy wondered whether he wasn't only a repulsive monster, whether he might also be destined to one day become a deadly threat.

He knew that his mother's great worry – it tormented her day and night – was that when her little Dengue Boy grew up and became Dengue Man, he would be unable to control his impulses. That he would begin to bite everyone and infect them with dengue, including herself or some friend from school. Not only would he be a mutant carrier of the virus, he would become its deliberate transmitter, its gleeful homicidal vehicle, dooming her to an even more terrible suffering. And so, when Dengue Boy left for school in the morning, his mother would hand him an extra Tupperware container along with his lunch, whispering sorrowfully in his ear, 'Remember, my little bug: if you feel any strange new urge, you can suck on this.'

Poor Dengue Boy would look down in consternation and nod, trying in vain to hold back the tears falling from his ommatidia onto his maxillary palps. Humiliated, he would set the box on his back and go flying off to school, enduring the shame of being thought a potentially dangerous criminal, contagious vector of incurable ills. Which is why, when he was far enough from home, he would angrily fling the Tupperware container in some ditch. And when the container hit the ground and came open, Dengue Boy, never looking down, his eyes still filled with tears, went right on flying. Dengue Boy didn't look down because there was no need to confirm, no need to verify what he already knew was in the mortifying container: a blood sausage, quivering, greasy and still warm, slowly coming apart and trickling into the cracks in the gutter.

Cooked blood, coagulated blood, black blood, thick blood.

Blood sausage!

That was what his mother thought would sate his shameful insect instincts.

And so poor Dengue Boy persisted as best he could, back and forth between school and home, until one day it was summer vacation. Since his mother worked all day and had no time to care for him, she sent him to a summer camp for boys along with the children of other working-class families. For Dengue Boy, the camp was an ordeal even worse than school. School might be a nightmare of persecution and abuse, the kids boundlessly cruel, but at least they were always the same kids. Dengue Boy was used to his classmates and could guess what they would do; he knew all their nasty tricks. Bloodsucker. Bug boy. Fly scum, they called him. He could even predict when they would spray his seat with bug repellant. But the camp was a whole new world with dozens of strange kids, and the risk was that they would be even more aggressive and spiteful, or at least unpredictable in their tactics.

The camp was on one of the dirtiest and most desolate public beaches of Victorica. For those unfamiliar with the southern reaches of South America, think back to 2197, year of the massive Antarctic ice melt. With the unprecedented rise in sea level, Patagonia (once known for its forests, lakes and glaciers) became a random scattering of little islands. But what no one could have guessed was that this long-foretold environmental and humanitarian catastrophe miraculously gave the province of La Pampa a new outlet to the sea, utterly transforming it. One day it was an arid, moribund desert at the end of the Earth, exhausted by centuries of sunflower and soybean monocropping, and the next it was the continent's sole alternative to the Panama Canal for interoceanic travel. This unexpected metamorphosis breathed life into the regional economy with a constant juicy influx of cash from port tariffs, while endowing it with idyllic new beaches that attracted vacationers from all over the world. But the best beaches, the ones closest to Santa Rosa, were the exclusive property of private hotels and the mansions of summering foreigners. Common folk like Dengue Boy were only allowed on the public beaches, near the Victorica interoceanic canal, where all the port debris washed up: a miserable repository of plastic and junk incubating all kinds of freakish things.

The camp was the perfect solution for mothers and fathers who worked from sunup to sundown, like Dengue Boy's mother. Crucially, the camp bus came by very early to pick up the kids and returned them punctually at 8 p.m. Since this was the camp's most important service, it was the best-oiled part of the business, and everything else took second place. So the kids got nothing but stale bread and boiled maté for breakfast, and buttered polenta and juice drink for lunch. As for the recreational activities the camp promised, they consisted of a paunchy retired gym teacher slouching in the sand smoking, blowing his whistle when he saw one of the kids swimming out too far or scaling a mound of sharp-edged trash.

And so the kids, far from watchful eyes, did whatever they wanted. They ran and played ball or swam and basked on the smelly beach. And in the absence of responsible adult supervision there was one kid in particular who became the leader of the pack. Everybody called him El Dulce. El Dulce was a fat, hyperactive boy, maybe twelve years old. His father worked at a chicken-processing plant, and El Dulce, who sometimes visited him at work, had won the admiration of the group by describing in great detail how the birds were slaughtered and gutted.

'At the plant,' said El Dulce, 'there's a remote-controlled super-robot machine called the Eviscerator 3000, and my father runs it. All you have to do is push a button and it sticks a hook up the chicken's butthole and pulls its guts out.' A reverential silence fell as El Dulce spoke. 'The crazy part is that the chickens are still alive. The only way to make sure the meat is tender is to steam their feathers off, then pull their guts out through their buttholes. Their heads aren't chopped off until the very end, when they get cut into pieces. That's why you have to use earplugs,' El Dulce went on, touching his ears, 'so you don't lose your mind listening to their death squawks while the Eviscerator rips up their buttholes.'

Once he had finished his story, and the other boys were quietly imagining the chickens' agonized shrieks, El Dulce, who by now had become a kind of master of ceremonies, led the group to a distant corner of the beach and without further ado dropped his trunks to his ankles.

'Speaking of meat,' he said.

And as everyone watched, El Dulce began to furiously jerk his weenie with his thumb and index finger. After a few minutes, before the group's riveted eyes, a skinny clear streamer shot from it, falling into the sand like a glob of snot.

'What about the rest of you? Aren't you going to beat the meat?'

Confused and terrified, the other kids, suddenly envisioning themselves gutted and plucked like chickens, proceeded to imitate El Dulce. They pulled down their suits hesitantly, and standing in a circle they brought their thumb and index finger to the zone and got to work. It goes without saying that this was a highly embarrassing moment for most of them, since they were at that in-between age when some have entered puberty and others haven't, and bodies start to change against their owners' will, turning erratic and clumsy. But for better or worse they were all human children, and their bodies, no matter their differences and idiosyncrasies, resembled each other. Except for Dengue Boy, of course. It is a well-known fact that the genitalia of male mosquitoes lacks a penis. Internal testicles in the abdomen connect to the cloaca, a small ejaculatory tract. And so Dengue Boy, horrified at the idea of revealing his difference, was the only one who didn't follow El Dulce's orders. Naturally, his disobedience did not go unnoticed. The little dictator, trunks still around his ankles and fists on hips, watched in satisfaction as each of the boys did as they were told. But when El Dulce's gaze fell upon Dengue Boy, standing there frozen and staring shyly at the sand, he jeered:

'What's wrong, Dengue Boy? Scared to show your dick?'

When Dengue Boy didn't answer, hunching instead over his four delicate legs and sheepishly poking at a few grains of sand with his beak, El Dulce dialed up the attack. And that was where things got out of hand.

'Look! Look!' El Dulce pointed, yelling to call the attention of the other kids, absorbed in their onanistic labors. 'The insect is a eunuch!'

In fact, nobody knew what *eunuch* meant – not even El Dulce – but that only made it more satisfying and effective.

'The insect is a eunuch!'

'The insect is a eunuch!'

'The insect is a eunuch!' they shouted over and over again gleefully, repetition making the words even more magical and mysterious. And so, unexpectedly, the glories of language called poetry by some were revealed to them, and with arms on shoulders and shorts still around ankles – though guided by El Dulce as if being led by Virgil into purgatory – they put Dengue Boy in the middle of the circle and began to yell in unison, unleashing a wealth of language they never could have dreamed they possessed, though it flowed from their hearts like divine bardic inspiration:

'Hermaphroditic bug boy!'

'Androgynous grub!'

'Dickless invertebrate!'

'Emasculated dung fly!'

And then all together like hooligans at a soccer match, in a chant led by El Dulce, who kept time with his baton-hand:

'Eu-nuch bug!'

'Eu-nuch bug!'
'Eu-nuch bug!'
And then the chorus again:
'Eu-nuch bug!'
'Eu-nuch bug!'
'Eu-nuch bug!'

O h how hard it is to describe the exact, fleeting moment of initiation!

Thousands of coming-of-age novels have been written, of course, attempting it with varying degrees of skill. But is it possible to account in words for the chilling instant when a child commits the decisive act, no matter how blind or muddled, that will braid together past and future, stamping him with the brand of fire or blood that some call destiny?

In any case, this time Dengue Boy didn't react as he usually did to taunts about his mixed parentage: he didn't despair, he didn't wish to be dead, and his hairy little antennae didn't tremble with rage or pain. The cruel chanting (rising to notable poetic heights, it must be admitted) of the circle of boys led by El Dulce didn't shake him at all. This time it was a very different kind of adrenaline that coursed through every branch of his veined wings. When Dengue Boy turned the gaze of his compound eye on El Dulce, who stood there with his pants still down, pointing and laughing at him, he no longer saw an antagonist, a peer, a human. All that Dengue Boy and his fearsome needle saw was a luscious gulp of flesh, a quivering slice of succulent blood sausage. Carried away by the thrill of this new and unquenchable thirst, a sudden idea crossed Dengue Boy's antennae with great clarity and sharpness despite the mindless babble all around. I'm not a boy, I'm a girl, he reasoned, perhaps with some incongruence. Dengue Girl. In fact, it is the female of the species *Aedes aegypti* – of which he (or she) was a singular specimen – that bites, sucks and transmits disease, while the male performs the routine business of copulation and procreation. With relief, with filial reverence, he realized that he'd been subject to a grammatical error all his life, and if he was Girl, not Boy, he could never rape his mother, nor repeat the crime of which his classmates accused his father. And so, blazing like one who discovers a humbling truth, Dengue Girl hurled herself at the body of El Dulce, naked to the ankles, tumbling him onto the sand. With surgical precision she immobilized him. She lowered her beak and like someone slitting a blood sausage to get at the insides, she sliced open his belly. Deaf to the hysterical shrieks of the other boys, who had swung from festive chanting to a state of terror and stampeded off in search of help (as best they could, of course, with their shorts still around their ankles), Dengue Girl stuck her beak into El Dulce's ruptured gut and pulled out a bloody portion of entrails. Before the horrified eyes of the gym teacher, who by now had appeared on the scene, too shocked to do anything but stupidly blow his whistle, Dengue Girl raised a beakful of El Dulce's clean, blue guts up to the sun as if offering a sacrifice to her god. Straight away, like someone flinging a top, she gave a jerk. A spurt of blood, excrement and bitter bile splashed the gym teacher's stunned face, then stained the sand, and, finally, the waves as they rolled slowly in and out.

Dengue Girl sipped at the luscious brew welling uncontainably from El Dulce's guts. El Dulce was shaking in a strange kind of seizure, surely from the sinister disease he had just contracted. Remember: mosquito saliva contains powerful anticoagulants and vasodilators that cause hemorrhaging, which is why the blood flowed ceaselessly like a great fountain.

Once Dengue Girl had swallowed the last drop from El Dulce's freshly dead body, she brought things to a close with something strangely like a bad joke:

'El Dulce was delicious!'

She looked defiantly at the gym teacher, who, frozen in horror, wasn't even blowing his whistle anymore, and declared:

'Not like the pathetic scrap of bread with maté you give us in the mornings!'

With sudden vehemence, Dengue Girl approached the dazed gym teacher, and, with a thrust of her beak, split his forehead open like a watermelon, sucking out the contents of his brain in a few slurps.

There was nothing left to do on that filthy beach.

Taking pity, or perhaps revenge, on the other boys, who by now had pulled up their suits but were still running and sobbing, she decided it made no sense to kill them. She just bit them. As soon as they felt the bite, they fell and were seized by the dread shakes.

She decided there was no sense saying goodbye to her mother either, since the poor woman would hear about her transformation from the newspapers or the other boys' mothers. All that was left for her now was to flee to the beaches of Santa Rosa in search of revenge, to kill and infect the rich people and foreign tourists who had caused her mother so much suffering, and so made her suffer too.

She took flight, shaking the blood from her wings, and set off enveloped in her trademark annoying buzz, until she was an imaginary dot on the gorgeous horizon of the Pampas Caribbean.

Hail, Dengue Girl! ■

A Girl Called Thunder

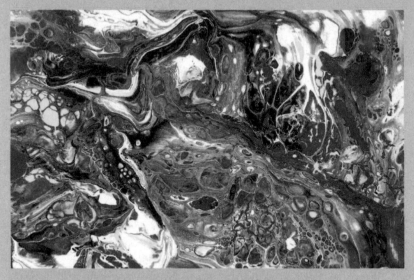

A novel by Waji

When the Department of Social Services takes
What The Thunder Said's little cousin away, the
17-year-old shaman is forced to seek out her father
in a last-ditch effort to keep her fragile family together.
But when she also asks for his help in fulfilling
a Lakota-Sioux prophecy, which involves ending
patriarchy in the world, he must first confront the
lingering demons of his own past.

However, will he have the moral fortitude to withstand
the pain of reliving those traumas yet again?

Available on Amazon

© Andrea Belmont

MATEO
GARCÍA ELIZONDO

1987

Mateo García Elizondo was born in Mexico City. He wrote the film *Desierto*, and has written for magazines such as *Nexos*, as well as graphic novel scripts for *Premier Comics* and *Entropy Magazine*. His first novel, *Una cita con la Lady*, won the City of Barcelona Award.

CAPSULE

Mateo García Elizondo

TRANSLATED BY ROBIN MYERS

Some time ago I got arrested and charged with three counts of first-degree murder. There's nothing special about how it happened: I used to own a real estate contracting business; some guys showed up one day with a front company and a plot of land in their name; they roped me into a dream project that ended up saddling me, my business and my entire family with debt. When they ran off with the loan money I'd taken out from the bank, I swore I'd find them. I searched for a while, and when I finally tracked them down, I arranged to meet them in a parking lot to get my money back. Not only did they refuse to hand it over, but they also started threatening my wife and daughter, so I stabbed them with this really long hunting knife I had, and once the blade was all the way in, I jiggled it around to make sure their innards would be properly scrambled and they wouldn't wake up on me in some hospital. It took me two thrusts to finish off the one who gave me the most trouble.

That's how I told the story in court, my audience of respectable citizens widening their eyes in fear and horror. They didn't seem to get that I didn't have much of a choice, or what it would have meant for my wife and daughter to spend the rest of their lives owing that kind of money. With three of the four shareholding partners dead, the circumstances are officially classified as extraordinary and the insurance company comes in to cover the debt. I may have got myself into a legal mess, sure, but at least my wife and kid can carry on their lives in peace. So if you ask me if I regret what I did, in all honesty I'd have to say no, it doesn't weigh on my conscience one bit.

Even so, I was found guilty on all three counts, and I became one of the world's first prisoners to be sentenced to the capsule: a new correctional method recently approved by the regulatory agencies of the United Nations and internationally lauded as the most humane means ever designed for dealing with lifers like me. The cheapest, too. Instead of having to house us, feed us and keep us entertained for the rest of our lives, some genius on the Penitentiary Commission had the bright idea of sealing us up in lead-and-titanium spheres measuring two and a half meters around and shooting us into outer space.

In the days before the launch, people from the commission turn up at the prison to explain what the sentence will involve, and you learn all sorts of high-flown terms like 'exponential rotational acceleration', 'non-specific ionic radiation' and 'large-scale distortion of the quantum field'. You don't understand much, but you appreciate the attempt to give you some kind of warning. Some people questioned the use of such cutting-edge technology to process whole-life inmates – until it was clarified that our upkeep cost millions of tax dollars annually. By contrast, dozens of capsules can be manufactured for a fraction of the cost of a commercial airplane, and once we're launched into space, the cost of keeping us alive is reduced to zero.

They still had to fund the gas for the initial propulsion, but they found a solution even for that. With a little advertising aplomb, the launches have become open-air, family-friendly events, and ticket sales are a considerable source of income for governments all over the world. It's the perfect place to take your kids on weekends. You can buy ice cream and cotton candy and beer, and the air crackles with wonder, a sense of closeness to the sky; people say it feels like you can reach up and touch the stars. And yeah, that's exactly how we feel too, the prisoners, when they herd us toward the elevators and whisk us up through the colossal structures until we reach the metal capsules, where they sit us down and solder our seat belts in place and give us a five-minute speech on how the machine works. We feel like the sky's right over there, a hop, skip and a jump away.

Outside, as the doors are sealed, the crowds anxiously wait for the engines to roar and the rocket to shoot upward in a cloud of dust and smoke, rising higher and higher until it cuts through the outer layer of the atmosphere. The impact is so strong that you can do nothing but throw up in your mouth. It feels as if your skin is a wetsuit being peeled off of your bones. As soon as the rocket emerges from Earth's gravitational field, the tip detaches and explodes like a fireworks display, and the capsules scatter out in riotous trajectories, releasing you randomly into the vastness of the void.

Of course you feel a little dizzy at first, as you watch everything you've ever known whirl and career away from you. That sphere of land and water suspended in nothingness, its seas and forests, its algae and flowers, where my daughter and my wife live, it all drifts off, slowly sapped of its bluish glow until it vanishes completely among the other stars. For the first time you realize there's no one to comfort you. It's a feeling you never entirely recover from.

Little by little the crazy rotations start to stabilize; the forward lurching eases and yields to weightlessness. Even though you're traveling at thousands of kilometers an hour, you start to feel like you're not moving at all. Without days or nights or any points of reference anywhere around you, your sense of time dissolves. I try to find solace in whatever I have on hand. I know every single centimeter of the capsule at this point. Being a real estate contractor and all, I was well aware that the final product would be a pitiful sight, but they outdid themselves on that front; it's basically a cardboard box. I wish I could entrust my life to a more solid structure, but whatever. It's not like anyone gets to file complaints around here.

The technology inside the capsule is based on 'cost-effective production', which means it's pretty primitive. I'm pinned to my seat by a set of tight belts, which are made of a Kevlar-graphene alloy and welded right to the chair, so that limits my mobility to some extent. I can use a lever to mechanically uncover an opening in the middle of the seat if I have to piss or take a shit. Then I just reach back and unfasten the Velcro patch in the back of my suit and I'm good to go. A system of automatic brushes and spritzes – probably the most complex machinery on board this thing – takes care of cleaning the shit off my ass. It never ceases to amaze me: they take absolutely everything away from you, and then they still grant you the dignity of an impeccable anus as you do your time.

Everything else is out of range. The capsule walls are one meter and twenty-five centimeters away from me in every direction, so there's no way I can touch them. There's nothing I can touch inside the vessel, actually. All I can reach are four buttons arranged on a panel in front of me: blue, yellow, green and red. The blue button fills a metal cup, my sole possession, with drinkable water. Then I have to return it through a little hatch. If I ever drop the cup, I'll probably die of thirst. The yellow button supplies me with bland, porous cookies I suspect are recycled out of my own excrement; my theory is the life-support system filters it through a culture of bacteria and microscopic algae before compacting it into little blocks, made of a substance that the stooges on the commission must have deemed edible at some point. They're all I have to keep me alive.

The green button is connected to a radio-wave transmitter with a single forgotten frequency. It's tuned to an astronomical monitoring service. If I happen to glimpse a comet or asteroid, or if I think I can make out a supernova in the distance, I can report it. Or not. It's not like they reduce my sentence or anything if I do. The radio operators are under strict orders to maintain absolute silence. In any case, I don't see a speaker for receiving messages. I know that no one is listening, but I need to talk; otherwise I'll go crazy.

The red button is the so-called S.H.I.T. (System for the Humanitarian Interruption of Travel). If I press it, a valve opens, and the sudden pressure change will make the capsule explode. I've been assured that in the improbable event I survive the explosion and my lungs haven't already burst, it won't take more than twenty seconds for me to suffocate to death in the bitter cold of space. Then you black out, they say, but it's just long enough to feel your blood and saliva starting to boil in the ultraviolet light, as if you'd suddenly walked into a giant microwave. For some reason I haven't had the nerve to press it yet. As I understand it, there were Secretaries of Human Rights at the United Nations who formally petitioned for the existence of this button, declaring it a 'moral imperative' before the new penitentiary sentences could be approved. It terrifies me, because I feel constantly, overwhelmingly tempted to press the button, but I always restrain myself.

A matter of equal importance: I owe my oxygen supply to *Polycarpus enoides*, a perennial shrub native to Australia that absorbs humidity and minerals directly from the air and needs no further attention to survive. Some specimens have reached the venerable age of 3,500 years in the wild, and the *Polycarpus* is likely to continue traveling through space long after I'm dead. My sentence is its sentence, too. This little shrub is my sole companion; we're cellmates in this saga. Isn't that right, *Polycarpus*?

At least they had the tact to install a small window in the front of the capsule. Or I used to think it was out of tact. Now I know they did it to torture us. The window offers a panoramic view of the universe: no matter where you look, all you can see is vastness. Someone who has never experienced vertigo would understand the feeling if they looked out my capsule window. The mind struggles to grasp the infinite, which is why we can only focus on it for a few furtive moments at a time. Any more would be unbearable. But I have it right in front of me around the clock, one meter and twenty-five centimeters from my face, and I know it's never going anywhere.

The people who put us here must have believed that we'd be forced to reflect on our heinous crimes. What they don't realize, though, is that the sight of the abyss only confirms my conviction that the lives of the guys I killed were utterly trivial. I don't think the judges really understood the magnitude of our punishment. Because whether or not your conscience is tormenting you, you're irremediably confronted with the primordial void. And that's not right. No human mind can stand it. I'd like to see them try. Them, the very picture of respectability, their Sunday jogs with their golden retrievers, their whiskeys before bed, their liturgies and good wishes and immaculate scruples, tidy and unsullied as my ass is right now. I'd like to see them sitting here, staring out at the big Nothing, trying to keep from shitting their sweatpants.

You learn things about yourself in prison, and the capsule is no different. I've learned that something very peculiar happens when your eyes can absorb the entire universe with a single glance. Consciousness is like water; it takes the form of whatever it observes, and it's impossible to look out at that jet-black immensity – empty, endless – without adopting those qualities yourself. That's how a prisoner's mind starts to encompass everything. They thought they'd be depriving us of sensory input by exposing us to silence and darkness. But what happens is the total opposite, which they might have realized if they'd tried subjecting themselves to this punishment for even five minutes: all the stimulus in the whole world, all of it, seeps into us with every passing moment, and from the smallness of our capsule we see it all, we contain it all. We turn into something like gods.

Anyway, I get to thinking about this stuff. Then I come back to reality and worry about these short circuits I have. Sometimes I'm flooded with images and memories of the life I left down there, or behind, or above, or wherever it is Earth's ended up. It happened to me in prison, too: they put me in solitary for stabbing a fork into some asshole's eyeball when he tried to nick my breakfast. You find yourself staring at the wall or the bars, and suddenly, in the sheen or the grime or the patterns and irregularities of the brick, you see flowers and cathedrals and your wife's boobs. Something similar is happening to me now, but it's not the same: I stare out at the stars and I start to feel like the universe has already gulped me down and digested me, that I've stopped existing and there's no difference or separation anymore between me and it.

Then I can clearly see my two sweet girls, sprawled out on a blanket in the grass, the sun shining down on them. They're wearing overalls and eating strawberries, which could also be raspberries or cherry tomatoes; tiny spheres of fruit that stain their mouths red. I'm not sure if they're memories or things I make up, or if I've learned to read oracles in the random geometric shapes cast by vapor and stardust as they mist up my window. I have the vivid sensation of being there beside them, but no matter how hard I search for myself in the vision, I never appear. My girls are all I see, and I envy them, because they can feel and smell the grass, and take steps on steady ground, and eat fruit. They have the solace of tangible things.

Sometimes I see stuff through the window, too. Traces of light, mostly; maybe glimmers of other craft, traveling along at speeds like mine. I've even seen giant brains floating around in the void. They look like jellyfish, and I zoom right past them, but if I really look, I can tell that they're brains, dangling their whole nervous systems along, drifting into the abyss by sheer force of inertia. *Polycarpus* thinks I'm crazy. I try to point out those intergalactic worms, those parasites gliding through space, nibbling at the fabric of reality, leaving black holes in their wake, but the visions are short-lived, and anyway, they couldn't care less about us.

I think this speed of travel is taking its toll on me. My mind is deteriorating, or maybe it's the non-specific ionic radiation; I can't be sure. All I know is that it's a very sophisticated kind of torture. No matter where I look, there's just infinity. There are crueler and more unusual forms of punishment than the death penalty; I'm convinced that this is one of them. In any case, I was sentenced to life imprisonment, not to death, but what could be more like death than this? Maybe this is worse, actually. At the end of the day, death only takes a moment, while this drift through oblivion, this perpetual plummet into nothingness, is never over.

Why are they doing this to me? I'm not a bad guy, I'm just a pragmatist. I don't deserve this punishment. Sometimes I feel like *Polycarpus* is mocking me, taunting the absurdity of my existence: a senseless, aimless, meaningless journey through the void. I look at the shrub and want to kill it; I'm glad to be bolted into my chair, because otherwise I would have done it by now. Sometimes I wonder what *Polycarpus* tastes like, what sort of texture the pulp of its leaves and bark would have, what it would feel like to sip the resin right from its stalk and chew on its roots, if only I could reach them. I'm sure it thinks the same. It's waiting for me to die and turn to mush, waiting for my body to release its reservoir of gases and water so it can feed on them in this hermetic ecosystem for the rest of its journey, like a tiny bottled forest straining toward the sun. I envy it. I can't do this, can't keep floating haphazardly along, hallucinating that the bush wants to kill me, eating nothing but my own shit, I can't. I can't let them dispense with me this way.

And I can't stop thinking about how to get out of here. I devised a method for removing the battery from the radio, extracting hydrogen from water and using the S.H.I.T. valve as an escape tube by propelling the capsule through a series of controlled explosions. I've even thought about how I'd use the toilet lever as a rudder. I could sail from one celestial body to the next, slingshotting along their orbits to guide myself back to Earth. Who knows how far I'd get before exploding or running out of water or oxygen. Besides, I'd have to get out of these graphene belts before I could even try. I'm ruining the cup by trying to file down the straps, which are still completely unscathed, but it's not like my teeth are really up to that sort of thing.

Sometimes I dream I'm a galactic octopus crossing the quantum ocean, planning to drop down onto land and shatter myself into a million pieces so I can infect humanity with some crazy idea. It feels so real that when I wake up, still here, I'm not sure if I'm myself, dreaming of the octopus, or if I'm the octopus remembering the prisoner I once was. In other dreams, vessels of a Galactic Federation come to my rescue and carry me away as a refugee to the paradisiacal planet of a humanoid species. They tell me I come from a brutal, primitive system, condemn the savagery of my treatment and praise my heroism in enduring space like the survivor of a shipwreck. I appear on holographic screens, I enjoy fame and food, and they think I'm crazy for asking them to help me make my way home. But that will never happen. At this point, I'm more likely to get picked up by a garbage craft, some enormous ship devoted to collecting space junk.

I travel hundreds of thousands of kilometers per hour. At such speeds the stars leave streaks in the sky, everything swells with light and the darkness is invaded by a pale, milky glow. You can see electron storms in the distance, and deep purple-and-crimson clouds that form when stellar winds make contact with the ambient radiation. Sometimes I feel the swampy give of matter as it changes states and assumes the nebulous, velvety texture of time, and I know I'm slipping along the waves that form on that border, like an insect suspended on the surface of a pond.

I think it's happening, *Polycarpus*. Something, a black hole, or maybe the very center of the galaxy, is pulling us toward its core. It vibrates with a deep, low thrum. Can you hear it? We're getting closer. I'm afraid it might want to dice us up, atom by atom; to pulverize our consciousness and sprinkle it over its breakfast. But I think we both fear the other possibility even more: that as we approach the enormous body that's luring us in, time will pass slower and slower, and we'll never get anywhere at all.

There's always the option of pressing the S.H.I.T. button and blowing myself up. How twisted can we get, as a species, that we do this to each other? I'm not sure why I keep holding back. It can't be fear; anything at all is less terrifying than this. *Polycarpus* thinks it's because I'm stubborn. Maybe so. It's constantly begging me to take the plunge. It says it doesn't want to spend eternity this way, that there will be no one else to make the call once I'm gone. It says it doesn't want to see, doesn't want to know. But I think I do want to see what's out there, on the other side of time. I hope it's not a long, sharp knife slicing out some poor idiot's liver. That would be incredibly disappointing.

Don't be a wimp, *Polycarpus*. What's the worst that can happen? Are you scared we'll get stuck in time? Tell me how that'd be any different from our current situation. It's a glorious opportunity: we can risk it all, because we've got nothing to lose. I'm not even sure we're still sane. But don't worry, we'll work with whatever we've got on hand. I'll try to keep my eyes peeled and my finger on the green button and I'll transmit what we see. My girls deserve to hear about this, they deserve to know what's above them, in the heavens. That's what we're here for, *Polycarpus*. To fling ourselves irremediably into the void and describe what we see as we fall. We've been traveling through nothingness since the day we were born, darting across time, feeling like we're going nowhere, advancing toward a colossal force that, eventually, will cause us to disintegrate. It's just that we realize it now; we can see things as they are. The correctional system has opened our eyes, *Polycarpus*.

Don't you see them out there in the distance? Those enormous beasts floating in the abyss like cosmic whales? They're slow, sure; they don't seem to be moving at all. But if you look closely you'll see them flapping their fins, propelling themselves through the ether, devouring stars. I know where they're swimming, what they're letting the invisible currents sweep them toward. Time never runs out, but it's flowing back toward its source, which is where the singing comes from, like a siren – can't you hear it? That's where the light is, the glow that ensnares everyone who rests their eyes on it. I see it. That's where we're going. That's where everything is going, knowingly or otherwise.

I already tried, but the laws of physics are irrelevant here, and there's just a mechanical retching sound when I press the red button. Nothing else happens. There's one other option left: just as the nucleus starts to swallow us down, I'll grab my metal cup and smash it against the window. I don't know what that would achieve other than disintegration, although that's probably the most practical solution. Look at the fissure in the firmament. Look beyond it at the light burbling forth like radioactive nectar. We won't take our eyes from it, even if they melt and drip out of their sockets like raw egg. It's not something mortals get to witness, it's not usually permitted to minds as small as ours, because when they do, they adopt the form of what they see, which means they stop being small. They learn what light knows and they turn into gods, *Polycarpus*.

Either that or the sight of the nucleus is driving us insane. But even if this is a hallucination, look at it: it's the only reality we need. This is the end of time. It's our way out. Loosen up, *Polycarpus*. Pain is the last thing we should be thinking about, now that our bodies are coming apart like a set of nested boxes flattening out onto each other and our entrails are unraveling and floating around in the weightlessness, still connected but jumbled up, in disarray. My consciousness is unraveling, too. It's unspooling into the entire capsule, which has shed its cocoonish quality and morphed into a kind of shell. We don't see the prisoner or the shrub anymore, but if we weren't looking at ourselves looking for them, we wouldn't be able to find ourselves, either.

What we do see are roots made of titanium, ligament and cellulose, burgeoning and spreading below the capsule like tentacles or antennae, which we can use to swim against the gravitational current. I wonder if this ever came up on the Penitentiary Commission. Now that we're shooting through the ether at a torturous speed, sipping the radiation that once fried our cells like a celestial elixir, maybe we can find our way home, wandering the stars, remembering the prisoner we used to be in occasional flashes of lucidity. They gave us too much time, *Polycarpus*, and they never imagined what we'd do with it. You know it's true. We're one and the same. We always have been; I know speaking with you is just another way of speaking with myself, I do. No, I don't think we've gone crazy;

I think we've evolved. We've attained enlightenment, or supreme radiation, I'm not sure which. You're right, maybe they're the same thing after all.

Something strange is happening to me. Despite the cruelty of this punishment, of having endured torture and exile until I saw my own consciousness disintegrate, despite all the doubts and all the wonderment, and despite this utterly new sensation of dissolving into every atom in the universe, I still can't bring myself to regret having killed those men, even now. I think it was written into the fabric of things; I think it was meant to happen somehow. Maybe I'm just stubborn. The shrub was right about that. Maybe I made some mistakes along the way and did some things that weren't entirely good and those things caused me problems I could have otherwise avoided. Maybe I should have poisoned them or run them over. But I keep thinking about it and I'm overwhelmed by a feeling I can't explain, a feeling of, I don't know, a sort of cosmic harmony; the certainty that things are exactly as they should be: my wife and our little girl in the yard, eating strawberries in overalls, and those assholes buried over there, comfortably crumbling into the earth. And for all that to happen I also had to be here. I guess that's what all those people wanted when they called for 'justice'. All those roads have led to this moment. It's as if the universe were perfectly arranged, as if my voyage through this place were fulfilling an inexorable purpose, and this crazy idea kept the whole world balancing on the tip of a needle.

Yes, this is how things had to be. When all is said and done, it's a good universe. A little nicked and dented, sure, with manufacturing defects and paint imperfections, but it's the only one we've got left. There are days when I look out and feel like I know it well and can't stand it. But then I surprise myself by clutching at it with all my strength, as if it might slip out from under me at any moment. It's a relief to open my eyes and see it there. Every time. You can depend on it like that. Otherwise, if all of this is just delirium in the end, then let this capsule follow its course until it vanishes into the galactic core. My body will still be inside it, hallucinating, but we won't be there any longer. They sentenced us to life in prison, but we've died and been reborn in a different consciousness, so I'd say we've done our time.

Polycarpus, we're free. ■

Courtesy of the author

GONZALO BAZ

1985

Gonzalo Baz was born in Montevideo, Uruguay. He directs the publishing house Pez en el Hielo. His first fiction book *Animales que vuelven* won the Ópera Prima Award from the Ministry of Education in Uruguay. His first novel, *Los pasajes comunes*, was published in 2020.

UNINHABITANTS

Gonzalo Baz

TRANSLATED BY CHRISTINA MACSWEENEY

1

The naval officer returns to the neighborhood, as he does every evening, but this time with a metal cone under his arm. He walks slowly so they can see him, as if he were taking a war trophy for a walk. The local children stop their game of street soccer to ask what it is. The officer eagerly holds out the artillery piece he's taken from the Armed Forces Materials and Armaments Service. The children gape, open-mouthed. An unexploded anti-personnel fragmentation shell, he tells them. At home, his mother and aunt are watching the latest telenovela. His mother nervously asks what he's carrying. He responds that it's a souvenir and puts it on the living room table, next to the two women. Ten minutes later, while the officer is having a shower, an explosion is heard throughout the whole block. The children interrupt their game again. Everyone comes out to see what's going on. Shards of glass and pieces of concrete are scattered along one side of the street. The explosion leaves a section of the roof hanging from a beam that will finally fall in the early morning, startling many people in the neighborhood awake with the memory of what they saw the previous evening: two charred women, ambulances, fire.

2

Eve told me all the stories about our neighborhood. And when they ran out, she invented others. She preferred accumulation to repetition because when things are repeated something strange happens to them, 'like when you see yourself in photos from different times wearing the same tracksuit, or when you go to someone's house and find they have a tablecloth identical to your grandmother's'. Her aim was to nourish my sense of having arrived late, when the events had already happened. The day we moved into the neighborhood, the house next door was in ruins, it was an inaccessible, absent place.

3

I'd seen her several times around our block and we were in the same high-school biology class. She was a keen participant when we came to study the anatomy of fish, which didn't fit with the image I'd formed from watching her jump between the roofs of houses, losing herself in the depths of our block or rummaging among the rubble in search of something I didn't immediately recognize. One day, following a collective foray into the park by the afternoon students to smoke weed, we walked home together. Her house faced onto one street and mine onto another, but from our roofs we could see each other's yards and, between them, what had once been a house. The walls were still standing, but since most of the roof was missing, there was a perfect view into the bedrooms, the bathroom and living room, and you could even see some moldering pieces of furniture. There was rubble in the yard, a barbecue area almost completely overgrown with the tall grass in which the ovenbirds had built a nest that my father liked to keep watch on through his binoculars. If you passed by the front door, it was like just another of the bricked-up houses to be found on any block, with nothing to indicate that behind those bricks everything was rubble.

On the way home, she told me the story of the naval officer. I watched her hands moving around as she spoke. She wore a number of bright nickel-silver rings, the sort they sell at the market on Saturdays. The effects of the weed made me think that her movements were leaving trails of light in the air. And that gave an added grace to her story. Occasionally I would wander away from the conversation, stroll through forgotten places, along dirt roads, among tin shacks and low concrete walls. Places that always return.

4

This morning, I woke to the sound of the lock in the house where I lived in those days. The grating of a metal key in the cylinder, the echo down the hallway, the bolts being pulled back. Sounds I heard thousands of times, imprinted in my memory. Fragments of that period are all around me in different forms, as if I had to reassemble them in order to know something. For a few seconds, in those early hours, I believed I was back in our childhood neighborhood.

5

Soon after we moved there, my father built a wall to block the view of the filthy mess left by the explosion in the yard of the house next door; to stop rats and insects getting in. As a young teenager, looking for somewhere to be alone, I began going up to the roof, from where I could gaze in fascination over that forbidden wasteland. I could also see the back of Eve's house, which looked more like a continuation of the ruins than a place to peg out laundry or have a barbecue at the weekends. After I started going to the roof, I was able to see what lay behind our neighborhood facades, and those early months of exploration were strange, as though someone had turned the lining of everything inside out, a sense of vertigo that wasn't coming from within me but from the spaces we inhabited.

6

Tacuabé, who we all called Tacua for short, spent practically the whole day hanging around the block. He used to beg for spare change and if you gave him a few coins, he'd hurl them back in your face. Local people, who knew him from before, gave him twenty-peso bills and he'd look at them as if the exchange were incomplete. I was scared of him at first because his scars were so repulsive, but then I got so used to him being there that his presence made me feel safe. Eve told me that the people from Pastor Jorge's church had bricked up the house because they said that it was haunted by the spirit of his dead mother, who had died in the explosion, and that she'd driven him mad, which was why he'd been thrown out of the navy and ended in the street, outside his house, outside everything. Pastor Jorge said that only his followers would be saved from the economic and spiritual crisis. Many people listened to him and started attending the temple – in fact just his house – where he'd be waiting for them with a buff envelope into which they could deposit their cash.

7

One day Eve asked me to help carry some things from the yard behind the house to the garbage can. There were piles of what I suspected to be her canvases, covered in shade netting and stinking unbearably of cat pee. Curious, I moved closer. I knew she painted because of the colors staining her hands and the smell of thinner that I initially found unpleasant but later identified as one of her characteristic scents: paint thinner, abandoned houses, cigarette butts, candlewax, earth and cats in the sun.

Can I see them first?

No way.

Fine, carry them yourself, then.

Go to hell, then.

8

When I asked why her yard was such a mess, she told me that her mother had left when she was ten and her father had let all the plants die. The autumn rains had turned the flowerbeds and planters into dark swimming pools where strange organisms flourished. I'd even seen some tiny fish there, occasionally coming up to the surface.

9

I'm behind the house, facing the wall my father built, kicking a football and receiving the pass as though there were two of me. My brother had drawn a circle on the wall and said that if I practiced getting the ball into the center, I'd be a good player when I grew up. My mother seems healthy, cheerful, she watches me play as she smokes a cigarette, the ashtray in one palm. With each kick, the ball comes a little nearer to the circle, the cigarette burns down, leaving a long tail of ash, always at the point of falling. One shot a little too lobbed sends the ball sailing over the wall and into the house on the other side. I turn my head to look at my mother and she's furious, she walks toward me, still holding the cigarette, and shakes my shoulders.

10

I saw Eve further up the neighborhood several times, walking almost as far as the local church, an impressive building that had to be viewed from the opposite sidewalk because the facade was in danger of collapsing. Mildew had eaten away at the walls like some strange fungal infection, producing a yellow powder not unlike pollen, which then settled on the sidewalk and the leaves of the lime trees in that block. The only things that functioned in the church were the regular Narcotics Anonymous meetings Eve's father and my mother attended. That building was where they ended up, trembling, watching the various structures crumble, braving the cold seeping in through the stained-glass windows broken by stones; it was the consolation of many local kids to watch the colored glass fall and shatter, sending a loud, mysterious echo through the old church.

I later learned that Eve used to walk around that part of the neighborhood two or three times a week on her way back from her visits to Estela, an art teacher who lived a block away. At first the idea was to watch her at work, because when you passed by outside, you could see the woman with her splattered shirt, layering paints onto a canvas that was always changing color. Eve was one of those people who liked to stare into windows as they pass, and so she gradually edged a little closer, driven by that urge of hers, which all of us in the neighborhood knew, to enter unknown places. One day Estela invited her inside. She showed Eve her latest work and asked what she saw. Eve answered: My mother. After that day, she began to visit regularly. Estela taught her the basic techniques of color and composition, loaned her books on art that Eve studied without understanding the first thing because the explanations came later. Estela had taken a liking to her and set her exercises. She once asked Eve to go to the registry office so she could see what it meant to fuse your body with a space: almost transparent office workers who formed a single unit with the green walls, the yellowing posters and artificial plants with dusty leaves. When she entered, wearing her red jacket, like a trail of blood in all that aridity, she understood why everyone there wore dull tones. Bodies blend into their environment. In Estela's house, Eve took her shoes off and walked on the floor to feel the grain of the wood on her feet, she stroked the flowers on the wallpaper, moved close to feel the heat of a red-hot wood-burning stove. Estela would watch her, lighting one cigarette from the butt of the last, blowing the smoke into the backlight to see what shapes it formed, toxic clouds, like the ones we saw from our windows, drifting over the neighborhood: Tacua in the middle of the street, looking up at the sky, the dark fish disappearing beneath the surface of the water in a planter. Once, before she left, Eve asked me to go to the hospital with her. I'll wait outside, I said. She stood at the foot of the bed, like someone passing by who stops to watch her house burning. Estela asked for a few drops more of her pain medication. This isn't me, she said, so you can stop coming.

11

During those days I didn't see her on the roof as I used to. She told me she was spending the nights in uninhabited houses. Her father would knock on our door every so often to ask me if I'd heard from her. I'd say that she must be with Estela. He'd walk up the street and, seeing smoke coming from the chimney, would feel less worried. Then he'd go back home and listen to the radio, drinking wine that he diluted with ice to make it last a little longer. My mother said he was a good sort who'd been through hard times.

12

I've imagined thousands of variations on the colors and materials Eve used on her canvases. But when I'm least expecting it, what come to me are the dark fish emerging like shadows from the mud, absorbing the light. I can spend hours in that state of total blackness, until I see a distant figure walking slowly among the rubble and I go to her. I always end up in the same place.

13

She left the neighborhood when the police arrested her father. They came one day with a search warrant and didn't need to turn the whole house upside down to find the half kilo of cocaine divvied up in the small bags her father had carefully sealed while listening to music, like those old women who knit while watching the news. The people in the neighborhood feigned surprise when they saw him handcuffed, being loaded into the squad car. Eve asked to be let stay in the house, but there was no one to pay the rent so she had to go live with an aunt outside Montevideo. On the last day, I watched her come out into the yard carrying a plastic bag, dip her arms into one of the planters, fill the bag with murky liquid and examine it, the sleeves of her jacket dripping. That action brought a period of my life to a close. New neighbors moved in, I started a course in auto mechanics but dropped out after a year to go abroad. Another family came to live in her house and cleaned up the yard, cut the grass, bedded out flowers, filled the planters with soil and within a few months had some flourishing rubber plants. And between the two houses remained the ruins of Tacua's former home, the place in which our shared dreams roamed.

14

I stopped going up to the roof. During those years, only my mother and I were living at home. Tired of her periodic relapses, her lack of willpower and suicidal tendencies, my father and brother had moved in with my grandmother. My mother used to smoke in bed and sometimes fell asleep with a lit cigarette between her fingers. There were small burn marks with hardened edges in the sheets. I'd stretch out beside her and we'd watch TV, by that time we didn't even bother speaking to each other. I sometimes went to the church with her for a Narcotics Anonymous meeting, and she'd return home with a glint in her eyes, as fleeting as something passing across the sky.

15

It was ten in the morning but looked more like night. Outside, the whole block seemed to be in a state of tension, as though it were remembering terrible things. Suddenly hailstones began falling to the ground, onto cars and the porches of houses. Tacua pulled his bomber jacket over his head. My mother, who was standing at the window, told me to take him an umbrella. I crossed the street wearing thongs so as not to get my sneakers wet, the hailstones thudding on my skull. At the sight of Tacua, jacket over his head, with the scars of burns on his face like centipedes sticking to his skin, I stopped short. Eve was the only person who ever actually touched him; she used to stroke his scars, kiss his cheeks. She was capable of doing that in spite of the stench of urine on his clothes, the grime encrusted in his pores, his hands covered in brick dust from scratching at the doors and windows of his house until his nails broke and his fingers bled. Spots of blood on the brick.

16

I lose myself among the pieces of concrete, the tiles covered in dust and mold. In our neighborhood, nothing ever broke the silence. Eve taught me how to understand it all: the gestures, the sly glances, the inaudible voices. After her departure, an ongoing rumor hovered in the air like a whistle after an explosion. Every so often the elderly ladies would ask if I'd heard anything from her and I invented stories: she'd become a nun, had married a count and was now reigning over a small Eastern European country. I never told the same story twice.

17

The women are absorbed in their telenovela. On the screen, two characters tussle but end up kissing. The women glance at the metal cone, something is making them uneasy. They look at each other. One has tears in her eyes, she seems to be about to say something but can't get the words out. The other puts a finger to her dry lips and leans across to look in the direction of the bathroom, where her son is having a shower. She moves closer to her sister and whispers something in her ear. Their heads are very close. ■

Courtesy of the author

MILUSKA
BENAVIDES

1986

Miluska Benavides was born in Lima, Peru.
In 2012 she translated Arthur Rimbaud's
A Season in Hell and her story collection,
La caza espiritual, was published in 2015.
She is in the process of completing *Hechos*,
the novel from which 'Kingdoms' has been
excerpted.

KINGDOMS

Miluska Benavides

TRANSLATED BY KATHERINE SILVER

San Juan de Marcona

The engineers used to say that before the establishment of the San Juan de Marcona mining camp, the locals and the outsiders from the high country – as opposed to the indentured labor brought in from the mines of the central Andean region – had no training in the processing of metals. The technicians complained that the 'Indians' had neglected the hilly plains for centuries, out of both spite and ignorance. They passed through without exploiting either the minerals or the marine species that lived in the cold currents, until the Peruvian government placed wise Raimondi in charge of measuring and mapping out the rivers and plains where the ore was hiding. After establishing the breadth and extent of the golden hills of San Juan de Marcona and their iron deposits, the Italian contemplated the waters of the bay, judged them deep enough for ships to carry the ore out of the country, and thereby deemed the hills profitable.

Juan Bautista arrived in Marcona with three coins in his pocket, intimidated by its reputation as a ghost town founded in the desert. He had been unable to descend the ancestral route used by his father,

Mario Bautista, to reach the bay where he would harvest *cochayuyo*, those thin strips of dark vegetable that saved his village when it was suffering from drought. They had blocked the route with fences that impeded access to the coast, and on the hillsides they were erecting steel towers and a myriad of wooden piles, heaps of rocks and clay, adjacent quarries no man could pass between without heavy machinery. By that time, word of the wealth of the coastal mine had spread: Marcona was no longer a humble campsite built by the first foreigners but rather a city being constructed out of sticks and reed mats.

Bautista was greeted by workers who had their own share of worries, though their ever-increasing hopes for a house and a savings account had, over the years, been drowning out the talking points of a union that had its martyrs, talking points that circulated through the alleyways of the camp at birthday parties, in cantinas and at meetings. They claimed that the new owners were worse, that they ran the camp as if it were their own little hacienda, that wages were the same as when they bought the place in 1995. He had witnessed lost battles fought during assemblies, which he stopped attending. 'Quit. This job kills, so let others kill themselves; not us,' he heard in a goodbye speech given by a fellow miner. It was his first meeting, and the solution seemed reasonable. They were upset that all the other miners were earning well. In San Juan de Marcona he could earn more soles than he'd ever seen in the countryside, Juan Bautista kept repeating, while the rest of his fellows wrote lists of grievances and signed declarations that gathered mildew and dust in the local offices.

The day of the explosion, Bautista made his way through the camp as he had the previous days, months and years. Upon waking, he saw the same cracks in the walls of his bedroom, the same damp patches on the ceiling tiles. Through his window appeared the same hints of morning light. In the washrooms, he nodded sleepily to Vélez and Calderón, who were working the morning shift with him; Janet, awake and still in her nightgown, was sitting and waiting for him in a white chair; his daughter was still asleep in her darkened room; the oatmeal had dissolved into the recently boiled water. When he stepped out onto the second-floor walkway on his way to the plant, everything seemed to be proceeding in unison with the rhythm of the sea and the slow advance of the cold fog, whose movements he had learned to decipher so that he could find his way blindly during the winter months. There was no indication that this day would be any different, not until hours later, when he acknowledged being part of a catastrophe. That day Janet said goodbye listlessly. 'I don't smell anything, just metal,' she answered when, before leaving, he had asked if she didn't smell something strange.

The plant was shimmering in the distance in the dawn light; the quarry scars had revealed the shimmer of the metals of the earth. That day was no different from any other; Bautista had dreamed nothing strange like that day in his childhood when he was almost swallowed up by the raging river and he'd dreamed about muddy waters. Calderón, he and other men in blue overalls gathered in front of the plant gates to clock in. A half hour passed while he and Calderón carried out their routine. Together they were working the pressure pump that extracted the ore. But when they turned it on, it exploded. Calderón was killed at once, his chest torn open. Bautista was saved by the distance of a few steps. He remembered being aware of the disaster for a few seconds before passing out, knocked down by the blast and pierced by iron rods. The following days went by as if he were deep in those muddy waters of his childhood dream. He woke up in an ambulance, where a paramedic told him that his only chance for survival was to be taken to a hospital in Lima.

Janet showed up in the hospital days later accompanied by lawyers and other men in suits. He barely recognized her, sedated as he was after multiple surgeries that would leave him immobilized for several weeks. In the meantime, his colleagues organized the imminent protests – they would block the highway that connected the camp to the rest of the world. He was not eager for them to see him in this state. With one leg almost healed and the other gone, he continued to assert that he had never saved or earned like that, and yes, accidents do happen. That's what he said to Alcides Espinoza, from the union, who came to his hospital room to ask him to sign their claim. He asked him to lend his support to their demands. When Janet came in to ask him what his visitors wanted, he shook his head and said:

'They tried to persuade me with their gift of gab. They sound like preachers.'

The television only ever devoted a few minutes to news from the provinces. One reporter described the incident at a rate of fifty words per minute, and at home nobody wanted to say much. But when Juan Bautista moved, against his wishes, into a dilapidated two-story apartment building near a forlorn hospital in Lima, the work stoppage – as the miners called it – continued strong. One day, while watching the morning news and eating hot oatmeal, he found out what was going on in San Juan de Marcona. Janet was talking to him about other things while she put away the groceries. His attention was focused on the report about the miners and the housewives pouring out of the mines and the camps to take part in the march of sacrifice toward the capital. On the screen he watched them with their flags and their uniforms in spite of the summer heat, their yellow and white helmets, their sunburned faces, their sunglasses, their bottles of water. One reporter spoke briefly about him and Calderón. People were walking along the highway that snaked through the desert. Janet had her back turned, was in high spirits and focused on the sound of her own voice. The buzz of the television and the presenter were left behind. He was overwhelmed by an internal buzzing, like a muffled roar that he hadn't heard inside himself for many years, and it forced him to remain silent.

A Singular Man

Mario Bautista held his hat in front of his belly and plunged into the crowd that was walking toward the cemetery, accompanying the dead with prayers and sobs. Father Cárdich sprinkled holy water on a row of coffins placed under the high stone arch that framed the funeral of the youths, victims of the cliff at the Laramati Curve.

Other drivers had told him about the accident when he'd stopped in Canta, and he decided to go to the cemetery to say his goodbyes, even though he knew that when he returned to the house of Sebastiana Narváez, reproaches awaited him. How could I not go? he said to his mother while she served him the piping-hot soup. 'And still you come here to eat? Go straight to the señora,' she told him. Bautista paid no heed. He had left the truck at the terminal without telling anybody he was leaving, then he joined the long procession that wound through the cobblestone street, the oldest one, where, they say, Cáceres, the Brujo de los Andes, and his *montoneras* passed for the last time during the war with Chile, and from there disappeared into the cordillera that rose steeply behind the cemetery.

When he finally showed up at Sebastiana Narváez's house, the double gates were wide open. In the middle of the large courtyard a tall tree with white flowers was in full bloom. Sebastiana, cheeks ablaze, was waiting for him, holding a whip that the men in her family often carried. Adela was also waiting for him, though she preferred to remain unseen, hidden behind one of the pillars in the courtyard. Everyone in the house said, with admiration and bitterness, that Sebastiana ruled over her kingdom without anybody's help. She had two sons she had sent to study on the coast; her younger brother had been sent to one of the more run-down haciendas in order to make a man out of him. She checked each and every bag of coffee he had brought from the valleys – one of the pillars of her business; this – they said – as well as her knack for hiring the best drivers, whereas the rest of the traders kept hiring novices and muleteers, like the one who drove off the cliff at the Laramati Curve.

'I have some urgent business to propose to you for tomorrow. Later,' she said to Mario Bautista, without greeting him, while the peons unloaded the bags and carried them on their shoulders to the storehouse. 'Let's talk later, after Mass.'

The Mass in honor of Justo Narváez, Sebastiana's father, was held against the protests of Father Cárdich, who suggested postponing it because of the drunkenness that would ensue in the courtyard of the Narváez house, where even outsiders would gather, drawn there by the news. In the priest's words during the service, Justo Narváez, the departed, was remembered as 'a singular man', a dreamer and a cosmopolitan in that backwater that was Santa Lucía. The priest stretched out his arms and invoked the saints embedded in the walls of the church to remember his friend. He was a man of great curiosity, the priest said, who repeatedly asked about the nature of God's kingdom, about whether the actual number of days till His return had been calculated, about when every promise made by Our Lord Jesus Christ would be fulfilled, and about how at some point the kingdom of the living and the dead would open and the world would become one. He also talked about how Justo had grown more pious after suffering a series of palsies, which did not stop him from asking questions about Our Lord. Sebastiana, alone and dressed in black, sat on the wooden bench in the first row, nodding.

Neither the sermon nor the party could silence the rumors about how strange Justo Narváez's death had been. As the women filed out of Mass, they whispered – after offering each other signs of peace – that Sebastiana had let him die. The rumor was gaining credibility. They said that shortly before dying, Narváez had shut down his silver mines in Cangallo, claiming the vein was spent. They said he may have asked the mountain itself to conceal its minerals or take them elsewhere, as had happened with the mines of a long-gone relative of the Narváez family, Catalina Astocuri, who on her deathbed told a brujo to ask the Virgin to hide the gold in her mines in order to prevent the sin of greed. It was not a coincidence – they whispered in church – that shortly after Narváez's death, Sebastiana brought in engineers to look for more silver in Cangallo. She knew about these and other rumors, but she chose to thank people at the door to the church, shaking the hands and the forearms of the attendees, the people who had worked for her or who had once owed something to her father.

Those who did not respect the mourning for the victims of the Laramati Curve went to the Narváez house. It was not the first time

Sebastiana ignored the mourning of others for her own needs. While the courtyard was filling with the deep and solemn sounds of the *huacrapucos* of Acocro – maestros of her father's favorite cornet – she discussed business with Bautista. He agreed to everything, right there in full view of the curious, who were moving their heads to the rhythm of the music, eating ribs and drinking alcohol. They had heard the promises that Sebastiana had made on other occasions to other drivers, even to Víctor Jaimes, only barely older than Bautista, to whom they had just bid farewell at the cemetery. She told them they were exceptional men, singular, and that they could make good money and marry a good wife. Bautista listened and agreed that at dawn he would take her merchandise to the edge of the jungle, where she traded with Franciscan missionaries, even though it meant driving past the same cliff over which the last truck that had left Santa Lucía had fallen. When the young man left the courtyard to go home to rest, some said that there were only two options: he would return dead or alive.

When the first hints of the morning sun began to find their way into the cobblestone streets, the distant sound of the *huacrapuco* musicians, departing along with the outsiders, barely pierced the silence. In almost total darkness, Bautista loaded the cattle onto his truck and balanced on the roof the bags he was supposed to take to the mission. Señora Narváez, didn't see him leave. Nobody, in fact, saw when the heavy truck, too heavy as Bautista feared, crossed the red bridge. He should have taken the shortcut that climbs then descends; but, instead of taking the high road, he continued along the river, which was flowing fiercely. Awaiting him around a curve was Adela, the young woman who visited him secretly at night; rather than tell her boss that she was pregnant with Bautista's child – she claimed – she preferred to leave that house. Hypnotized by her nocturnal visits, he ignored the promises he had made the night before, and the sound of Sebastiana's voice, which had almost convinced him to drive along the Laramati Curve, still fresh from the dead. The woman boarded the truck, and together, silently, they disappeared at the base of Cerro Moroqaqa, which was said to spirit travelers away, in the direction of towns where the cattle and the truck would be sold and all trace of them erased.

Visits

Outside – a summer's day – the day goes by slowly; the driver comes to a stop at the yellow light so he can pick up the waiting passengers. Her mother is waiting for her on the corner, uncomfortable in the heat. They walk two blocks, empty except for a few children playing soccer in the street.

'I'm going back to the store from here,' her mother says, 'so you bring this package.' She hands her a pair of pajamas tied with plastic ribbon. 'Then take the clothes down from the line so they don't get faded,' she tells her, as the waves of heat appear on the two o'clock horizon.

Juan Bautista's house is only half built; on the second floor, with no glass or roof, the windows are bare. The woman is leaving through an iron door and lets them in. He waits for them inside, sitting on a chair in a hallway with unplastered walls. He stretches out the leg, which for a long time they thought was healthy, on a wooden bench. He complains about the intense pain, how he thinks the pins in his hips have come loose, and how they won't give him an appointment. The scars on the stub of his other leg are covered by a shortened pant leg. She holds the cotton and the hydrogen peroxide while her mother cleans the open wound, which has still not healed since the beginning of the new year. There are gangrened sections on his leg, which seem to be advancing along the entire surface of the muscle. They've explained to him that two veins have burst, possibly from the loose pins. They've told him that he has to wait for surgery because there are still no beds.

She walks away. For the sake of modesty, she always looks for
something to wash or put away in the kitchen so as not to see her
uncle unclothed while her mother is giving him his injection. 'Why
does she make me come?' she wonders when the dishes are done
or when she can't find any, and they are still talking. She doesn't
want to go anywhere else because she might run into the woman
who is usually hanging around the courtyard and the living room.
Everybody says he is still young, but to her he looks very old, at least
she knows that he is the oldest of her uncles. She is curious about
what that woman is doing there. She knows that when Aunt Janet
arrives from Marcona, she'll have to leave. She has even heard that
the woman who comes to take care of him has a husband and family.
They've told her the mine sent her and they pay her wages, which,
according to the aunts, is a pittance.

'Next time just give me the packages at the corner,' she complains
to her mother as her mother boards the bus. She suspects that she
obliges her to come out of fear or discomfort, so as not to be alone
with that woman, whose footsteps can always be heard when she
approaches to overhear their conversations – complaints that Janet
abandoned him at the worst moment, that kind of thing.

She drops off the packages an hour later. She doesn't plan on
going home until after she loiters around the avenue for a while. It's
summer. She amuses herself looking at the shop windows full of
clothing and shoes, the casinos guarded by men wearing suits in that
heat. She walks down the avenue bursting with shops, food stands
and small storefronts, with people coming and going; she makes
her way past chaotic street corners and through traffic and finds
herself in a run-down park with broken pathways. She decides to
wait on a concrete bench in the shade of a tree. Around her, mothers
are strolling by with their children; some ride in plastic wagons. A
couple, about her age, talk on the bench facing her. Lima's opalescent
afternoon is unfolding, imposing itself; overhead, the thick leaves
of the trees – she notices – offer the best moment, and – she tells
herself – all that's missing is for something to simply happen. She

stares at the corner she'll have to turn to return home. Then she hears the booming of certain afternoons, or, better said, the great booming that has now caught her off guard. Over and above the noise of the traffic that increases as the afternoon wears on, she hears the familiar sounds of trumpets playing from out of the depth of the sky, a sound that comes down from above – she says when she describes what she hears – and that she always hears in the afternoon. People are focused on their own affairs and show no sign of hearing it. The mothers, standing around with their arms crossed, talk to each other while their children run around in circles. The couple are whispering, their faces very close to one another. A few minutes pass before the noise stops and she decides to return home. Whenever it comes – she tells herself – it's because something is about to happen.

'How could you not hear it, it's so loud,' she tells her mother at dinner.

'It's the train crossing the river, and that's just how it sounds,' her mother says.

Her brother looks at her. They never bought the explanation usually given on the nightly radio show her aunts used to listen to when they reported noises in the sky. 'It's clouds colliding,' the announcer would always say toward the end, after transmitting for half an hour the so-called sounds of the final judgment, which could be heard in Tel Aviv, Australia, everywhere. That night they look for videos on YouTube, and they learn that the sound can be heard in different places simultaneously, even if in different versions: trumpets, a sustained booming, a crash. A video from Jujuy is most like the noise she heard in the park. Another video says that it's the sound made by an aurora borealis. A voice solemnly asserts that the aurora borealis splits the earth open, as if it were making an incision: 'It's the portal for a universe that's nearly fifteen billion years old.' They get frightened hearing this. Their mother takes their phone away; she sends them off to bed.

At night the silence is not uniform, at least not until the cars and buses stop driving along the avenue around midnight. Her room is dark; the door is open. Her brother and mother are sleeping, or that's what she thinks. She hears the cats walking across the roof. She has difficulty sleeping; she changes her position every so often, until she sees a shadow come in through the half-open door of her room. Like other times, she lifts her head to see better, though she knows that she will see nothing more than what she's seen or believes she's seen. Afraid, she puts the sheet over her eyes. It's the spirit of Grandmother Adela again. She knows it and isn't surprised. She promised her so many times she would return. One could say that she is coming as she has come on other occasions. She doesn't really know, but she recalls the booming that afternoon, which always foreshadows something. She remembers the words. Surely there's something her grandmother wants to tell her.

Mayu sonido
[The river that spoke]

I

The adults had taken Grandmother Adela behind the door. One of the girls stood there staring, her eyes wide open, trying to decipher the whispers. A few minutes later they brought her back, and though the girls were afraid, they settled into their chairs to shell the peas and listen to a story often repeated with very few variations. But the old woman did not pick up the story she had been telling before they interrupted her. She pursed her lips.

'What I'm going to tell you is not a lie, it's reality,' she said. 'I was their age when I arrived at the house of a very good woman, strict but good.'

She looked at them with her blind eyes and added:

'My mother had seven children and said, "I can't keep my oldest daughter with me." My family sometimes went to sell wool that the señora thought highly of, so I met her. "Come Adela," she said, and promised me she would take me in. I cried when I said goodbye.

'I stayed there for years. I learned to cook, to iron the clothes of the señora's father, a very respectable and pleasant man, Señor Justo Narváez, that was his name. The señora's mother had died of her stomach, they said, many years before. I was at peace. I had my room; the men pestered me, but the señora warned them: "Nobody touches her." The señora's sons also loved me like I was family. One day, many years after I arrived at the house, Señor Justo complained that he had a headache here in front and at the back of his neck. The señora sent someone to bring herbs. They gave him some pills for the pain. Then her father said, "Daughter, it hurts a lot . . . call the doctor." She didn't. "It will pass, Papá. Don't make so much of it," she said. The days passed, we gave him some pills, and one day the señor could no longer get out of bed. I had to support him on my shoulder, otherwise he couldn't stand. "Oh, señora, let's call the doctor," I told her. I was very young, but I realized that the señor was in a very bad way. We didn't call the doctor, and the señora warned us: "Don't tell people on the street or in the market that my father is sick. My father doesn't want people to find out." Nobody said anything, and there was the señor, with his dry hands, so pale, as if his insides had been sucked out. One night, the señora said to us, "Our Lord took my father." We sobbed. They came from all over to say goodbye to him and then the rumors started. They said the doctor never came. "He woke up dead," the señora said, tears running down her face. Who would dare contradict her. In the house we realized little by little that the señora had hoped that her father would die and didn't call the doctor. That was her hope. Some say they had problems. Because of what she hoped for, her father died. She wanted him to die. That's when I decided to leave, to go far away.'

The old lady coughed, then added, 'That woman had a lot of power. They said a lot of things I can't tell you right now. I left the house with my first intended, Don Mario; we didn't know where we were going. He – may he rest in peace – told me, "If I stay, I'm going to end up with nothing or die." That's what he said when we left.'

The old woman grew quiet and looked toward the door. The

adults were walking by in a hurry – lunch was being served.

'And then what?' the girl asked.

'And then we went far away. Don Mario became a miner, and died from his lungs. Then, after many years, I met my new intended in San Damián, and years later we came here to Lima, to a place that was nothing but desert. One day, walking in the city center, I ran into a friend from my town. We greeted each other, then she said, "The señora says that you stole from her. And she also said that somehow or other she's going to find you, that who knows what you might be telling people." "Mario died. I have a new intended. And I had a son with Mario," I told her. "So take good care of him. You know how the señora is, don't you? She's looking for you and she's very spiteful," she warned me. "Why should I care that she's looking for me?" I said. And she walked off without saying goodbye. I always remembered this friend who warned me.'

The old woman stared fixedly.

'Though the señora must be dead by now.'

By then they'd finished shelling the last peas. A woman came in shortly afterward and threw the vegetables in the pot. She offered the old woman her shoulder to help her into the living room, but the old woman rejected her with a brusque movement. The girls shook out the party dresses they had put on for the visit and joined the troop of cousins running through the hallways, in the courtyard, out on the street. They were waiting to eat the lunch they had helped prepare and they left the old woman alone at the table mulling over her memories.

II

When torrents swell at the mountaintops, they descend the slopes and announce their presence with a loud booming that then subsides. The mountains announce their descent. At first the waters descend in silence, then they gather strength when they join with other waters from neighboring peaks; then the current turns fierce. They were warned so many times about the sound that announced the arrival of the raging river. It could bring mud, stones; it was also said that it unearthed the cadavers of animals, even of musicians and drunkards, and the children knew to get out of the way as soon as they heard a sudden roar that didn't stop.

They say that Adela often talked about how she saved Juan Bautista from those turbulent waters, as if by miracle. How she pulled him out of the river. The children had not been able to cross safely in time, in spite of being warned by the booming, which came as if from the sky. Nobody knows how, out of the whole group, he was the only one who slipped into the water. They weren't paying attention, trusting that the water wouldn't flow through there, even though the earth itself, furrowed like an enormous serpent, was the vestige and proof that a raging river had been there before. She and some others took a shortcut and saw him in the middle of the river. His body was covered in mud, a caul of mud blinded him; the boy was barely able to keep hold of a log that advanced slowly in spite of the strength of the river. She didn't despair, and she followed him along the bank until the log, pulled by the current, got caught in a spot surrounded by stones just before the vertiginous descent. The child was clinging to the log and it held in place; the water splashed around him. They tied Adela around the chest and waist with strong ropes, and the locals held on as she plunged forward. It was difficult to reach him, so she grabbed him from behind. By the time they reached the bank, they were exhausted. He had difficulty breathing because of the mud; the stones and branches had lacerated his body.

Juan Bautista has difficulty remembering what came next. For a long time, he thought he held inside him the great booming that announced the river's frenzy that day, which on some nights didn't let him sleep. He claimed that in the afternoons he'd hear a protracted sound, something similar to the warning of the raging river; at other times he'd hear what sounded like faraway cornets. He'd turn toward the mountains; he'd look for the sound in the sky without finding it. It seemed to exist only in his ears. Whenever he asked, people around him said they heard nothing. Nor could he remember the moments before the incident, and ever since then he figured it'd be better not to invoke the memory or its sounds.

But one day, Juan Bautista is woken by a booming sound that rises out of his dreams, and for a few minutes he feels his absent leg. He thinks he can move it, but he opens his eyes and recognizes his body: the shadows of dawn bring back to him the shapes of his healthy leg and the stub lying next to it. At that threshold where lucidity is fast approaching, he remembers for the first time in a long while that day in his childhood when the river almost swept him away, and it occurs to him that perhaps he should have died then. The memory returns to him sharply like a bolt of lightning on the horizon of his childhood, much brighter than the timid light peaking through his window. He feels a throbbing in his temples and in the diseased veins that are already contaminating his healthy leg and his belly. He is overwhelmed by a sad suspicion that, according to what he heard from rumors and confessions, they had always been looking for him and perhaps now they had finally found him. ∎

EUDRIS PLANCHE SAVÓN

1985

Eudris Planche Savón was born in Guantánamo, Cuba. He is a doctor and writer. His first novel, *Hermanas de intercambio*, won the *Pinos Nuevos* Award and the 2019–20 World Literary Excellence Award. His story collection, *Cero cuentos*, was published in 2020.

TRAVELLERS INSIDE THE MARQUEE

Eudris Planche Savón

TRANSLATED BY MARGARET JULL COSTA

'Probably we had something in common which I shall
never find in anyone else.'
– *The Diary of Virginia Woolf*, 16 January 1923

For Katherine M. with my LOVE and devotion.
For Claire Tomalin, for her excellent biography of K.

La Première Voyageuse

I

S he is sitting beside me. She takes a packet of biscuits out of her
handbag and offers me one.
'No, thank you,' I say.
In fact, I'm as hungry as a biscuit-crazy she-hound.
'Go on,' she says, 'I can't possibly eat all these on my own.'

My hand says *Yes* as I take a biscuit.

'No, take more!'

I smile awkwardly. But my biscuit-craving hound of a hand is hungry and demonstrates this by grabbing six biscuits or possibly seven, I can't remember now.

A man in uniform approaches and asks to see our tickets. He is fat, ugly and his dental hygiene is just atrocious. I feel for my ticket in my pockets.

'Here,' I say, but he is too busy staring at her to hear me.

She really is beautiful, even I could happily spend my life studying her. And those eyes . . . heavens! She has 'the look of a Japanese doll'.

'Just like Katherine Mansfield,' Virginia would say if she were here.

She takes the ticket out of her purse and hands it to the man.

'Would you like one?' she says, offering him the packet of biscuits.

He accepts. I look at him with utter loathing, not that he notices. My she-hound of a hand tries to bite him, but, thinking better of it, merely gives him the ticket.

He leaves. The young woman is looking at me and gnawing her lower lip, which doubtless tastes of French cuisine.

'*Bon appétit, madame!*' I think, but am interrupted by a new offer of biscuits.

My she-hound of a hand takes two, shares one with my mouth and keeps the other one.

I remember that while looking for my ticket, I came across a small book in one of my overcoat pockets. I take it out and settle in to begin reading.

'Oh, *The Garden Party!*' she says. 'I so enjoyed that story.'

'Me too,' I say, meanwhile thinking that her accent, when she says the word 'party', is similar to that of the girl who recites poems at the nightclub.

'You like it, do you?' she says.

'I like you,' I think, but manage only to lisp out a *Yes*.

I imagine standing in front of a mirror, giving myself a slap around the face for such gaucherie. I decide to say something, but she gets in first.

'I'd love to read it again.'

I hand her the book.

'You really don't mind?'

'No, not at all,' I say.

She takes the book and starts to read. Katherine Mansfield has just stolen my chance to begin a conversation.

II

I closed my eyes and fell asleep. In my dream, I recalled her inviting me to have a cup of tea at her 'garden party' . . . that girl with the look of a Japanese doll. What a crazy dream! She really could be Miss Mansfield! She's so beautiful. Her boyish haircut, among other things, really does remind me of her . . . sitting on the lawn . . . the taste of sweet tea and the tang of ginger fill me with joy . . . Suddenly, I don't know how, we're in a different place, behind the rose bush. You're naked and dreaming, rather like the *Sleeping Venus* in the paintings by Giorgione and Titian, in precisely the same pose, with what looks to be a silken sheet in the foreground. One of the most beautiful pictures I've ever seen. You're a goddess. I move closer. Now you're Titian's *Venus of Urbino*, but instead of lying in a luxurious room as you are in his painting, you're still there in the garden, wide awake and looking at me like a very alluring geisha.

I like her hands. They're touching me. At first, this gives me goosebumps, but only at first. I run my tongue between her fingers, as they caress my face . . . then my neck, my earlobe YES my shoulder YES my breasts YES my back YES my buttocks YES then my face again: beautiful fingers . . . they slide down to my . . . I'm alarmed to find, right there in front of us, various characters from Mansfield's garden party: Laura giving instructions to four workmen on where to place the marquee . . . Another Laura, who was in fact the same one, eating a slice of bread and butter while she gazes at a boy. Then she runs off . . .

They don't appear to notice us. They vanish, and we are left alone.

Now that I analyse it, those characters from the 'garden party' were only here in order to underline the sense of intimacy, the splendour, rather like the two servants working away in the background of the *Venus of Urbino*.

I caress her. I hear the playful tinkle of piano keys and someone singing a sentimental song. We are sitting inside the marquee now, sipping tea. I offer her a sprig of lilac, which she accepts, smiling, as she holds it to her nose, enjoying the scent.

'I love this part,' she says, interrupting my daydream and turning to me. 'Listen:

'He bent down, pinched a sprig of lavender, put his thumb and forefinger to his nose and snuffed up the smell. When Laura saw that gesture she forgot all about the karakas in her wonder at him caring for things like that – caring for the smell of lavender. How many men that she knew would have done such a thing. Oh, how extraordinarily nice workmen were, she thought. Why couldn't she have workmen for her friends rather than the silly boys she danced with and who came to Sunday night supper?'

We both laughed out loud. Our eyes met. This time, I savour the taste of my own lips, rather shyly. Not that she noticed.

'That's such a great scene,' I say, and she nods. 'You know, we haven't even introduced ourselves, I don't even know your name' – although I only think this last part.

'It's better like that, exchanging names might break the spell,' she would say.

She resumes her reading. I watch her discreetly. While she's reading, I have the distinct impression that she's also watching me out of the corner of her eye. God, I'm ridiculous!

III

You look like her, like Kathleen or Kass as almost everyone calls you. There you are, reading your own stories . . . You like German and French . . . You spent your childhood in a house in the country, Chesney Wold it was called. You were probably fat when you were a child, and the others made fun of you. The odd one out in the family: 'Kass the difficult one', 'Kass the sentimental one'. You were the third child, like Chekhov. Later on, when you were already a writer, you were accused of plagiarising a story of his; that would be one of your misfortunes.*

Oh, I'm such a fool! Of course, you're not Kass and your life wasn't and isn't like that at all, you just happen to resemble her. Little Japanese doll! If you really were Kass, then I would be Marion, your best friend from childhood. I remember the day you went with your siblings to welcome 'Dear Mama', who was arriving home by ship after a long time away. There you were, eager to see her. 'She's arrived! Mama's arrived!' you cried. Yes, there she is and I hear her say to you: 'Well, Kathleen, I see that you are as fat as ever.' I look at you: my friend Kass blushing scarlet . . . on the verge of a tantrum . . . stomping off, head down, the wind ruffling your hair.

And then you look at me, and I come back to earth. You ask me something, which I barely understand, and you repeat the question.

La Deuxième Voyageuse

IV

'Did you know that the author died young?' I ask, but she doesn't understand and I have to repeat myself.

---

* One day, I would like to write an essay on all the things you share in common with him, and his influence on your work. I will talk about Chekhov's siblings and yours. You had the exact same number, though the genders were different, and, obviously, you were born into very different times. Chekhov had four brothers: Alexandr and Nikolai were the eldest. Mijail and Ivan were younger than him, as was Maria, the only daughter. Six in total. Both of you died of tuberculosis. You had four sisters: Vera and Chaddie were the eldest. The younger ones were Beauchamp (I'll call her that, by the family name, because she died prematurely and was never given a name of her own), Jeanne and Leslie, the only boy. Six in total, or rather five. But no matter.

'Yes, I did,' she says.

Her answers are always very brief. She's shy. I realised this the first time I offered her a biscuit. Perhaps she lent me the book out of shyness. She looks rather like Ida, Katherine's lover. And despite her long hair, she also reminds me of the handsome John Middleton Murry with his boyish face. He was Katherine's other lover or husband or whatever.

'Have you read the whole thing?' she asks.

'Yes, here you are,' I say, holding the book out to her.

'No, no, you carry on reading. I just wanted to point out a description towards the end, which might just be the best ever.'

'Which one?'

The Murry girl leafs through the pages.

'This one,' she says, running her finger over the paragraph in question.

'Yes, you're right. It's a beautiful description of death. It makes me cry every time I read it.'

'It's the best I've ever read,' she says, as our eyes meet. She isn't beautiful, but she has a very piercing gaze. I like her a lot; she has a pleasant, thoughtful face. And her rather pale skin gives off an air of freshness and joy. She really does remind me of, yes, a photograph of Murry.

'May I?' she says, and I notice she is blushing.

'What?' I ask.

'Read the description out loud.'

'Yes, of course! Lovely.'

'Who's lovely?'

'Why, the description,' I say, laughing.

V

She comes closer. Our faces are almost touching. The book is there between us, resting in my hands. She starts to read. Her voice is soft as a whisper. I sigh.

'There lay a young man, fast asleep – sleeping so soundly, so deeply, that he was far, far away from them both. Oh, so remote, so peaceful. He was dreaming. Never wake him up again. His head was sunk in the pillow, his eyes were closed; they were blind under the closed eyelids. He was given up to his dream. What did garden parties and baskets and lace frocks matter to him? He was far from all those things. He was wonderful, beautiful. While they were laughing and while the band was playing, this marvel had come to the lane. Happy . . . happy. All is well, said that sleeping face. This is just as it should be. I am content.'

'It's just perfect,' I say, wiping away my tears and quietly observing the sweet tears running down her face too.

'Have all the biscuits gone?' asks the ticket man. I hadn't even noticed he had come back.

'No,' I say, meanwhile feeling for the packet in my bag.

'What about you . . . aren't you feeling well?' he asks, with a nod in the direction of my Murry girl.

'Me? No, I'm fine,' she says with a defiant look on her face.

I offer him the biscuits. He takes a few and leaves, perhaps alarmed by that look. I realise they loathe each other. But why?

VI

If I didn't have the distinct impression that my Murry girl really isn't much of a talker, I would tell her that Katherine's story has certain autobiographical roots: apparently, her parents were giving a summer party and sent Vera, Katherine's older sister, to take some food to the family of a young workman who had died. And Vera, like Laura in the story, set off in her party dress and hat to the backstreet located behind Tinakori Road where the young man had lived.

But, no, you wouldn't be interested. Perhaps you enjoy poetry as much as I do! I could talk about that too. As well as my love of flowers and parties . . . In time, we could become very close. We will live in my apartment, furnished with rugs of assorted textures, on which

I sit each evening laying out my tarot cards: they told me I would meet someone from another life. Could that be you? My interests: French films, making love in French, speaking French – if only I knew how! Friends: Gerardo and Paulette, a pair of parrots. French women seem so wild and adventurous. Two qualities I absolutely adore! If I could, I would decorate my apartment in French style, but I know nothing about decor. My dreams: to be a singer, although what I actually do is paint. I would like to collect men of rare beauty, my Murry girl, but I would never tell you that. I would prepare a room just for them and shut them up in there until I needed them. *La Chambre des Marionnettes*, I would call it. And there's also a fantasy I would like to live out before I die – 'If I die, but what am I saying? No, I will never die' – which is to play the prostitute for a night, then come home and fall asleep naked on the rug. Then wake up and watch a French film, it wouldn't matter what. And masturbate while I watch the actors. Later, I would take a man out of my special room in order to satisfy my need to paint naked men. I would shave them first. The painting would be something along the lines of Michelangelo's *Creation of Adam*, with his perfect physique, like that of a Greek god. Then I would make love with my *marionnette* and, finally, smoke a cigarette while gazing out to sea from the balcony . . . Now and then, you will go back to your own apartment, and I will be left alone. I don't like living with people for too long. I love being alone. Then, when I need you, I'll give you a call. You will visit me under the sobriquet John Middleton Murry. I will greet you wearing the kimono I bought after visiting a Japanese exhibition. We will sit on the rug to talk: . . . the thing you can hear purring is my cat Wingly. And this is Ribni, my doll-daughter, a recent arrival. Later, the three of us will drink *une tasse de thé*.

La Première Voyageuse

VII

The train is coming into the station. I stand up and smile. My little geisha does the same.

'Enjoy the rest of your journey,' I say.

'Thank you,' she says.

If I wasn't so shy, I would say:

'By the way, my name's Marion, like Katherine Mansfield's friend.' She'll laugh and so will I. 'But not Marion Ruddick, my name's Miller. Although, of course, if you've ever seen photos of Murry, Katherine's husband, you'll have realised that, given my looks, I would be the ideal choice to play him in a Hollywood biopic.'

She will say:

'Yes, you're right.'

I'll laugh again.

'Here's my address and telephone number,' and I'll hand her my card, 'write to me or call. Oh, forgive me, I'm talking so much I haven't even given you a chance to introduce yourself. Quick, tell me now, otherwise, the train will leave and I'll miss my stop . . .'

I leave. The ticket man walks past me in the opposite direction.

La Deuxième Voyageuse

VIII

She really is very shy. The Murry girl left without telling me her name. I should have introduced myself, thus prompting her to do the same.

Don't sit there! Don't sit there now! What a pest the man is!

'Has your friend gone?'

'Look, I don't have any more biscuits!'

'What's your name?'

God, I was stupid. Oh, Katherine, why didn't you think of that before? Of course, you were too captivated by her innocence and her resemblance to John Middleton Murry. She might have talked more if you had told her your name. She would say:

'What a coincidence! But your surname isn't Mansfield, is it?'

'No, what gave you that idea?' I would say. 'My name's Purcell, Katherine Purcell. Here's my card. Give me a call sometime.'

'What's your name? Hey, you kind of disappeared for a moment there.'

'Look, I don't have any more biscuits!'

'Has anyone ever told you how pretty you are when you go all thoughtful?'

'No, they haven't! And regrettably I don't have a single biscuit left.'

She would have laughed and said:

'Yes, I'll call you.'

'Enjoy the rest of your journey. And remember, give me a call!'

And who knows what else would have happened afterwards.

La Première Voyageuse

IX

I open the front door. As usual, I'm alone, no dog, no cat, no tortoise. I turn on the TV. Laura Pausini is singing one . . . two . . . three beautiful songs. I feel tense. I turn up the volume, I sit back and remember the ticket man, imagine him walking past me in the opposite direction, then sitting down next to the young woman and flirting with her. They kiss, oh, please, not that; his teeth were just disgusting. Enough to make you throw up.

I'll meet her again one day. Then, as well as my name, I'll tell her I'm a writer. Needless to say, I won't mention that I was unjustly accused of plagiarising Mansfield's 'The Garden Party'. We'll talk a little, while I smoke a cigarette. You'll say that you enjoy reading Maupassant in the original, as well as Dickens, Flaubert, Austen and the Brontës. You'll ask:

'What do you think of Emily's *Wuthering Heights?*'

You know, I imagine you all dressed in pink, like the girls in Proust's *À l'ombre des jeunes filles en fleurs*, who won him the Prix Goncourt. You'll say that, sometimes, you dream of being surrounded by butterflies, and I'll laugh. I'll invite you back for tea and we'll be happy.

X

I want to dream that I'm in love with a Katherine who has the look of a Japanese doll, a Katherine who lives in BUENOS AIRES. I've always dreamed of visiting BUENOS AIRES, making love in BUENOS AIRES, being a famous writer in BUENOS AIRES . . . I'm tired and feel like crying. Feel like climbing the walls. What are you saying? Are you mad? Why not use this whole incident to write a good story? Write, Marion! Write and cut the bullshit!

If this were a story written in the style of Katherine Mansfield, it would be called 'Something Childish but Very Natural' or 'Minor Loves'. Or who knows what else. In that case, I will write it tomorrow. The most important part is there already. It's all in my head, so now I can stop. 'When you stop you are as empty, and at the same time never empty but filling, as when you have made love to someone you love. Nothing can hurt you, nothing can happen, nothing . . .' old Hemingway used to say. Yes, I'll do it for her and for our moment of passion in 'The Garden Party'. I'll carry on tomorrow.

If this were a story, Katherine would begin like this:

She is sitting beside me. She takes a packet of biscuits out of her handbag and offers me one.

'No, thank you,' I say.

In fact, I'm as hungry as a biscuit-crazy she-hound . . . ∎

DAVID ALIAGA

1989

David Aliaga was born in L'Hospitalet de Llobregat, near Barcelona, Spain. He has written about the question of Jewish identity in literature for *Avispero, Jewish Renaissance, Mozaika* and *Quimera*. His fiction books include *Y no me llamaré más Jacob* and *El año nuevo de los árboles*.

INSOMNIA OF THE STATUES

David Aliaga

TRANSLATED BY DANIEL HAHN

'I start to give an account . . . because
someone has asked me to.'
– Judith Butler, *Giving an Account of Oneself*

Later, when I was back at the hotel, wakeful as I invariably am in the small hours, I would ask myself if the whole thing had really happened, the snow and the night, the flashing red and blue of the police car, and my doubts and the cold, that whole nocturnal tangle. I thought I had heard one of the agents call the other Valjean, and I considered googling the nearest police station, calling up and asking if Officer Valjean was on duty, but I didn't. I left the episode to get muddled in my memory until I could no longer tell whether the recollection was real or dreamed, and it was not until months after the trip that I told Daniela about it. She didn't know whether to take the account as accurate or to be infected by my doubts. She just said: Man, sounds like you lived out one of your stories.

It happened the night it finally started snowing. I'd been in the city for four days already and people hadn't stopped saying that the storm was going to hit our group of Salon du livre guests before we got our flights back home. That we were going to see Montreal pulling its winter cloak over its shoulders, that the fair usually coincided with the first snow of the year, bestowing charm and authenticity on the experience of the fifteen guys who, like me, had been invited by the Quebec government to discover the city and its literary talents.

It did occur to me, as I wandered distractedly along rue Notre-Dame Ouest without realising that in the damp, all-enveloping chill, fragile stars of ice had started to stir, that in a sense, whenever I spoke of our group in Spanish, it would have been more precise to refer to our group of 'guys' collectively not as fifteen *tipos* but fifteen *tipas*. To a Spanish speaker like myself, normalising a mixed group to a collective feminine wasn't standard in linguistic terms, but if from nine in the morning, as we visited the offices of the city's main francophone publishers, to the afternoon in the meeting room of the conference centre and right up until I invented some excuse not to go for dinner with the others, we were bound together by that condition of invited guests, professional colleagues, trawlers for brilliant and sellable texts, and circumstance really did require – did it? – a defining of the group's collective gender, then a group comprising thirteen female editors and two male editors was undeniably feminine.

Not fifteen guys, then, not fifteen *tipos*, but fifteen *tipas*. Of course, the words publishers or editors, as we designated ourselves every so often in our lingua franca, English, were lexical units that did not present this problem – I've always thought English a language that offered greater possibilities for confusion, for blurring the edges and for breaching, falling even after the final hurdle, the gap between the event itself and what gets recounted. But in Spanish, in my head, I needed to choose. In French, too. The Parisian publisher, Marie, was an *éditrice*, not an *éditeur*. And I couldn't help referring, when I did so, to us as fifteen *editores*, again generalising to the masculine, not *editoras* – invited *editores*, European *editores* – but I was not at all displeased by the thought (and I discovered this when something cold and featherlike smudged my left cheek with sleet) that those days challenged the possibility of an identity that was monolithically masculine.

I had learned that to get back to the hotel all I needed to do was find one of the main roads that cross the city from north to south or from east to west and walk down it until I recognised a metro station – Sherbrooke, Square-Victoria-OACI, Rosemont, Bonaventure – that would reorientate me and allow me to stroll on towards rue McGill, which I recognised in reverse by the dreamy impression that the ochre light of the street-lamp reflections in the pale brown facades produced in me, and because some of the restaurants stayed open late, among them a fish and chip place where I ended up having dinner on the subsequent nights, as well as a twenty-four-hour convenience store managed by a Sikh man where on the three previous ones I'd bought a bottle of water and some packets of liquorice before retiring to my room. But at that time, when I thought about the fifteen *editoras*, I was still far from rue Saint-Paul. Some forty-five minutes away, maybe forty if I picked up the pace. This was a less busy street with hardly any stores, and barely any cars at that time, and often the few light bulbs that were still lit on the other side of the windows would melt into darkness and night and dream as I walked past.

I'm not really sure why, but I decided to leave rue Notre-Dame Ouest, one of the streets that served as a guarantee on my night-time walks, and turned right. Rue Guy, according to the sign on the corner. It was a slightly darker street. The lamps on both pavements were more spaced out than on the main road, and it appeared that the men and women who lived in those three-storey houses had decided to go to sleep even earlier. Except for one woman. She must have been ten or a dozen years older than me, though I might be wrong. She was sitting beside the window in a relaxed pose, with her hair tied back any old how, comfortably dressed and reading. I found the picture strangely satisfying. It was somehow reassuring to watch her for a few moments, as if I were sitting in that living room myself, in baggy trousers and a sweatshirt with a book in my hands, feeling the central heating at a temperature that allowed my body to call it home.

I tried to make out, from all those metres away, what book it was that she was reading. My eyesight did not, of course, reach that far, but I got it into my head that she was reading Annie Ernaux. Or at least, that is how I wanted to complete the scene. I don't know why Ernaux and not, oh, Modiano, say, who's much more melancholy and nocturnal. Maybe because the woman who'd been sitting on my right on the plane from my stop in Frankfurt to Montreal had been reading *The Years*, and I had snooped indiscreetly over her arm and thought Ernaux seemed like a writer who was powerful and delicate at the same time, discovering that her books were inhabited by rage and subtlety . . . But then I hadn't read any more Ernaux than the four furtive paragraphs from the flight and I couldn't ultimately know why I'd placed one of her books into the warm hands of that woman with the messily tied hair and comfortable clothing who was reading in her apartment on rue Guy.

The reader must have noticed that there was somebody watching her from the street, and while if she could have seen the look in my eyes she would have found, I like to think, a frank, almost tender curiosity, she nonetheless moved away from the windowsill, turned off the light and went to read somewhere else because, though the room remained in darkness, its contours continued to be illuminated by the blaze of a lamp somewhere deeper in the house, in a room my curiosity couldn't reach.

I set off walking again, and a couple of blocks later it occurred to me that perhaps I ought to retrace my steps and ring the doorbell to apologise. Who would be happy having some stranger's gaze intruding into their private space? To have a pair of eyes questioning a scene from our lives, asking who are you and why are you reading by the window, at this time, in those clothes, with your hair untidy like that, and what book are you reading, why that book and not some other, what are you doing alone and awake when the others are sleeping, what does all this say about you and what can I imagine, I who don't know you at all, except that I've started to create your portrait, to enclose your existential possibilities around these queries that I express with the absurd legitimacy of someone looking from the street into your apartment? But that would only have been weirder still.

I turned another corner on a whim. Rue Ottawa. I'd not walked this one before. Or at least I didn't recognise the road, the landscape. The snow was intensifying, and despite that, beneath the chill, I think I was able to smell the sea closer than on any of my other Montreal wanderings. The black sky collapsed into tiny winter feathers that were impossible to count and that were now refusing to turn into moisture on the sidewalk and were instead covering it in white, and they were making it slippery. Montreal was becoming smudged with snow and night.

The first person to warn me about the storm had been the taxi driver who'd picked me up at the airport. A big, very dark Haitian man, who spent the first fifteen or twenty minutes of the journey listening to a strange radio station on which somebody very angry was giving a speech in French, occasionally prompting fired-up shouts from the crowd. I asked him something in that same language, which when spoken by me did not much resemble that of Ernaux or Modiano, nor that of the political agitator coming through the speakers, and then, as if bashful, he turned the volume down on the radio. *D'où êtes-vous?* he asked me. His French didn't sound like the writers I love either. He talked in a voice that was different to what I expected from Bergounioux or Volodine, more cavernous and bewildered. *De Barcelone, d'Espagne*, I replied, though these coordinates didn't really explain all that much about me. *Je viens de la Méditerranée*, I should have said, and perhaps that way my response would have had more meaning for me. But I said *Barcelone* in the first instance, and then *Espagne* – I silenced a *Catalogne* that I suspected would have been entirely useless to a Haitian cabbie in Montreal – and the driver located me on his map according to those two geographical reference points and whatever Barcelona and Spain meant in his head, which were, of course, very different things to what they meant in mine when I spoke the two place names. For example: *Ah, Barcelone! Football, Messi, Griezmann.* I smiled, nodding – what polite comment would I have made if he'd explained to me that he was Haitian instead of my having discovered it from the radio station he was tuned in to? Ah, Haiti, yes I saw a documentary once about the houngan and those powders they use to transform human beings into demented zombies! Football, Messi, Griezmann, he said. At least one of my grandfathers was a Barça fan. Sometimes, when I go past the stadium or when, hopping cable channels, a match happens to pop up, I think about my *pappous*, and about the times we went to the grounds together, and how with my first pay cheque I bought him a blue-and-scarlet shirt because he'd never had one before and he put it on to go watch the club play that day, even though he was embarrassed to be wearing sports clothing on the street. After all, if this taxi driver also had a football team, especially if he'd inherited it, with no possibility of renunciation or reason, or if he followed the Montreal Canadiens because his first landlord in Quebec had been a fan, or his Canadian wife, or because when his father arrived from the Caribbean he'd worked at the rink cleaning the seats or selling popcorn, but at the same time maintained his association with some Haitian institution or other, in his chance comment I had actually begun intuitively to understand some of the links that just happened to bind me to Barcelona.

From Barcelona, but that's not where your roots are from, right? One of the three German editors in our group, speaking English, was trying to work it out. *Your surname isn't typically Spanish, is it? I've not heard it before.* A woman with grandmotherly charm, a look in her blue eyes that was crystalline and genial, who had lived in Madrid for two years and from time to time did venture to talk in Spanish. I shrugged and smiled back at her. Could be, I started to explain, rather tired from a whole day spent switching between English and French, not knowing in which of the two languages I felt clumsier, more caged. My father's grandparents were Jews from Thessaloniki who arrived in Spain before the war. Thanks to that, they survived. Just about. Of course they fared better than the family they had left behind. Muzzled, but alive. And about how there are Jews in Spain, a lot of them, who've forgotten that on the afternoon when the Falangists took Barcelona, they went to plunder the synagogue on Calle Provenza, they unrolled the Sefer Torah in the middle of the asphalt and pissed on it . . . That's how philo-Semitic the fascist and his dogs were. Any one of my four grandparents – my maternal ones were Sephardi from Morocco, from Tangiers, do you know Tangiers? – who arrived when the dictator was already about to die would have cut off both their hands sooner than vote for the extreme right just because they happened to hate the Moorish bastards more than they hated the filthy Jews, and because they sang praises to Israel – to only one part of Israel, the part they had an interest in – as a shield for the West, I'd started to tell her, sounding angry, because I always end up telling anybody who asks about the marriage between the Spanish thing and the Jewish thing or between Barcelona and the Catalan, sounding angry, that Spain is full of idiot Jews. But yes, my surname could be Spanish after all, I resumed, when I realised that my words and my overexcitement were casting a pall over that endearing gesture of hers, which didn't deserve to be tarnished with rage or with concern. Why not? After all, in the fourteenth century there had been thousands of Jews who left Barcelona, Girona, Tortosa . . . also Toledo or Cordoba, headed for Europe and North Africa. Perhaps I'm the product of a return trip.

During the welcome dinner, the Portuguese editor Soares asked who our favourite writers were, to break the ice at our end of the table, where we sat along with the Bulgarian editor, Annetta, and the Venetian, Flavia, and the Parisian. I squirmed in my chair. I never know how to answer this. Or rather, yes, I do know, but I also know that I'll regret it tomorrow, or only a short while afterwards, there'll be other writers I prefer; depending on my state of mind that evening I'll arrive home and start rereading some book by Charles Simic and I'll stand on the sofa, and I'll read lines out loud, and Daniela will come into the living room and laugh, and she'll call me a clown, and I'll laugh too. And another evening I'll be reading the French writers, Modiano, Quignard, Michon, and I won't want to talk until quite some time after I've closed the novel because I'll still be living in it a little, in a spectral Paris, in a spiderweb of

betrayals during the occupation, in the search for a murdered girl
in the camps, faced with a prophetess from whose eyes a river is
flowing, in the tobacconist's in a town in Languedoc or crossing a
bridge in a Brittany village. And so I went with the French, whom
I tend to prefer when among readers for whom Thomas Pynchon
or Richard Ford would be too obvious a choice. Marie opened her
eyes a little wider and said something like, *Vous lisez des auteurs
complexes, des grands écrivains!*, which is what I wanted her to say,
because sometimes I'm a reader of *Spider-Man*, of *Doctor Strange*,
of *X-Men*, a reader who only wants to be left alone with forty-eight
pages strewn with onomatopoeia in his hand, and at others I'm the
still-young writer and editor who hasn't yet finished his doctorate
in literary theory but who reads *des auteurs complexes*, the ones not
everybody's heard of, and who does like to impress a fellow editor,
though straight after that he doesn't want to have to play the part of
a sophisticated kind of guy, or of an intellectual, and gets fed up with
himself, and who on arriving back at the hotel needs to call a friend
so they can laugh about something he said a couple of hours earlier.

This time I gave up in a matter of mere seconds, I shattered my
portrait, or the mask, or the mirror, and they no longer knew in which
fragment they'd really be able to find me, in the remnants that no
longer made up a single reflection they sought out my eyes or my
mouth with their questions, though their interest was only transient
and polite. The atmosphere was relaxed. Neither Flavia, nor Soares,
nor Annette, nor Marie were measuring me up as blatantly as the
Dutch woman was, and I redefined myself: *Pense pas. Grant Morrison
et Steve Englehart font également partie de mes favoris. Englehart?
Morrison?*, pronounced with the stress on the second o and an arched
eyebrow. Authors *de la BD*. I'm writing a doctoral thesis on superhero
comics. Guys in colourful tights who save the world from troubled
individuals like Baron Mordo or the Mole Man. And they burst out
laughing. All of them surprised – Soares genuinely amused, slapping
the table – reacting to what they find curious. Then the food arrived:
pizza, salad, pasta. Someone asked Flavia, I think I remember it

wasn't me – I hope it wasn't me – her views on the lasagne, and she said, of course, that it wasn't a patch on the one her mother made.

The salad was for me, the habit of not ordering even the four-cheese pizza I fancied due to the suspicion that they'd handle the cheese without washing their hands after putting the pieces of speck on Soares's pizza, the mincemeat in Flavia's lasagne. And I found that unpleasant, too. I had tried, on other occasions, once in Washington when I was travelling with my first partner – I've made myself use the word partner, at the time I said girlfriend – to eat a pulled-pork burger with Cheddar cheese sauce. But then a feeling of discomfort, an urge to throw up, had emerged from someplace, my grandmother putting her fingers in my mouth, between the chewed-up pork and reaching to the back of my throat, jabbing at my oesophagus with her index and middle fingers, and I had thrown the hamburger onto the plate, angry, with a feeling of unease in my chest, and now she's looking at me funny, my angry grandmother, perhaps pretending to be angrier than she really was, saying to me: we're Jewish and we don't eat pork or cheese together with meat. And me not eating it, and asking myself what the hell it meant that we were Jewish, that I was Jewish, and if for me it had something to do with – as it did, of course . . . sometimes – with the way I looked at food, with not eating the same as other people and them asking me about it, and my sometimes simplifying things or disguising them by saying I was a vegetarian, or at other times that I didn't eat meat or, finally, that I was Jewish.

A young Jewish writer like Jonathan Safran Foer, Soares wanted to compliment me. I stammered some kind of affirmation. We did at least share some reference points related to the Jewish question and to the literary. In Barcelona, in Spain, where I'd told the taxi driver I came from, the place where I *was* from – but how could I be? and yet how could I *not* be, at least a bit? – a Jew was, as a friend of mine said, a unicorn, a fantastical creature of the kind my neighbours had heard of, but when they discover one right in front of them they look for the horn or the tail, and say the strangest and most regrettable things, even if they're trying to be friendly. Are you Jewish? And what is that, being Jewish? Do you believe in God?, or, more troubled, You don't believe in Jesus? And in addition: do you Jews do this, or do you not do that? And even: are you circumcised? But also: how can you possibly like Michon and Englehart, Pynchon and *A Song of Ice and Fire*, Aronofsky, Wagner and football, all at the same time? Why don't you come have dinner with the rest of us? Why did you order pulled pork, child? Aren't you going to be parents? Why have you chosen to sign a name that isn't the name we gave you? Why do you lend it to your characters? Mind if we ask what you're doing wandering around on your own at this time of night, with the way it's coming down? Are you okay? What's your name, *monsieur*?

The Montreal municipal police car was lighting up the street, the black night and the white snow, in blue and red. The two officers were looking at me with a certain pre-emptive cautiousness – I might be a madman or a drunk, or both those things, and I have been both those things, the former more than the latter, on certain days in my life. The one called Valjean asked again: *Ça va, monsieur?* And right away his partner added: *Are you okay, sir?* In case I didn't understand. I was sitting down. I suddenly saw myself, with no memory of how I'd ended up there, on the stone plinth of a granite sculpture, with very straight lines, bulky, on which the snow had settled. I tried to recognise the guy who was being depicted in the stone, but neither his shape nor the inscription on the plinth meant anything to me. I turned to the officers and nodded. I would have said *oui* or *yes*, I suppose.

How long had I been there? They helped me to my feet and bit by bit I returned to reality. All of a sudden my body became aware of the cold. The total black and white that I remembered from right before the officers arrived had evaporated. Are you a tourist? And with my head clearer, afraid I might have a problem, I explained that I was an editor, that I was in the city for a few days as a guest of their government for the Salon du livre. They exchanged a look, Valjean and the other man, and then they turned to me again. Passport? The other asked, and I groped around in the pockets of my overcoat and held it out to him. He opened it with hands much more adept at operating in gloves than mine, he glanced at it and asked: So, you are Mr David Aliaga?

The one who wasn't called Valjean and whose name I would never know handed my passport back to me. ∎

AURA
GARCÍA-JUNCO

1988

Aura García-Junco was born in Mexico City.
She is the author of the novel *Anticitera, artefacto
dentado* and a forthcoming collection of essays
about love. 'Sea of Stone' is an excerpt from her
forthcoming novel, *Mar de Piedra*.

SEA OF STONE

Aura García-Junco

TRANSLATED BY LIZZIE DAVIS

Even the ~~gods~~ can't avoid fate.
Under the crossed-out word, a response by another
hand, in another color:
Unless the gods are men.

Found on a wall on the Paseo de las Estatuas,
Colonia Centro, Mexico City, 2025.

Federal Law Against Missing Persons Takes Effect.

WEDNESDAY 30 NOVEMBER 2011, 12:51 P.M.

Within three days of being passed, the controversial federal law against missing persons, which ends any ongoing investigation in the event that a missing person be found in statue form, has been enforced for the first time.

Nearly four months after the disappearance of Eloísa Montiel, a history major at the Universidad Nacional Autónoma de México (UNAM), relatives of the student confirmed that her statue has been found on the Paseo de las Estatuas, formerly known as Avenida Madero, in the center of the capital. Montiel's relatives offered no further comment.

Accordingly, the student's case file has been officially closed, amid a large number of public protests against the law, endorsed by majority this month. Given the growing number of statues, it is expected that this law will halt most similar missing persons investigations in the capital.

After

Two encounters on the Paseo de las Estatuas
(formerly Avenida Madero), 2025

Life moves along as routinely as it does on any Sunday. Only one person can be seen. Statues fill the entire avenue; they cover the pavement once meant for cars. Their presence paints the space gray. Gray: the mood in the air, like a graveyard, a shipwreck, like rubble. Figures of men, women, even children, all of them standing, their assorted outfits made uniform by the color of the stone. There are fat ones and thin ones; some are unusually tall (the old man with the mustache, nearly seven feet), some can only see the others' chests, their rigid necks don't allow them to look up.

There's a man, standing in front of a statue of a woman in a dress. She's a little smaller than he is, and thin, so light, he thinks, she almost seems to float, though she clearly can't. He wouldn't be able to pick her up even one inch from the ground. How much could she weigh? A ton? He imagines the short, loose-fitting dress ruffling in a breeze of bluish wind, the brilliant colors he's sure once adorned the fabric. He imagines the skirt, in that waft of air, lifting just a moment to reveal a bit of thigh, how her youthful skin must have quivered. He imagines the elusive warmth of what no longer is. The man looks at her and thinks, only thinks, of touching her; he intuits the texture under his fingertips: slippery, cold and stern.

I've been dreaming of this moment since I was a kid. I would tug on your hardened skirt and it would turn to cloth; a lock of hair would slip down your forehead. Your stare so piercing, I'd freeze in place. Your eyes – sometimes brown and sometimes blue – would blink, and you'd give me the most beautiful gaze I've ever seen, either dreaming or awake.

From inside the lull, I would become aware that something wasn't right. My eyes were dry, I couldn't close them. I'd start to panic; I'd try to move my arms and run, skip, anything. Impossible. But you'd blink, and my silent scream suddenly turned into pleasure again, I didn't need to close my eyes anymore; I wanted to look at you forever. Solid already, I became the one you adored.

I had that dream a thousand times as a teenager. I lost it for a while, when I lost myself, too, in my wandering; but now, here, I remember it as though I'd dreamt it last night. One significant difference: I could touch you in the dream. It's not that I can't here. You're closer to me than a lot of things are, but you're like a museum statue here, thousands of years old. It would be like touching something sacred. I reach out, pull my hands back before they touch your stone skin. The magic of an instant: This is the Moment. The Meaning. Mana.

The man almost expects the statue to respond to his inner monologue. He avoids blinking, as in his dream, for fear of missing something. Stone and flesh face to face in the same immobility. If it weren't for the colors, it'd be hard to tell which one was breathing. Such is the perfection of the statue.

His eyes narrow. He knows in that instant he's in a state of complete awareness, which almost never happens, but which allows him to sense and perceive things he normally can't: vibrations, signs, responses. That's how he senses now, even before it's visible, another presence approaching. The stillness is broken. The look on the face of the woman who walks up behind the statue expresses surprise: she wasn't expecting anyone. Those who are able to look at each other, do, and frown with their supple lips.

Now

Sofia

Is she drunk already? She doesn't think so. Though maybe. Very possibly. When the once vague desire to kiss Ulani moves further into the realm of possibility, the answer tips toward an emphatic *yes*. She's drunk, and it's dangerous. *Control yourself, Sofia.* Before

Sofia's thoughts can go much further, Ulani returns; she starts sitting down, but instead leans in to kiss her. Sofia has no time to think about anything but the texture of her lips.

'There are lots of people here. Should we go to your place instead?' Ulani murmurs softly, a hint of shyness. Sofia's inner voice blares: *Absolutely not, say no.*

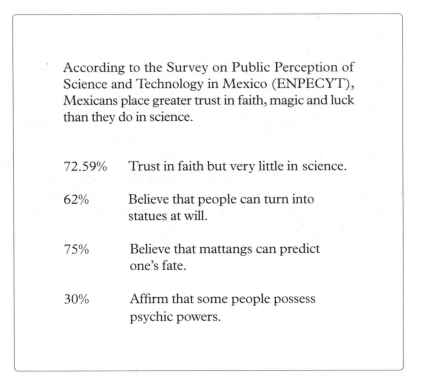

According to the Survey on Public Perception of Science and Technology in Mexico (ENPECYT), Mexicans place greater trust in faith, magic and luck than they do in science.

72.59%   Trust in faith but very little in science.

62%   Believe that people can turn into statues at will.

75%   Believe that mattangs can predict one's fate.

30%   Affirm that some people possess psychic powers.

Sofia looks into her eyes: they're green, small, like a sea concentrated into one point. Closer, closer still. Their noses brush, and her field of vision is overwhelmed. They hesitate, not daring to touch lips, but the distance, so small now, is charged with a caress that spreads over their entire bodies. The taste of wine on their breath mingles, and their tongues, timid, glide over unfamiliar teeth. The tangle of their arms tightens as their need becomes more urgent. Their breasts press together, crushed, distorted by the pressure. She feels dampness. She feels that fine face in her hands, as they now navigate downward, toward her small, slender shoulders. Neck, clavicles, shoulder blades, armpits, chest rising, straps falling, cleavage, flesh spilling over her hands. Eyes: a student. Unwelcome moment of recognition, of doubt: *This is bad, it's awful, I'm her professor. How old is she? Twenty-three? Twenty-four?*

Ulani sits on her lap. She kisses her deeply and sways her hips, lowers her shirt again, which had risen back up, and exposes her breasts, lifted by the elastic band of her top, just in front of Sofia's flushed face. Her eyes take in the brown skin, bristling, the fine hairs velvet to her touch. Her belly tightens, her body becomes rigid, but Sofia can't. She begins formulating exit strategies. She gently takes hold of Ulani, adjusts her shirt. She kisses her, brushes her cheek.

'Forgive me.'

Ulani looks at her, confused, her eyes two green flashes.

'I'll be right back,' Ulani says, and gets up. She leaves a wake of tiare flowers behind that rocks Sofia's thoughts. Ocean under her clothes. The tides of her mind shift toward one view of Ulani: the way she laughed at dinner, the slow choreography of their bodies, the comments she made, so surprisingly witty. *Barely more than a teenager. Well, no, not quite that, but a student, yes. What's happening to me, Eloísa? Why did I bring her here?*

'I'd like to talk through some things that I'm not clear on, about the relationships between women in the tribe you mentioned today.'

'Sure. Why don't we meet during my office hours?'

'Actually, I was thinking we could go somewhere closer to your place, so you don't have to waste your time on the commute.'

My professional filter quit working, and I could see her: her brown skin, her green eyes, that slightly crooked smile, standing in front of me in the faculty lounge. I don't know if what she said qualified as flirtation, or if she was simply asking me out. What do you think, Elo? No one in the department knows I'm a lesbian, at least I haven't told anyone. Is it obvious?

Sofía throws back what's left of her wine and pours more. She hesitates for a moment and doesn't fill Ulani's cup; she's on her way back from the bathroom already, cheeks newly washed. She sits back down in the chair and holds out her hand.

'Did you do this?' She's brought over a small framed drawing.

'A friend of mine did.'

'Why are you keeping it in the bathroom, collecting dust? It's really nice.'

Sofía is surprised; so many years on the wall have turned it into one more invisible object in the apartment, the kind she has learned to ignore.

'I'll tell you another time.'

'Ah, so we *will* be seeing each other again.' Ulani shoots her another slightly crooked smile and takes a drink from the only cup that isn't empty.

Sofía doesn't know what to say. From the midst of her violent self-disgust, the desire to kiss her surfaces again. She's not thinking clearly, and the tingling of the wine weaves a fine layer over her skin. Instead of stopping herself, she bends toward Ulani and guides her backward. When the girl is lying down, she holds her arms and lowers her shirt with her teeth. A sigh.

Definition

A mattang is made by interlacing small wands of coconut fiber. It's a map of the waters of time assigned to you by the cosmos. A bit of shell might represent an island, a person, something that makes you sad; or it might be a current, a path, the solution to a problem. If you look at someone else's mattang, you won't be able to interpret it, even if you understand your own very well. Don't despair. Unlike other maps, each mattang is made to be deciphered by just one pair of eyes. Your mattang is yours alone, the keeper of your destiny. Decode it with the help of time and mana. It's not easy, and sometimes what appears obvious – that curve in the rod that compels you to turn around, make a decision, end a relationship, quit a job – is something totally different: an invitation to weather the waves and avoid the obstacle, stay the course. One must read one's destiny very carefully. Trust yourself: in the end, you're the best and only captain of your life's vessel.

– Mattangs: A New Spiritualist's Handbook for Reading the World. Third Edition.

In bed, their bodies a downy mass of skin and Ulani's sweet scent, Sofía considers staying another hour, until the next day, the next month. She shudders at the idea, the bitter taste of wine still on her lips. Slowly, she pulls her warm arm out from beneath the sleeping girl. She's boiling hot, but a certain modesty compels her to look for a cotton sweater, a black one that's covered in Clío's white hair; the cat meows in the kitchen.

Now in the living room, she drops onto the sofa. Something digs into her tailbone. She feels around with her hand: it's the drawing from the bathroom that fell between the cushions. She dusts it off with a wrinkled napkin. The drawing is of an open hand with a shell in the center. The shell is so tiny it nearly gets lost in the palm, as if it were floating there. The pencil lines are delicate, and over time they've begun fading into the yellowing paper. On the back of the frame, it reads 'For Sofía', and there's a lattice of smudged lines.

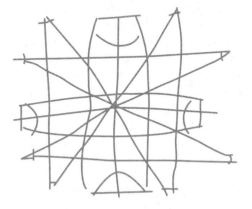

She never understood why Eloísa signed that way. When Sofía asked her about it – their first year of college, if she remembers correctly – she said, jokingly, that it was a map of herself.

'A mattang?' Sofía asked, suspicious. She had noticed that more and more of the people around her now believed in those maps like horoscopes or spiritual guides. The mattangs were showing up in unexpected places – her mother's coffee table, her roommate's bed – when only a decade ago, no one in Mexico knew they existed. She was missing something. In the books on navigation she'd consulted, there wasn't a single account of a spiritual use for the maps, much less were they made out to be some kind of crystal ball. No one had ever been able to explain to her how it was that one's present life and one's future life could be there, in a mooring of shells and branches.

'I don't know yet,' Eloísa said in that decisive tone she used so well, indication that there was nothing more to say.

In retrospect, with the drawing in front of her, she finds it ironic that Eloísa went around devising mattangs for a future she wouldn't have. Just as scientists look for the genes that cause premature death, cancer, baldness, could a mattang, she wondered, be used to find the precise moment of your death? *Maybe the secret of what happened to you is right here within these lines, Eloísa. Maybe your death is named here. Or maybe I'm completely losing my mind.*

It was ironic. The one certainty is that mattangs gave Sofía, who didn't believe in them as tools for divination, a future: becoming a scholar on the topic, if only to understand how the hell they'd become what they were for her Guadalupe-loving Mexico. After all those years and books, sometimes her only conclusion was that the appearance of the statues had caused a kind of collective insanity.

She hears Ulani's groggy footsteps; she's already dressed. Silent, her face one big smile, she throws herself onto the sofa. It's unclear who sets the first kiss in motion.

'In high school, we had this game where we used to look for map pairings. Did you ever do anything like that?' Ulani asks while contemplating the drawing Sofía is holding.

'No, I don't believe in that kind of thing.'

'Sure, that's what everyone says. You teach Polynesian and Micronesian history, but you only believe in its culture and geography. You collect mattangs, but you only see them as objects. You even study Kaula Aranda, but for art's sake alone. Want to know what I think? No one would spend her whole life on something unless she could see the magic of it, the mana. Otherwise, what are you keeping this drawing around for?'

Sofia's lips clench, her temples throb. Her hands tighten like claws on the frame. Ulani strokes them and opens them gently. She takes the drawing.

'No need to get upset. All I meant to say is that my friends and I thought it was fun to look for pairs of maps. We went to a technical high school in a neighborhood you've probably never been to, it's that ugly. After school let out, we'd ignore the older guys strutting around like peacocks outside and spend our time looking at mattangs and constellations instead, matching them up, sure our destinies were somewhere in the tangle – ridiculous things, like becoming millionaires, or famous actresses, or literature PhDs.'

Ulani pulls her backpack out from under the coffee table. She digs around inside and takes out a book. Sofia recognizes it: *Atlas for Understanding the World: New Oceanic Legends*. She wrote one of the essays in the collection, though she isn't proud to have contributed; Serratos, the man who edited it, is a fraud. Ulani flips to a page covered almost entirely by an image of the sky. Sofia is taken aback: she wrote about that set of oral traditions but never noticed the resemblance between the constellation and Eloísa's drawing. What are the odds of two parallel images appearing by pure chance, in a mattang and in the stars? Surely Eloísa's drawing was inspired by the one woven into the night sky, but that was so many years before the book that it didn't make sense either. An unexpected and inexplicable mirror. The small coincidences that make Sofia uncomfortable and make everyone else believe.

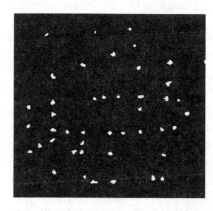 A new constellation appeared in the starry sky over the island of Rapa Nui, a very clear sky, pristine like none other, on that night of all nights. A young sailor's eyes remained open in his sleeplessness. Lying on his straw mat, he casually glanced up at the sky, and was overwhelmed to see a spectacle of celestial fireflies. They flitted about for a while until they fell into line, some side by side, some above or below. Fixed there in the firmament, they showed him the path he needed to travel to reach the first of the Pitcairn Islands.

Serratos, Marco Polo, Embleton, Sofia, et al., *Atlas for Understanding the World: New Oceanic Legends*, Santillana, 2022.

Ulani left an hour ago, more than enough time for a torrent of self-criticism and joy. Sofia drags her bare feet to the bathroom and hangs the drawing back up. It's suddenly become a strange object again, out of place despite years hanging there, since the spring of 2010. The room is so small she has to stand over the toilet to look at it. *Leave it there or take it down, that's the question. What do you think, Elo? You're the one who made it.*

She looks closely at the pencil marks. The hand is hers; the shell is the artist's invention. Something stirs in her reservoir of memories. She turns the drawing around, hangs it so the backing faces out. Eloísa's handwriting, the mattang that never was. It looks better that way, the 'For Sofia' says goodbye as she walks out of the bathroom.

Her phone buzzes: 'I'm running a little late, will get there closer to 7.30. Bringing wine and a little something for you.'

Only two hours away. A flash of excitement, an impulsive smile. Sofía sets the phone face down and returns to the printout on her desk, but realizes her concentration is gone.

Ulani is once again getting between her and her work, like she has these last few weeks, since the day they met. The classroom has become something else for her now. When she's teaching, the secret tension makes her heart beat harder; she's aware of every move she makes, how she looks at different angles. Ulani's eyes have become the center of a panopticon, and Sofía, the suspect of a crime. *Guilty* of a crime. Every day in front of the class, she wonders if anyone else knows what's going on between them; she looks for clues or confirmation in the students' faces. When she thinks about Ulani and the chance they'll be discovered, she feels a strange quickening between her legs. What scares her the most is to think she wouldn't be all that upset by it. She thinks about Luis, the most attractive boy in the class. Sofía's always thought him a bit of a jerk, though her only proof is the cocky tone he uses with his female classmates, who get flustered when they talk to him. She imagines him slightly humiliated, surely a little excited, should he find that the beautiful, gentle Ulani (Sofía has seen him looking at her) is not only indifferent toward him, but in fact prefers the teacher, a woman not so young anymore, somewhat boring, who could never compete with him in looks.

She's caught herself more than once imagining Ulani naked while teaching, the feel of skin against skin, her fingertips tracing the contours of her belly. When that happens, she has to contain her trembling and refocus attention on the class, which, despite her distractions, always seems to go according to plan. At other times, obvious signs of her predicament manifest themselves; she's sure she can pick up Ulani's scent, or feels something akin to a bright, balmy day in her chest, awash in the memory of her cascading laughter. She's beginning to feel intoxicated. All she can do is think of Ulani, of getting caught, or, worse, falling in love like an idiot, and Ulani leaving her, vanishing from the face of the earth, shattering her into a thousand pieces again. *What if I end it once and for all? I'll spare both of us my suffering; we won't destroy each other's lives.*

She breathes. She shoos the cat off her lap and ignores the strategic meowing. Then she tears a page from her notebook and writes: 'Be kind to her, it's not her fault that you're broken. Be kind to her, it's not her fault that you're broken. Be kind to her, it's not her fault that you're broken.' She walks to the bathroom, takes a big, dusty candle – sea-breeze-scented – and lights it, burning the page little by little, repeating the mantra inwardly. The smell of singed paper keeps time with the dancing embers, and tickles her nose. She can't help but sneeze, and her sneeze sends the embers flying.

She picks at one of the black spots flecking the sink, but it turns to dust between her fingers, and spreads a stain. She looks at her face; there's a smudge on her cheek. She leans in to brush it away, and a wrinkle under one eye catches her attention. *What if this is the last of my beauty? There wasn't that much to begin with.* The wrinkle seems to mark a trail across her skin, and she follows it with her hands, all the way to the laugh lines around her mouth. Her cheeks are dotted with black specks. Sofia takes off her shirt and her pants and stands in front of the mirror in her underwear. She evaluates her body part by part, dissects it like a butcher would a cow. She compares her slack stomach with Ulani's firm, sculpted belly, her graceless backside with Ulani's round, perfect buttocks.

She turns to one side, and her eyes catch on the little drawing hanging backwards on the wall: 'For Sofia', it recites. The hazy silhouette of 22-year-old Eloísa enters the bathroom and stands beside her. Sofia feels the pain of those first days after she went missing wash through her, press against her viscera. A pain that has been absent for fourteen years. *Invisible for so long, and now I can't stop looking at it.* She realizes Eloísa has always been there, she's a moat that surrounds her sealed castle, the void that guards her.

Sofia leaves the bathroom without getting dressed and goes to her room, just a few feet away in that tiny apartment. She rummages in the closet, digs through useless papers. Finally, she takes out a green box. It weighs more than she remembered, and trying to unlatch it she notices how the wood is warped by humidity. The box pops open with the sound of compressed air, and the dank smell intensifies. A photo: in the background, huge triangular prisms of rough, gray stone; down below, a valley of magma hardened into whimsical shapes. The campus sculpture park. In the image, Sofía smiles with a lightheartedness she hasn't felt in recent memory. A few inches away from her, though not touching, the Eloísa on paper smiles, yes, but her lips don't give the impression of lightness; they look rigid. *Lips holding back a secret, that's what I said to you once, and you laughed at me. In the end, your secret-keeping lips, the ones in the photo, held the secret of your disappearance.*

Too many memories. It's 6.30, and Ulani will be there at 7.30, and she hasn't written a single sentence. She sits down in the living room as is, mascara running, naked. She lets a minute go by.

'Today isn't going to work. I'm sorry, I'm just not feeling well. I'll let you know when I'm doing better.'

She sends the message and turns off her phone.

The photograph whispers in her hands. *Where are you, Eloísa?* Sofía feels a pull: toward the only location where Eloísa exists. She sets off on a furious race to where she swore she'd never return.

Three months later
Two encounters on the Paseo de las Estatuas
(formerly known as Avenida Madero)

Sofía

Who knows how the hell it happened, but I ended up here, in this cafe. Such a simple route, what could have gone wrong? After all, the other Eloísa has been grounded in that spot for eternity. Why should anything that involves her change? Everything's continued on exactly the same these three months. Going to see your statue is as ordinary as picking up something to eat. But against all odds, here I am. I had walked up from behind. I'd been thinking about Ulani the whole way, and when I realized that, it made my stomach turn: I was going to see my stone Eloísa with another woman (of flesh) on my mind. And my stomach jumped again, in response to the first time around. It is a mere statue, I thought, and you, Eloísa, are either dead or lost, and I need to accept it already and move on. I was nearly there, at my new sacred place, with all of these thoughts crowding my mind, when a head of tousled blond hair came into view on the other side of Eloísa's statue. He was wearing a suit, about thirty, upscale, looking at her spellbound – little calf-eyes, completely bovine. I felt like turning away, but curiosity won out. No, that's not true; I'll admit it. Crazy me, I was jealous. Of what, for fuck's sake? Jealous? It makes me a little sick, really, to think I can feel so possessive of a statue. But yes, that's just what I have to tell myself over and over, dear Eloísa, because the idea that it's only a statue is not automatic anymore: it's made of stone, a mere figure in the middle of the paseo, one among many others. And here I am at this fusty cafe, stirring a green tea, searching for an answer in the cup's watery folds like some pathetic believer in signs and omens, as if I were saying, *All right, little teacup, tell me who he is and what he's doing here, tell me if he isn't The Guy.* The tea, of course, stares back at me, its water-eye impassive, and I run out of time to think.

Luciano

We spent an hour in that cafe. I'd say she was in her mid-thirties: she's starting to show her age, but you can tell she was good-looking enough in her youth. She said her name is Sofía, and she was sucking on a cigarette from the moment we went to sit at an outdoor table. She surely wouldn't have skin like that if she didn't smoke so much, wrinkles, big pores. Such a shame when women let their vices destroy them. That's what I always tell mine, not because I plan on spending a lifetime with them, just so they're aware of what they're doing to themselves. No woman over thirty should be allowed to smoke. Her voice was deep and cocky, very masculine, really. Strange, since her long, dark curls and honey-colored eyes didn't strike me as particularly butch. She told me about Eloísa: she said that's her name. They were college friends, and one day she vanished. No one knew what happened, and then the statue showed up. That one, the same one I've visited since I was a kid. It took me less than a second to realize it was impossible; the years don't square.

'Are you sure that one – that exact one – is the woman you're talking about?' I asked.

The whites of her eyes said it all, she rolled them back hard as if to say, *Yes, you idiot, it has the face of someone I knew: I'm sure.* The tone of the conversation shifted then. I told her that was impossible, because that statue, mine, had been there a very long time, since I was a kid, and I'm already thirty-three. Her mouth twisted into a sneer: now she was laughing at me.

'Look, I can assure you that's the statue of Eloísa Montiel, *missing* since 2011. Fourteen years ago, to be exact, *disappeared.*'

'*Petrified*, in any case,' I answered.

'If that helps you sleep at night, then fine, *petrified, turned to stone.* Look it up, I'm sure you'll find something on the internet.'

We didn't get anywhere. But that's her – 'la Eloísa' – that's who I've been dreaming about all these years. The image of her face is as clear to me as a photograph, even though other things have faded away. It's not a trick: a harbinger as strong as a dream can't be false. I was more confused than upset by the things she said. I want to know where Sofía is in my mattang. I don't care if the reasons aren't clear to me yet, the answer always comes to those who know how to feel the sea. Mana. ■

MARTÍN FELIPE CASTAGNET

1986

Martín Felipe Castagnet was born in La Plata, Argentina. He is the author of the novels *Bodies of Summer* (translated into English by Frances Riddle) and *Los mantras modernos*. In 2017 he was selected by Bogotá39 as one of the best young Latin American writers.

OUR WINDOWLESS HOME

Martín Felipe Castagnet

TRANSLATED BY FRANCES RIDDLE

Swimming was prohibited in the lake at Little Pass: too many archaeological remains at the bottom. This didn't keep the local kids from trying to reach the lakebed in a single plunge, with all the air they could fit into their lungs. It was during one such dive, surrounded by the crumbled faces of a lost civilization, that Euphrates decided he wanted to become a woman and a sculptor. She emerged clutching a translucent stone that she had taken blindly from the muddy depths and she kept it for the rest of her life.

The stone was sitting on her desk as a paperweight when she opened the envelope, and it was the first thing she saw when she finally peeled her eyes from the test results. The puncture of the thick needle, the X-rays, the surgery, she didn't want to think about any of that: she had been through too many operations. Better to think only of the little ancient stone, her constant companion, or of the idols carved from marble and wood crowding the table, the statues, complete and incomplete, of people and animals, the carvings with their hypnotic waves all around her studio. Against one wall was the bed, a sofa really, where she slept (she had moved out of her bedroom, which now served as storage), the wool blanket grazing the floor. Her apprentice would put it in its place on her usual rounds . . . and tidy the piles of books even though no one ever asked her to . . . but how far was the blanket from actually touching the floor, she wondered . . . that one centimeter made all the difference . . . when Haydée says to her, You've left it on the floor again, she'll respond: No, it's not touching yet . . .

The sculptor blinked and resurfaced, her mind clear. She put the envelope in the third drawer of her desk. The news was expected, it didn't take her by surprise, but she had many issues left to resolve. She remembered all too well her writer friend, probably the most intelligent person she had ever known. But even though he was in bad health, he hadn't left a will and now his books were being published in shamefully bad taste: they'd printed his drafts, notes taken on napkins, even some of his grocery lists. That wasn't going to happen to her. She had a strong distaste for the legal side of things but she had resigned herself, just as she'd resigned herself to the doctor's appointments. It had already been decided that the final resting place for her body of work would be the regional museum which she had helped set up in Little Pass to exhibit some sculptures rescued from the lake. It wasn't the most prestigious museum or the one that would attract the largest crowd but a place filled with respectful hands, careful caretakers. They had yet to settle the final details but they were so close to reaching an agreement, with enthusiasm on both sides, that she wasn't really worried.

She touched each of her statues, one by one, or at least all of those she could reach. They were the few that were left, the ones she had been able to avoid selling off; if it were up to her she wouldn't have gotten rid of a single one: they were like family, silent relatives. Each one communicated a different feeling, like the one that brought to mind a steaming cup of tea, or the one that absorbed the heat of the day, no matter how cold it was. It was important to touch them, a ritual to wake them up and keep them alive. The swimmer crouched in diving position, completely doubled over, hands disappearing into the water or the air. The perfume seller, one of her first pieces: everyone swore they could smell the half-open box the young woman held with her head bent (she still ran into the model from time to time, now matronly with sagging breasts, working at the local paper shop). And the blind dog lying on his pedestal beside the studio door, perking up his ears but with an unfocused gaze. She stroked him: the bronze was smooth and worn. Her friends always petted him, at her insistence, for good luck.

Then, she said to herself as she left the studio, there's the issue of the headstone. She'd been working on it for the past few months, since the pain first started, even before she went to see the handsome doctor in the city. Haydée Ricci, her apprentice, had frowned at her pessimism (she should see the test results, that'd show her, the sculptor thought). A headstone is no small matter! It's a sculptor's final piece, like it or not. After thinking it over for a minute, Haydée asked, So it's going to be a sculpture over your grave? No, Euphrates responded, just a headstone, which is more than enough. That's fine, Haydée said after a while, everything an artist like you does can be considered sculpture. Euphrates smiled. In reality . . . I'm not going to sculpt it on my own. But it will be mine, she assured her. And even if she didn't sculpt it herself, what did it matter? A true artist, Euphrates had learned, could use anyone's hands. Where are my keys? Is there cider left or do I need more?

She put on her coat and hat, pausing to smell it first like she always did: a mix of firewood and onion. At the last minute she grabbed a container from the cabinet, a bottle wrapped in straw with bits of apple pulp stuck to the glass. She closed the door without locking it and set off down the hill. She greeted her milk cows and tipped her hat to the pigs, the fat mama pig with her piglets, good morning, good morning. The news in the envelope had set her free. She could no longer put off the inevitable, the thing she'd always saved for later. The regional museum, the fate of her home and her work, the needle, the headstone she was making and unmaking as she pleased from that lump of stone. After half a kilometer she turned and cut through the dry pastures to her neighbor's house. She left the empty bottle beside the door and continued downhill on the path that led to the main road.

But there was something else bothering her. Yes, that was the real problem. The issue of the ring. Let's consider the ring, she said to herself. But the sky was more interesting, the birds of prey gliding over the pines in imperfect circles, and when the clouds dispersed the lake gleamed in the distance . . . and under the surface of the water, the silent heads, the perpetually eroding stone.

Half an hour later she was off the mountain. The first bus stop was the cemetery, entered through a wrought-iron gate on the edge of Little Pass, the town straining at its borders but still too small to be considered a city. One corner of the graveyard had been lopped off by the railroad tracks and this was where the headstone workshop stood. It had been opened by her friend Hermes, many years ago, and was now run by his son, Marcel. An enormous sign that the father had carved read: HERMES AND SON, STONEWORK. And underneath the son had added a quote from the sacred ancient texts: THE SWEET PRIZE ON HIGH.

Marcel worked outside as often as he could, but when it got too cold he moved indoors since, as he said, an engraver wearing gloves was worse than one with a hook for a hand. That day he was in the front courtyard, wearing a scarf that he'd wrapped around himself several times. He was sitting in a wicker chair reading a book, his back to an unfinished slab. Euphrates sat in one of the other chairs and shared her unsurprising news. Well, Marcel responded after a pat on the shoulder, we must all eventually go to live in our windowless home. Does that mean that you have to hand over the ring? Do you know who you're going to give it to? When she shook her head, he added: You must at least have decided what your blank slate will say. That's what they called the gravestone, to make it sound less grim. She laughed and answered: It's going to say: WITH NO HURRY AND NO MONEY. But they both knew that neither of the two things was true. Marcel was her closest confidant in town, the only person who had a key to her house (not counting Haydée, who lived in the city and commuted by train every day except her day off).

On her way uphill Euphrates turned off the road to swing by the neighbor's house. She picked up the bottle beside the door, now filled with cider, and left a few random coins in the green can. Back in her kitchen, she poured out a mugful and heated it on the stove. She went into the studio and sat at her desk. From the third drawer, way in the back, she removed a small case. For a long while she sat looking at the Ring of Ruirving. It was a simple circle that didn't quite close, dark gold, like molasses, until it was placed in the light: then it looked as translucent as her stone. The ring was lighter than she'd remembered.

I wanted to take my time to design my headstone, but now . . . I could always choose at random, she thought, but that wouldn't be fair. Had old Chairo chosen her at random? Among all the artists of such a large place? He had visited her twice at her studio in the mountains: once to meet her and the second time to bequeath her the ring. The first time he came alone; the second with a lawyer even older than him. She had been chosen all those years ago; now it was her turn to choose.

It had been the biggest surprise of her life. Euphrates was still a young artist, promising, with some followers, but not yet widely acclaimed. She had managed to become financially stable and move to the house at the foot of the mountain, with its back to the village where she had been born. Every once in a while she received visits from talented friends, possible patrons, even students who traveled from the nearest city to take classes with her. But nothing had prepared her for that visit. In all of Portent there was no actor better than Chairo; no rising star could compare to the legend of the seasoned performer with his foxlike presence. Euphrates had seen him many times onstage, during the short while she lived in the capital as a young artist, when she'd studied at the Academy of Art and Design. And now here he was at her door asking her to show him the secrets of her sculptures.

The first time he visited she didn't know what to offer him (she didn't drink alcohol) so she served him some of her neighbor's cider. Chairo asked for seconds and thirds and ended up taking the large bottle home with him. He never explained the reason for his visit;

just that he needed to meet her in person. A collector friend had introduced him to the work of this young artist, and he had even attended, incognito, a small exhibit of her work at a metropolitan gallery. Euphrates showed him her kiln and her forge, her workshop and her personal collection. Would you like a piece? she offered, drunk with happiness. Chairo let out a long peal of laughter that would remain etched in her memory. I can pay for it, he clarified seriously, and the sculptor insisted: It's a gift or nothing. Maybe another day, the actor said.

Seven years later, an unfamiliar voice called to announce the arrival of Chairo that evening. The sculptor ran down the hill, but instead of leaving the empty bottle she knocked on her neighbor's door until she woke him from his nap, startled. Please tell me you have some cider on hand, she begged. It was the end of spring and Euphrates returned home with the neighbor's last three bottles, one in each hand and another tucked under her arm. She put the bottles in the fridge and that night they once again drank cider. The lawyer politely refused a glass but did accept the chair Euphrates offered: his knees couldn't hold out. Chairo, on the other hand, could hardly remain seated. Not yet, not yet! he said to his lawyer. Euphrates had no idea what was going on and she thought: He wants to buy one of my statues, no, he wants to buy all of them.

The old man finally explained: The Ring of Ruirving is a prize given to the best living artist, and now I will hand it down to you. It's a secret prize and no one must know of its existence, except for the foundation that finances it. Your only task is to continue dedicating yourself to your art, and when the time comes, hand the ring down to the only artist you feel truly deserves it.

The lawyer took the little case from his pocket and opened it. A month later, Chairo went to live in his windowless home. When Euphrates received the news she tried the ring on for the first time.

She called Haydée into the studio the following day. Her apprentice was a nice girl, even though she had the habit of hiding the negative reviews. Euphrates found it funny: the critic who had picked apart her last exhibit was a newborn babe; he still had so much to learn about life that the sculptor took his bad review as a triumph. If she wanted to improve as an artist, Haydée would have to learn to read criticism more carefully.

I need to schedule a meeting with Maestra Brasi, she told her apprentice. Haydée was used to important names but this request surprised to her. Euphrates didn't want to go into detail. Doing so would mean explaining about the envelope in the third drawer. It's a kind of job interview, she said vaguely. Later Haydée poked her head in: Brasi had accepted. Euphrates was feeling increasingly feeble, so they arranged the visit for that very week, on what ended up being one of the coldest days of the year.

That morning Euphrates woke up with a knot in the middle of her back. She went out to the barn, her footsteps crunching the snow. She was slightly embarrassed by the amount of filth. Haydée cleaned, and had cleaned up especially for this visit, but it was never enough: the sculptor would rather excavate an entire mountain than wash a single plate. As she ate breakfast she looked at the utensils and dishes she ate off of, as if seeing them for the first time: she noticed a duck hiding in the reeds, a bee carved into the fork handle. There were fatty glops floating in the milk: the most delicious part, she decided. Haydée had the idea of scheduling a breakfast with Brasi, but Euphrates always got up so early that it was still dark out, and she wasn't going to wait for the other artist to arrive.

Fifteen minutes later she was vomiting her breakfast into the kitchen sink. If only I had time to dedicate myself fully to my blank slate, she thought. But she had to meet with Brasi: she couldn't leave her the ring without being sure. The old man had put his faith in her, and she had risen to the challenge. But then she thought: Risen to what challenge? For the first time she rejected the simplistic notion that had exerted so much influence over her for all these years. And so she asked herself: But did I rise to it, or not? Did I pass the test or did I fall into the trap? She turned the faucet on and rinsed her mouth out with water, then changed her shirt and sat in the studio waiting for her guest to arrive.

B rasi must've been perplexed by the invitation, Euphrates thought. They had been rivals since they'd first met: they were practically the same age and their careers had run parallel, competing for the same grants, the same awards. But Maestra Brasi, as everyone called her, had no idea about the Ring of Ruirving, and on that point Euphrates had her completely beat. Their rivalry hadn't impeded a particular form of friendship, forged through regular contact, as polished as Euphrates' stone, and just as hard at the core. Brasi criticized Euphrates, to her face and behind her back as well, but as far as Euphrates was concerned the competition had been beneficial to them both.

There was always something that seemed a little out of joint in her rival, as if she'd learned the language but not the courtesy. Euphrates summed it up by saying: Brasi is missing a screw; maybe that's what makes her a great artist. In their younger years, the capital of Portent was experiencing a period of rapid growth: new neighborhoods sprung up overnight, the result of agrarian reform launched by the government. From the midst of these neighborhoods and settlements emerged Brasi Siraise, a young foreign woman who was amazed at how the citizens of the capital moved through the city without signs or any way to orient themselves.

The day after her arrival, the first thing she did was to go in search of a transportation guide, something that would allow her to familiarize herself with the city and learn how to get around, which lines took her where. It wasn't just that she couldn't find a copy in stock, they told her no such thing existed. That's when she thought: I know what it is I came here to do, she explained twenty years later in a radio interview that Euphrates had listened to sitting beside her wood-burning stove. Brasi bought the only map available for sale, a drawing of the old town with no transportation signs, and she did the most obvious thing: she hopped on the first bus that passed. The ticket collector asked her where she was going. And Brasi responded in her precarious language: Final, final. At the end of the route there were some food stalls, with people sitting on stools to eat at a table in the middle of the street. She sat down and had lunch, and then took another bus. The next day she did the same thing. Her landlady helped her get ahold of a land registry map, the kind used for construction. She traced it onto rice paper and sketched her daily journeys on it. When the first draft of the map was complete, she rode every bus line again, this time with her eyes closed, to feel each curve of the road.

When she took her project to the Department of Transportation for confirmation, the employee called his co-workers over and said: Look, it's just what we've always needed! They didn't even have a map of bus routes. The design was intuitive to the eye, with all the lines in different colors, like the maps people are used to these days.

The success of that map brought the friendless foreign woman into contact with other graphic designers in the capital; that's how she met Euphrates, who was part of a collective of young artists who gathered in an abandoned soap factory. And that was the very map that Euphrates, the future sculptor, purchased when she moved to the capital, the first time she had been able to dress as a woman without anyone saying anything, the first time she'd felt that she was finally on the path to becoming someone thanks to that pocket-sized map which guided her over unfamiliar territory. Euphrates wasn't surprised that she and Brasi had ended up in the same place; she admired and envied the other artist in equal measure.

Some years later, Brasi impressed her with another ambitious project: a city in miniature, at one-quarter scale, large enough to walk around inside. I could duck down and look into the windows, Euphrates remembered, spotting more and more details the longer I looked. But what she'd liked best was that Brasi had built a real city inside the soap factory, a vibrant metropolis that looked nothing like the sprawling capital outside. To complete the project she had allotted portions to the other members of the collective, each sector with its own time period, unique architecture and planning. The city in miniature grew and changed as the neighborhoods evolved.

All of Brasi's projects shared that same logic, centered on physical space and collaboration. This was something else Euphrates recognized and admired, that Brasi had a brand of talent that was totally inaccessible to her. It was the money, the system of shiny, symbolic prizes, that had pitted them against each other; also the bullying tone that Brasi employed, which Euphrates couldn't stand: she'd dealt with enough of that in her youth as a boy. Their interactions became increasingly hostile, until one night, when no one else was around, Brasi told Euphrates that if she didn't leave she would break her face open with an iron rod, that the collective had become her team, whereas Euphrates, the promising young sculptor, didn't work well with others. They shouted insults at each other: extraterrestrial pretty boy, social-climbing vulture. They later made up, but by then Euphrates was already planning her return to Little Pass.

Over time Brasi cannibalized every discipline to become a total artist, with endless exhibitions in galleries and museums, but for Euphrates she'd always been exceptional, ever since the pocket-sized map. Wasn't that what art was for? What good do my statues do, Euphrates thought, except decorate a world that has no use for them? Who needs someone like me to hack up a perfectly healthy stone? Why me, why not someone else, she'd thought on Chairo's last visit, why me and not her?

B rasi arrived by bicycle, a feat the sculptor admired: uphill, pedaling with maximum effort, first one leg, then the other, as if in slow motion.

As she'd expected, Brasi was not tempted by the cider, neither chilled nor warmed. Why have you invited me, she asked straight out after the requisite small talk. Euphrates told her part of the truth: I'm dying and I wanted to make peace. Her rival didn't seem fazed. So young! Brasi said to her, and she took her hand (what huge hands I have, Euphrates thought, just like my square knees). They'd both recently entered the first years of old age which are the start of something else, the maturity of an artist, but one of them was going to have time and the other wasn't. We're both old, Euphrates answered with a hint of malice, as if decrepitude were something contagious.

They talked all morning, sharing memories of the past, reminiscing on the times in the fast-paced capital and their vague attempt at reconciliation. Euphrates reminded Brasi of her zoological exhibit, which Euphrates had visited outside the scheduled show hours, and how furious Brasi had become when she uncovered the head of a sleeping cat, gently suggested by two curved lines that intersected to form the nose, and Euphrates couldn't help but pet it, her hands leaving a stain on the metal forehead. Brasi glared at her and said: You can't just do that. Euphrates didn't tell her about how later on, one of the security guards told her that the fish made the sound of bells. She walked over to one that was struggling against the current, and rapped it gently with her knuckle. It made a beautiful sound, not at all metallic: it was the hum of marble, sanded and polished to a state of extreme tension. Two rooms later, as the exhibit went back in time to extinct animals and sculptures increasingly more abstract, Euphrates heard that same sound again, coming from somewhere behind her; it was the security guard, enjoying the exhibit as much as she was.

I almost didn't come today, Brasi confessed. The reason for the meeting intrigued me, but it also interrupted my work: in fact, this morning I woke up fully intending to cancel. What do two old bags like us have to say to each other? Sit around comparing scars? Your surgery and my C-section? We each have our own traumas, and I've had enough of the past. But I imagined you had something important to say. Although I never would have guessed . . .

Haydée knocked on the door to offer them more coffee, which

Brasi happily accepted. When they were alone again, she asked Euphrates why she kept Haydée on as an apprentice, since she wasn't a very good artist. I mean, she's not bad, but anyone can learn to make coffee. Euphrates knew Brasi was testing her, but nevertheless it was true: Haydée had talent and determination, but she lacked the need or desire to impose herself, to say, *Here I am*. She was better as a collaborator than as an artist. She'd come to Euphrates through the scholarship program she had set up with the money from the foundation, granted to kids from the interior provinces who wanted to study in the capital, and she realized too late that the girl wasn't going to be able to absorb everything Euphrates was capable of teaching. But Haydée was joyful, she filled the studio with life, and Euphrates enjoyed watching her grow: how her features became more defined as she left adolescence behind, a living sculpture, the first face Euphrates was aware of watching age day by day.

After breakfast, Brasi wanted to tour the barn, where she asked questions about the cows. Why does that one have a clipped tail? How do you know which one gave birth? Euphrates explained and talked about other ways of raising cattle, like how in the feedlots their faces would be shaved bare from constantly rubbing against the rails (both were against it), or about playing them classical music (both were in favor). And then Brasi, nonchalantly, dropped the bomb: So you called me here about the Ring of Ruirving, didn't you?

Euphrates felt like she'd been duped: by the foundation, by Brasi, by herself as well, but mostly by her rival. You shouldn't have said it, she thought, even if only to let me keep believing the secret. Brasi must've seen it in her face because she shrugged her shoulders and said, with a shy smile: Everyone knows everything in the art world, at least everyone who wants to know. They walked back past the piglets, hiding behind their mother.

Where did that city to scale that you built end up? Euphrates asked her. In a private museum, Brasi answered, they always take the best pieces and all they give us in exchange are useless bills. Well what do you want the ring for, then? Euphrates asked. For the prestige, Brasi answered. But no one will know about it! The people who matter will know. So you're the only one who matters? I could pay my entire team, Brasi answered. Was it wrong that I told you I knew about it? No, Euphrates said, it was wrong that you knew about it.

Before leaving, after putting on her coat, Brasi bent over the statue of the dog, but didn't touch it. I always liked your deaf dog, she said. What makes you think he's deaf? Euphrates asked. Maestra Brasi sighed: Has there ever been a dog that didn't look to the door when their owner came or went? The next time you have news about me, Euphrates said, maybe . . . But she didn't finish the sentence. Brasi said: You don't have to say anything, and getting on her bike she went back the way she'd come, now with the incline in her favor. The sculptor stood in the yard with her arms crossed. The animals were outside the barn and cowbells clanked intermittently. Snow fell over the cattle as their warm breath steamed.

S he wished she'd never received the ring, she thought, but she didn't want to give it up, either; I have to decide who to give it to, but I hate my decision. Brasi had seen through her: the money had made everything much easier. You could've bit your tongue, she thought, but instead you made it harder for me. That's why we were never friends.

Euphrates went to bed with her mind made up: she would return the ring, even give back part of the money if she had to. But then she woke up feeling nauseous and saw things differently. She'd cherished the secret pleasure of having been chosen; giving up the ring would be an insult. She could just die without giving it to anyone, feign ignorance to the foundation, Sorry, I died! They couldn't take back the money she'd lived on all these years, the money she'd used to finance the scholarships, the money she'd saved to leave to Haydée along with her studio. Or could they? She hadn't signed any kind of contract; she just billed her expenses like she would to any other patron. It had become a bureaucratic process: a resource she could put to good use, but at the same time a burden for a person who wished to dedicate themselves purely to beauty, to making sense of the world. Sometimes these attempts were small and went unnoticed and sometimes, with luck, they stood the test of time. The money had pulled her into philanthropy work, and now she was trapped. She had never been able to determine the origin of the Ring of Ruirving, but she was certain it must've been some old artist who felt guilty about his bank account and was too much of a narcissist to invest the money in a better way.

At least her headstone was on track. She spent her days talking with Marcel. As they worked she told him about her childhood as a boy and the lake crowded with the weathered smiles of fallen empresses, when it was still possible to dive down and explore the lakebed; about growing quickly and rising to the top in the capital and the relationship she'd had with Marcel's father, Hermes, when she moved back to town and he'd opened the headstone workshop; about shared memory and individual transcendence, about the role of art and the mystery of creation, the secret history of her sculptures. Marcel listened attentively, nodding from time to time, sympathizing, though without interrupting his ceaseless drawing in his sketchbook.

Why is it so hard for you to leave the ring to Brasi, the engraver asked her one day, if you've already chosen her? It's not that simple, dear, we're talking about my legacy. I thought that's what the museum collection is for, Marcel answered, and your headstone, which is what everyone will see when they come to visit you. If I could leave the ring to you, Euphrates said, it would be so much easier. And you can't? I can't. Why? The chosen person has to have relevance. And I'm not relevant? Euphrates laughed.

As she returned home, uphill and with her hat pulled low on her head, Euphrates remembered the time her grandmother took her by train to the opera and how she'd been dazzled by the fierce presence of the singer onstage. At the side door outside the dressing rooms, the singer gave her a yellow rose from her own bouquet, a rarity in those days . . . she'd held it up to her grandmother, who had agreed to wait with her despite the cold, and whose glasses seemed to shine, strangely. . . they said thank you to the singer, from the bottom of their hearts, but she had already walked away . . . Though many have come close to that perfection, I've never heard anyone else sing quite like her, she said to herself as she stopped on the road to catch her breath and admire the dusk settling over the lake, precisely because it was a formative experience for me. Talent only goes so far; the rest is up to us.

The next day, Haydée embarrassedly asked for time off, as she did every year: she wanted to visit her family on the islands to the west of Portent. Of course, Euphrates answered, staring blankly out the window: it was the perfect opportunity. Will you be able to take care of the barn on your own, will you wash the dishes, sweep up the shavings? Yes, the sculptor assured her in the firm tone she used whenever she was telling the truth, I promise to clean everything that gets dirty. The next day she called the foundation: the number which up to now she'd used only for accounting-related questions. I need someone from the team to come out, she said.

That same afternoon a notary arrived, hurriedly, in a car with a driver. It wasn't the lawyer who had accompanied Chairo so many years ago, naturally, although Euphrates had held out faint hope. The notary kneeled beside her chair to remove the papers from his briefcase; he was young but balding. Have you made a decision? he asked. Euphrates took a deep breath: I leave the ring to Maestra Brasi Siraise. And then she added: I'd imagined myself laughing when I said it, but I've never felt so serious. The only condition is that the foundation be the one to notify her once I'm deceased. I don't want to do it myself. She signed two copies of the form certifying the succession and handed one to the notary. She took the ring case from the third drawer and gave that to him too.

As the notary checked the Ring of Ruirving, Euphrates picked up her stone to use it as a paperweight, but instead kept it in her hand. She traced its outline with her fingertip, it felt like a hoof, smooth and lustrous as an acorn, and she sniffed it, hoping to catch the scent of her childhood on the lake, which she thought she remembered as a mixture of pine and rust. She didn't smell anything, just felt its usual cool density as she touched it to her nose. Tomorrow I'll return it to its rightful home, Euphrates decided, I'll put it back with the statues on the deep lakebed, and she tucked it into her pocket.

The next day, when she was about to head down to the lake, she received a phone call from the museum in Little Pass: they had officially accepted her collection and wanted to interview her on film about her body of work. That's fine, she answered with an empty cider bottle in one hand, but first I want to make a change to the bequest, a small one. And now, old lady, she thought, you can stop holding up these tired bones.

Haydée fainted when she heard the news of Euphrates' death. I abandoned her, she said to Marcel over the phone, I had a gut feeling but I left her to die alone anyway. She didn't want to return for the funeral or to take over the house. I have to rethink what I'm doing with my life, she said before hanging up.

They buried Euphrates beside the railroad tracks in the town cemetery, which was crowded with friends and strangers alike. The sculptor was the only famous person in all of Little Pass, and that was enough to make people come together now that she'd died. Brasi sent a handwritten letter of condolence:

> My work keeps me from attending, but I would like to express my admiration for my colleague, Euphrates. We were always depicted as rivals, and we were, but despite our public differences, we were also united, in private, by our secrets.

Marcel had the headstone placed on her grave, incomplete, just as she'd left it. It was a somber piece, a wall of ivy bordered along the bottom of the slab with a kind of incision, as if a surgeon had sliced into it. Each leaf of the vine was intricately engraved, except one that had not yet been carved. The lines under the name had been left blank.

After the funeral was over, Marcel walked up the main road, which was less steep. The people from the local museum had given him the message: the statue of the blind dog was for him, the final change Euphrates had asked for, and they'd agreed. They hadn't expected her death to take place so imminently, and in that way. They hadn't even gotten the chance to interview her or film her beside her work. Don't worry, Marcel told them, I have hours of conversations with her. She talked and talked, and when she left I transcribed everything she'd said.

He thought about the statue of the little dog, which had always brought him good luck since he was a boy, when he went to visit Euphrates' studio with his father. There was something in that unseeing stare that spoke to him: the dog couldn't see because it was blind, not because it was made of bronze. It would look good on my tombstone, he thought, when my time comes, and he promised himself that later that afternoon he'd prune the squash vine that grew wild over his father's grave.

He reached the sculptor's house. He didn't hear the clanging of cowbells, which he found odd. The freeze had killed the last of the hay that had been left uncut. Marcel opened the barn door. The cows, desperate with hunger, rushed out to feast on the morning grass. ■

CARLOS FONSECA

1987

Carlos Fonseca was born in San José, Costa Rica, but spent his teenage years in Puerto Rico. He is the author of the novels *Colonel Lágrimas* (*Coronel Lágrimas*) and *Natural History* (*Museo animal*), both translated into English by Megan McDowell. He teaches at Trinity College, Cambridge University.

RUINS IN REVERSE

Carlos Fonseca

TRANSLATED BY MEGAN MCDOWELL

1

The page, cut from an old newspaper and clumsily glued into the notebook, relates an event that occurred in the Balkans. It was the winter of 1991, the war between the Yugoslav factions was entering its most savage phase, and many of the inhabitants of a town on the outskirts of Zagreb reported suffering from insomnia. More unexpected was a symptom that the Croatian doctors hastily chalked up to the traumatic stress of the bombings. The insomniacs, when they finally did manage to fall asleep, dreamed of a color they had never seen before: a kind of phosphorescent blue, halfway between sky and arctic.

The article went on to reference a coincidence that happened months later. That spring, residents of the Serbian village of Deronje witnessed how the petals of the Asparagaceae flower that dotted the nearby fields turned a lucent blue, very much like the color their Croatian adversaries claimed to have dreamed. The column, other than mentioning that the color was possibly due to the use of chemical agents like sarin gas during the conflict, merely reported that the cause of the occurrence remained a mystery. On the lower part of the notebook's page, beneath a photo of the luminous flowers – perhaps faked or staged but certainly convincing – was a handwritten line: 'Prophecy: Chaos cross-dressing as destiny.'

2

The confluence of the newspaper clipping and the quotation, which I found today while I was looking through the unpublished notebooks of the Honduran poet Salvador Godoy, made me recall the chain of coincidences that had to occur two years ago so that, in the long and agonizing aftermath of the hurricane that had just thrashed the island, I would come to take an interest in Arno Krautherimer and his dreams. In that instance too it was a combination of chaos and destiny that led me to the figure of the Austrian architect, in whose remote deliriums I thought I recognized the image of our ruinous present.

In those days I was still living in Puerto Rico, in a small apartment that had belonged to my grandmother and whose particularity consisted in being the only residence in the whole tower without a balcony. Someone forgot to build it, she used to say with a laugh, while she looked out defiantly from the rocking chair she'd placed before the picture window. More than once, during the chaotic weeks that followed the storm, I would remember her laugh, stop bustling around and sit down to look out at the view through that window. There it was: the devastated island, but the island nonetheless. From the tenth floor I had a bird's-eye view of the rubble of nearby houses, the way the storm had dissolved the sharpness of the panorama with all the force of a child scattering the pieces of a puzzle with one swipe. Further on I saw the lake, placid and steadfast, and beyond it the city stretched out, roofless and covered with the artificial blue of plastic tarps, looking for all the world like a wounded and bandaged body. I'd sit there to rest a little, until the heat grew thick and I felt I could truly fathom the sense of listless ennui in which we were surviving. This was not the tedium of boredom, much less indifference, but more like the feeling that the world had returned to a primitive state where time was once again as torpid and sodden as one's own sweat.

I was thus sitting in the rocker when three knocks startled me one morning. Three raps that reverberated through the dark and inhospitable space the storm had left behind, through whose hallways, crammed with emergency supplies, I had learned to move with the sober diligence of a medieval monk. To reach the door, I skirted assorted bits of debris, boxes of potable water and dozens of half-reassembled devices. On the other side of it, I found my friend Gabriel Piovanetti, sweaty after climbing ten flights of stairs. Since the hurricane, Piovanetti had become a kind of mobile radio. He left his apartment every morning for long walks, seeking to fill out the scant information we subsisted on in those days. After around six or seven hours, at about three in the afternoon, he'd retrace his steps, bringing news of the images he said he'd seen: the devastation in Cataño; La Perla reduced to a tangle of cables and wood; Fernando Botero's enormous sculpture of a nude woman dragged to sea by the winds. We'd hear him knock at the door – in my case always at three on the dot – and we knew that even in the midst of catastrophe, we could count on the constancy of his stories to make us forget our distress.

It was because of his stubborn punctuality that I was startled that day; the characteristic knocks on the door came at eleven, and not at three. But there was a reason for the schedule change. Piovanetti said he had found, outside the Visual Arts School, a set of boxes that bore my name: FOR CARLOS FONSECA. In hindsight, it's become clearer that those boxes were not addressed to me. I was not the intended Carlos Fonseca, but it didn't much matter at the time.

Excited by this unexpected discovery, thinking perhaps it would set off an unexpected spark in a world where time seemed to stagnate, I retraced the route my friend had followed a few hours earlier, until I located the boxes amid so many fallen posts, toppled trees and useless rubble. Piovanetti was right: not without a thrill did I recognize my water-smudged name, never stopping to consider that the name also belonged to others. Little could I have imagined

that this mistake, or presumption, would give me the gift of Arno
Krautherimer's delirious architecture.

3

It's shocking to think how many stories end up in the trash.
Discarded, ignored, forgotten. I'm sure that would have been the
fate of those two small boxes had it not been for my friend's eagle
eye. Clearly battered by rain, they were part of a long line of similar
boxes. Someone, convinced they'd be ruined by the floods, had taken
them out of the school's basement storage room. And certainly, that
someone wasn't wrong, as I confirmed once I'd returned home
and opened them up to find a bunch of wet papers, damaged and
illegible. I remember I tried to read some of those pages but failed in
every attempt: the passage of years and inclement weather were too
much for the tired eyes of this poor unemployed historian. I could
only make out a few lone words – blueprints, dimensions, bases – that
reminded me of geometry tests I'd taken in my adolescence. I was
about to give up, when at the bottom of the second box I found what
I first thought was a small, mildew-infested strongbox, wrapped in
several layers of packaging that seemed to have kept it from sharing
the ruinous fate of everything around it.

Now, as I remember all this, I relive the emotion of the discovery:
the feeling that beyond the gloomy limbo it had sunk us into, the
catastrophe had an offering for me. An old box made of carefully
carved Brazilian mahogany, with a forged inscripton whose golden
letters were darkened by time: E.C. 1945. When I opened it, I found
about a hundred pages, yellowed but intact, with a blend of images
and text that was confusing at first, but that little by little I started
to shape into a possible story. On elegantly stamped pages – the
heading, in tasteful blue ink, read: ENRIQUE COLÓN, PSYCHOANALYST,
AVENIDA ASHFORD, SAN JUAN, PUERTO RICO – a man's emotional crisis

was detailed. The file initially referred to him as 'the patient', but soon moved on to call him 'the architect'.

I sat down in my grandmother's rocker, perhaps in need of a horizon for what I was reading, and there, before the slightly cracked window, I began to read the file, wondering all the while who this architect was. When I was nearing the end, I found a page that said: *Patient: Arno Krautherimer, Session notes: 1942–1943*. I remember thinking how strange that name sounded in my happy tropics, and how odd that such an old and personal file should have ended up in storage at the Visual Arts School. Then I remembered a fact that provided a possible explanation: looking at the series of hallucinatory architectural sketches that accompanied the notes, I figured the most likely thing was that the pages had arrived during the transitional years when the building went from being the old Island Asylum to housing the then newly inaugurated Visual Arts School. I couldn't remember the dates, so anything was possible. Most likely, in the move, someone had confused the patient's sketches with those of an artist and the file had snuck in to become part of the institution's cultural heritage. I laugh now at the thought that I owe my initiation into the oneiric architecture of Arno Krautherimer to that confusion between art and madness.

I must admit to feeling a certain reticence at first, as I began exploring the universe of confessions uttered under an oath of confidence. I had the impression I was accidentally sticking my nose into someone else's private business, as if I'd found a door ajar and decided to enter a neighbor's house. Curiosity, legitimized in part by the fact that those boxes were seemingly addressed to me, ended up winning out over any sense of delicacy. I gradually let myself be caught up by the unexpected image of that man with the exotic name lying on an unlikely divan almost eighty years ago and spilling his dreams and fears to one of the island's first psychoanalysts, while on the other side of the ocean the world was laying its bets. I pictured him blond, with blue eyes and an evasive gaze, hesitant at the questions the Caribbean analyst would be asking him with a smile that betrayed admiration. And I wondered what any of it had to do with me. Me, an unemployed historian, a professor whose career had already been seeming like a blind alley for some time when a hurricane came to deal it a death blow – though I didn't know it yet – while giving me the story of a life.

What did those dreams and those childhood memories have to do with me? What did I care about some Austrian's lamentations? I remember one note in particular caught my attention that afternoon, amid the countless annotations filling the psychoanalytical file. It said:

> The patient claims to dream of buildings that are the opposite of those he consciously imagines during the day. He feels like a fraud, since when awake he advocates for spaces built according to the simple harmony of reason, but at night he dreams the inverse. When I ask about his childhood, he remembers the cracks that grew so patiently in the oak and beech floorboards of his childhood in Vienna at the turn of the century. He admits that this image of the cracked floor has become an obsession. I suggested that, in order to lessen the effect of his nightmares, he should try to sketch out the buildings he sees in his dreams.

Then on another page appeared the transcription, this time in first person, of one of the dreams:

> I dreamed again yesterday. I dreamed we were in the old house in Leopoldstadt, and I went over to the window trying to escape the cracks I could see growing around me, and struggled to peer outside, as children do. Just then I felt a gust of cold air that made me turn around, and suddenly I saw my mother, who was leaning over and submerging her hair in a tub of cold water. Her hair, now heavy, hung over her face, and I intuited that the

weight of it would end up collapsing the house. The worst part, however, was my acute awareness that I was dreaming, though I desperately wished to wake up.

Guided by those scenes, I began reconstructing the image of that Austrian child crawling across oak and beech floorboards, playing with the debris that the passage of time would have left in the fissures of the floor. I pictured him growing up in that Vienna of cold and monumental architecture, and tried to draw the line that would link him to the man who years later, now an architect, sat across from a Caribbean psychoanalyst to recollect his childhood. I had the sense that this man was looking for heat, and I smiled at the image of him doing battle with the island mosquitoes. Maybe the nightmares he spoke of were nothing but the byproduct of island inertia.

The many sketches the file contained interrupted my harebrained digressions. Looking at them made me think the architect was right: they seemed like the product of a feverish delirium, the nightmare of a builder suddenly aware of how fragile reality can be. In the first ones, dated early November 1942, the alterations were slight: the minimalism held firm, though cracks began to appear. Slowly, however, the fissures demanded ever more room and by the final sketches, from February 1943, the structures seemed to lose their initial shape and the cracks threatened to encompass everything. In these final sketches the architect appeared to go mad, and the buildings, more than buildings, took the form of the contrasting strata of rocks in the desert. Then they took a step further and even the straight lines seemed to give way, morphing into sketches that recalled marine shapes: the sinuous and elusive silhouettes of corals, octopuses and anemones. Beneath one of them, Krautherimer himself had jotted down an idea that caught my attention: 'I have always thought that architecture is the faithful reflection of nature, the order of what is stable, of harmony, of repose. I'm beginning to intuit that the reverse may be true: architecture as a space of opposing forces, like tectonic plates about to collide.' The mention of an imminent tremor epitomized an intuition I'd had when I saw those designs: I'd felt something in them resonating perfectly with the aftermath of catastrophe we were living through at the time. Before me, the landscape framed by the window seemed to confirm the presentiment. I was surprised that, given the dates, none of the notes mentioned the war that was breaking out at that time, or Austria's role in the conflict. As if it were enough to understand that nature was not the coveted, peaceful garden of dreams, but a world of forces battling for primacy. Examining the nature of architecture was an oblique way of talking about history, I said to myself, and for the first time all afternoon I felt it made sense that those papers had fallen to me of all people. I went on reading and looking at the notes and sketches until around six, when I felt the sun going down behind me. With no electricity to light it, the house returned to darkness.

4

Over the following weeks, my fascination with the figure of Arno Krautherimer and his extravagant dreams somehow came to fill the great void that the hurricane had left behind. In the mornings, in the asphyxiating swelter of the Caribbean autumn, I did what I could to help friends and family with the tasks that kept us afloat amid the lack of electricity, water and information. I fixed broken windows, installed generators, repaired roofs. Then, at noon, I'd sit in the rocker and give myself over to reading and analyzing the psychoanalytic file. I spent the hours trying to understand the Austrian architect's intrepid designs, dreams and ideas, until three o'clock rolled around and I heard Piovanetti's knocks at the door. I'd invite him in and, without going into the discoveries that in some sense I owed to him, I'd let him talk about the world that lay outside my door. That world of rubble in which, little by little, I had begun to see a cruel reflection of my architect's nightmares.

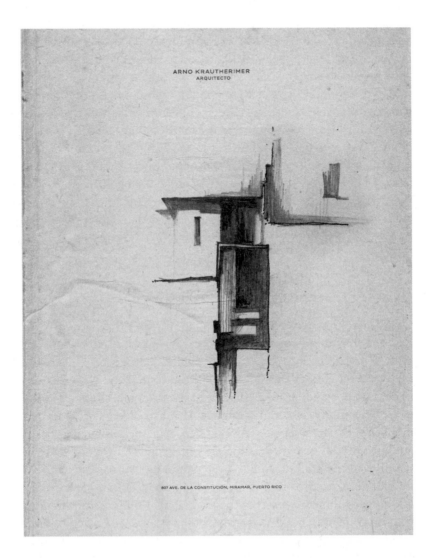

ARNO KRAUTHERIMER
ARQUITECTO

807 AVE. DE LA CONSTITUCIÓN, MIRAMAR, PUERTO RICO

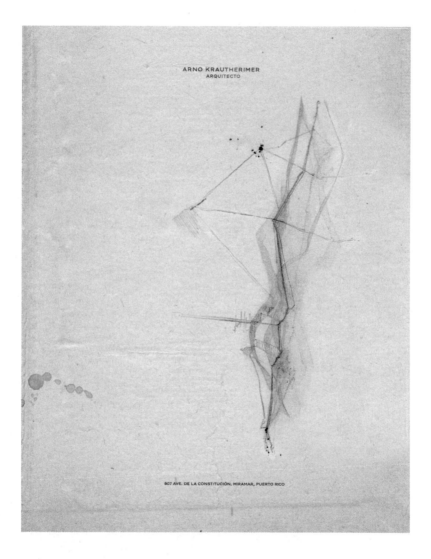

ARNO KRAUTHERIMER
ARQUITECTO

807 AVE. DE LA CONSTITUCIÓN, MIRAMAR, PUERTO RICO

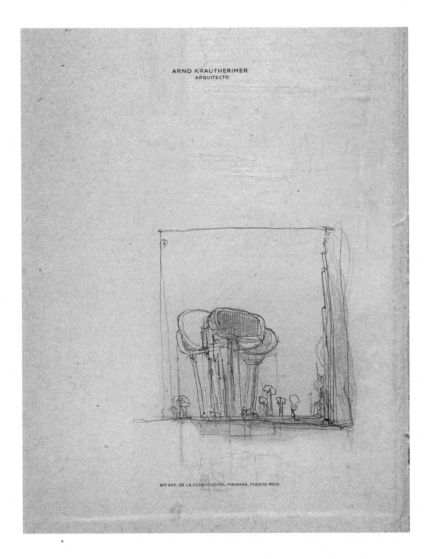

In early December, Gabriel closed one of his reports in an unusual way. He invited me to a party another close friend of ours, Karina, was throwing to celebrate the return of electricity to her house. Accustomed now to the dark nights, I considered refusing the invitation, but then I remembered something: our friend had studied architecture. Perhaps by talking to her, I could clarify the origins of those enigmatic papers I had accidentally inherited. So, I accepted.

Hours later, when I got to Karina's party, I felt as though I was entering one of Krautherimer's dreamed structures. I remembered that her house had been abandoned for more than a decade, during which time it served as a flophouse for addicts. Karina and two other architects from the college had decided to remodel it. There was no question they had done an exceptional job, but the house's charm was due in large part to the traces that remained of its more ignoble past. It was strange, I thought, to see it like that, lit up and full of people, as if deep down none of it had happened; not the abandonment, or the drugs or the catastrophe. Obviously, I had it wrong: we were there precisely to celebrate the fact that at least one of us had won the battle against the storm. But I couldn't help feeling that in some way, the party was a mere simulacrum of familiarity or closeness. The hurricane had left us roofless, our secrets exposed to the elements. Afraid people might think I lacked solidarity, I kept my thoughts to myself. I chose instead to surrender to the party and the beer, which was miraculously cold, until after midnight, when I finally found Karina alone, smoking on the balcony. I approached her casually and, after the initial greetings, ventured to ask if by chance she had heard of an Austrian architect named Arno Krautherimer. To this day I remember her broad smile in the night that was illuminated at long last.

I remember thinking how that smile – with its perfect mixture of mischievousness, irony and insouciance – was what had attracted me to her ten years ago. Then I thought how little remained of the kid I'd once been. I saw her laugh, make a vague gesture and disappear into the crowd still filling her house. She came back a minute later carrying two books. She put one of them beside the ashtray, and opened the second to a page she had marked with her index finger.

'Here it is,' she said with another smile. There was my architect's name, beneath a photograph of a man with thick eyebrows and a profuse mustache. His look was more playful than I'd imagined, and his dark hair contradicted the image I'd created of a blond European waylaid in the tropics. 'You can take them, I know them by heart,' she told me. And without asking for any further explanations or providing any more details, she disappeared again into the crowd. It was the last time I saw her that night. I went home around one, carrying the books. I had an inkling – maybe under the influence of the party and the alcohol – that those books held the key to unlock the hermetic world I had accessed three weeks earlier.

5

The life of Arno Krautherimer, as I read in the two books, was an example of what we all know so well but prefer to ignore: that our dreams do their best to betray us at times. Born into a Jewish family in Vienna at the turn of the century, his life traced a perfect arc through twentieth-century modernist architecture. Heir to the ideas of Adolf Loos, he had decided at a very early age to leave the ornaments of old Vienna behind, following the path of the two men who would become his great teachers. In the twenties, he crossed the Atlantic in search of Frank Lloyd Wright's prairies, only to encounter the elderly, weathered figure of the all-but-forgotten Louis Sullivan. The United States was, for Krautherimer, the land of simplicity. When the First World War ended and the Hapsburg Empire along with it, he had come to America seeking to distance himself from the Old World's cold monumentalism. And he had done it. Or at least he thought he had.

In the first of the books that my friend gave me, called *Modernism in Architecture*, there were photographs of some of Krautherimer's projects from the thirties: geometrical structures, guided by the horizontal minimalism of broad roofs that confused inside with out. I remember looking at those buildings with surprise, recognizing certain features I'd seen in sketches in the psychoanalytical file, mutated into nightmares. That book, however, had not a single mention of Puerto Rico, or any sojourn of the architect's on the island.

I sought in the following weeks to fill those details in by reading the second book, an old copy of the history of architecture in Puerto Rico, whose pages fell out with frightening ease. Guided by the table of contents, I turned to a chapter dedicated to the role architecture had played in the political reforms of the early forties. I read that at the start of the decade, future governor Luis Muñoz Marín and current governor Rexford Guy Tugwell had worked together on a plan for modernizing the island. A project for an economic and social future that included architecture: new hospitals, new schools and social housing. Krautherimer had come to the island as part of the so-called Design Committee for Public Works, tasked with drafting that renewed infrastructure. Little could he imagine that in the heat of those restless tropics, the minimalism of his designs would risk mutating into ruin.

Few details were offered about his life, but one of them resonated with me. It was mentioned in passing that when Krautherimer was young, he had been a close friend of Ernst Ludwig Freud, son of Sigmund. I thought it was funny that a man who'd been so close to the father of psychoanalysis, one who had likely even walked and dined alongside him, would years later seek a cure for his disquiet on the divan of one of the first Puerto Rican psychoanalysts.

So I riffled through the old papers to find one I'd read that very afternoon:

A dream, glimpsed clearly at mid-morning while I was working on a couple of sketches for the school plans. I looked out and saw snow falling on the fronds of the virgin jungle, and the contrast led me to think of the crackle of hot water hitting ice. Then I realized this was precisely my nightmare from the night before, and that, in the small hours, I had felt it was Europe itself that was slowly snapping.

It would have been easy to read those dreams, I thought, as nightmares transferring the collapse of his childhood Europe to a personal plane. More difficult and interesting, though, was to read it all in a Caribbean key.

I preferred to imagine that, just as some dreams prophesy the future, those of Arno Krautherimer augured the fate of that delusion of modernity that was starting to die even before it was born. And I again imagined him in the winter of 1942, sweaty and exhausted, struggling during the day to raise the foundations of a modern present, while at night he dreamed of its eventual collapse. I thought I saw him briefly in his tropical delirium, reliving his experience of years before, in the impeccable Vienna of his childhood, when he'd looked at the floor and found there, in the oak and beech boards, a world of silent cracks. Our sad fortune, I thought, was to live amid those ruinous landscapes that he, more restrained, had merely dreamed.

6

When you look for signs, oracles turn up everywhere. I don't know at what point that architect's agony became my own. All I know is that little by little, my reading of that file ended up inundating my reality. I looked around and saw cracks everywhere, dreams run aground. As if the island was the ship whose stability we had never questioned, but whose fissures were revealed now that the storm had flooded solid ground. The startling thing, I understood then, was that the disaster only unmasked the flaws that were hidden but omnipresent. During those days I came to think of myself as yet another failed project. It seemed to matter little that when I was young, I had done all the things the older folks suggested: get good grades, earn a scholarship to a US university, graduate with honors and return to the island, ready to triumph. I'd done it all according to plan, but when I returned six years later, it seemed there was nothing left for me. Just a job as a waiter in a local bar where the tourists arrived already drunk. More than once, chatting with one of those tourists, I'd ventured to comment on my situation, only to hear them say the solution was clear: I should make the most of my passport and travel north – to Orlando, Chicago or New York, one of those cities that in the past had welcomed the Puerto Rican diaspora. I bit my tongue and thought of my brother, who had left the island almost a decade ago now, headed for the Gran Manzana. Every time we talked, he tried to convince me to move. He promised me a room for free until I found work. I always turned him down, the same way I demurred with the tourists. Puerto Rico was my country, and anyway, I had my job at the bar and my routine. Now the hurricane had taken that, too, and my patience along with it.

Unemployed and with nothing to lose, I went deeper into Arno Krautherimer's life: like someone lost in a desert who thinks he sees an oasis in the distance and the mirage becomes his fate. I began to think I could turn it all into a book, a monograph depicting this uncanny episode in the architect's life and the history of Puerto Rico. I even came up with a title: *Rise and Fall of a Modernist Dream*. On my most optimistic days during that endless winter, while I watched how the island struggled to return bit by bit to normalcy, I saw that book as a possible way out, a redemption. Its publication would bring me some recognition and grant me a future as an academic. But every time, the treacherous logic of dream and nightmare would waylay me again, and after a few hours my optimism would evaporate before the evidence of devastation.

One of those days, excited about the project, I decided to take a walk around the university. I took it all in; the rubble of the buildings, the limpid vegetation just starting to regrow, the absence of the parrots that used to cheer the landscape with their song. Even with the book, I thought, little was left for me there. I walked through the halls, where the students now seemed to move with more caution and fatigue than before, distant replicas of those Giacometti sculptures I'd liked so much in another time, until I reached the theater and noticed a small crowd. I got closer, thinking I would find a musician or maybe a clown, but I quickly realized my mistake. In front of the group, a photographer was snapping pictures of a ballet dancer posing on her toes amid the remains of an old structure. Looking at her, I thought that Krautherimer was right, true beauty is only reached when it risks collapse. 'Architecture: Defiance of Gravity', I remembered having read beneath another of his sketches, and the precision of the phrase helped me understand the scene I now had in front of me: that ballerina on pointe who, at least for the brief instant turned eternal by the photographer, was exposing the vertical thread that ties us to the gods. We stood there for a few minutes until the photographer finished the session, and I had the odd feeling that a cycle was ending. Two days later, the electricity finally reached my house, and, when I saw the lights go on, I knew the time had come to leave the island.

7

In the months following that sudden decision, I sought with sad determination to leave behind everything tying me to the island, and that included Arno Krautherimer. I clung to the practical details of the move, aware that surrendering to the weight of today is another way of burying one's sorrows. I focused on packing my things, confirming my brother's offer of a place to stay in New York, searching for possible jobs in the Big Apple, saying goodbye to family and friends. I thought about taking the file with me, but instead decided to leave it with Karina. She – an architect, after all – would know better than

I what to do with those pages that had kept me company throughout the long aftermath of the disaster. Tired, feeling a bit like a traitor, I left the island in early April.

Five months later, I was walking the Manhattan streets alongside a new girlfriend when I was brought up short by a poster advertising a current exhibition at a nearby museum. The subject: modernist architecture. Without divulging the true reason for my interest, I convinced her it would be fun to have a look. The walls of that enormous hall were lined with the names of the past century's great architects, along with their iconic projects. I recognized Fallingwater by Frank Lloyd Wright, Louis Sullivan's Wainwright Building, Richard Neutra's Miller House, the designs of Le Corbusier, Walter Gropius, Marcel Breuer, and so many others from the Bauhaus. Each one of those famous architects had a full wall dedicated to the exhibition of their works. I was pleased to recognize certain traits in those designs of that properly modern vision that Krautherimer's tropical dreams had transformed into their opposite. We were on our way out, in the final section of the exhibit, entitled 'Aftermaths of Modernism', and I was astonished to find a photograph of a project of Krautherimer's. It was the Von Kaufman House, a mansion the Austrian had built in California in the fifties for the famous producer Hugo Von Kaufman. A limpid and minimalist house that seemed in total concordance with the designs Krautherimer had made in the thirties, before his stay on the island. Same simplicity, same harmony, same ode to reason and minimalism. I alone knew the convulsive undercurrent that throbbed treacherously beneath the affable surface of those designs.

I must have peered very closely at the photo or its plaque, because my girlfriend asked if the piece was special. Wary of exhuming the catastrophic reality I thought I'd recently buried and left behind, I shook my head and kept walking, eager to find the minimalism of forgetting. And truth is I found it, for years, until today, as I was reading Salvador Godoy's notebooks and came across the article about the unexpected coincidence between Croatian dreams and

Serbian flowers. Then the blue of my childhood sky came back, and I remembered how, after the storm, everything seemed to have changed except for the clouds. I reread Godoy's astute words, 'Prophecy: Chaos cross-dressing as destiny', and in that instant, I understood how I had tried to steal the fate of a man who shared my name.

ps: After publishing the first version of these notes, a historian friend called to tell me that the old Island Asylum had closed its doors in 1928 and the Visual Arts School hadn't opened its own until 1967, so it was impossible that the papers had been transferred from one institution to the other. I told my friend that that was exactly what this brief recounting is all about: the possibility of confusing dates, of mixing up causes and effects. That has always been my problem with historians: they don't know how to twist straight lines. They don't know how to dream history. ∎

AUTHOR'S NOTE: I would like to thank Gabriel Piovanetti-Ferrer, who provided me with the materials and the vision that gave way to this story.

ANDREA CHAPELA

1990

Andrea Chapela was born in Mexico City. She is the author of the tetralogy *Vâudïz*, the essay collection *Grados de miopía* and the fiction books *Un año de servicio a la habitación* and *Ansibles, perfiladores y otras máquinas de ingenio*.

BORROMEAN RINGS

Andrea Chapela

TRANSLATED BY KELSI VANADA

Every three months, we cross the ranch to check on the solar cells and test the antenna on a different frequency. This time we're trying something new, angling the antenna toward the sky so the radio waves will bounce back. After transmitting for twenty-four hours, we'll come back to see if anyone has responded.

All our previous attempts have gone unanswered.

We're like those scientists of long ago, who sent signals into space in search of life on other planets. We're searching for life too, but here: beyond the isthmus, beyond Mexico, hoping to find out who or what survived the collapse.

By the time we get back to the main house it's already getting dark, and we head straight to dinner. The antenna uses so much electricity when it's switched on that we have to light the dining hall with candles, as if we were living in the olden days. The conversation around all the tables centers on today's effort: whether it will work, whether it's worth spending our precious resources on the search, how much longer we should keep trying. Clara (it was her first time going to the antenna) asks who each of us would call if we managed to establish communication. The answers vary: names of cities, relatives, institutions that probably don't exist anymore. Mamá says she'd dial our old apartment in Mexico City. Hearing her made me realize I'm not interested in calling our old house: I came to terms a long time ago with the fact that Papá didn't survive. I wouldn't choose a place in Mexico: if I could make just one call, I'd dial the bar in Madrid.

I think *the* bar and not *a* bar, because it's the one where Susana worked, right below our microstudios. I spent so many hours of my year in Spain there (reading at the bar with a beer or drinking coffee in the afternoon, talking with Manu after work) that in my memory it's the only bar in the city. That's where I spent the final heat advisory. The three of us were there in lockdown for twenty-two hours, not knowing it would be the last time we'd be alone together.

I haven't thought about that day in a while, but this simple question takes me straight back.

The siren went off at 8.25. I leapt out of bed. An earthquake, another big one like the one in 2031, I thought, and my body reacted before my brain. I rushed to the door without even putting on pants or shoes: that's when it dawned on me that this alarm was just one wavering note, instead of the *waow-waow-waow* of my childhood. I was in Madrid, not Mexico. There were no earthquakes here, just days of extreme heat. Days of lockdown. It was the third day that summer when temperatures had soared above fifty degrees Celsius. Up till then, countries had adapted to every climatic catastrophe: winter freezes, summer heat, the lack of rain in some areas, terrible hurricanes in others. Daily life, above all in places like Europe, had gone on without much interruption.

During the previous heat advisory, Susana had said: Next time let's come down here, take over the bar, and hide out till it's over. But would they remember that now? What if I went down and no one was there? Then what? It would be so embarrassing to have to remind them of our pledge to spend the day together. I hesitated by the door till I heard my name. Susana was calling me from the street below.

I opened the window. The alarm was still sounding, but its intensity had lessened, and beneath its sustained note I could hear the voice of a woman repeating every two minutes: *Excessive heat advisory. Expect temperatures above fifty degrees. Citizens are urged to take precautions. Excessive heat advisory . . .*

During heat advisories, only essential workers were allowed to move around the city. Transportation was reduced to a minimum and driving private cars was prohibited. Even in our neighborhood south of Madrid, outside the M30 motorway, we had to take precautions to protect the structure of our building as much as its occupants: keep the windows closed, use minimal electricity, turn on the regulators responsible for controlling the climate of our tiny studios.

There I was flaunting the instructions, leaning out over my balcony in the middle of an advisory. Susana stood on the street below, dressed in shorts and a strappy top, hair pulled back in a half ponytail. If the siren hadn't gone off, Susana would've had to open the bar that morning, I thought. A stroke of luck.

'Angélica, are you coming down or what?'

My heart skipped a beat. The plan's still on, I thought. They remember, they do want me to join them. Now I realize (though perhaps I already knew it then) how attentive I was to every expression and sign of affection, looking for proof that they loved me in the same way I loved them, something that would explain what was happening between us. I was convinced that even the tiniest gestures were full of meaning. Like that time when I fell asleep in Susana's bed, my head in her lap while she read. Later she scolded me: You say you come over to study, but actually I think you come here just to take a nap. I laughed, kissed her on the cheek, and told her she was right: I slept better when I knew she was watching over me. Or when I'd go to watch TV in Manu's room: he'd spread out on the couch with his head propped on my thigh, my hand on his hair, his hand on my knee tracing circle after circle. I tried to sound out the limits of our relationship. There was something between us, something I needed, but I wasn't bold enough to ask for it.

I never knew what to do with that desire.

I want to say I met them the same day, but that's impossible. I know I met Manu first. When I got in from the airport, dragging my two suitcases, he was pulling boxes out of a taxi and piling them at the entrance to our building. Our microstudios were next to each other and I didn't have anything to do, so I offered to help him carry stuff upstairs. In return he bought some beers, which we drank sitting on the floor of my studio. He told me he was from Seville, and he was going to work as a lab technician while he waited for a spot to open up in the doctoral program he wanted to get into. I told him I was in Madrid to get a master's degree. We made plans to go to El Rastro together to buy the furnishings we still needed. I was relieved to find a friend so fast: and my next-door neighbor, no less.

If I were to tell the story the way I remember it, I'd say I met Susana that same night, when I went down to the bar for dinner, but I can't have been drinking beer with Manu at my place and talking with her downstairs at the same time. It must have been a different day when I sat down at the bar to order a bocadillo, and she asked me where I was from. She said she'd been living in the building for a few months, and promised to show me around the neighborhood.

Weeks later, the three of us ran into each other at a party on our rooftop. It was the last party before the cold snaps started and the bitter winter frosts kept us from spending time outside. What sparked things off for us was some partygoer's passing comment, which I overheard just as Manu and I went up to the drinks table to pour ourselves more wine. Susana was talking with a big group of people near the table, and someone told her that she seemed like one of those people who have a favorite figure of speech. Of course I do, she said, laughing, don't you? Her answer intrigued me so much that I turned toward her. I don't know whether I was emboldened by the wine or the late night, but I said I liked synecdoche. Because of how it sounded and because of the movie: I wasn't even positive I knew what it meant. Manu asked what a synecdoche was. Susana responded that it was a type of metonymy, and he asked for an example. We clicked. Little by little, the others moved off until it was just the three of us, captivated by our shared curiosity. We forgot the initial question, which led to other questions, which gave way to increasingly ridiculous examples, until we'd polished off the bottle of wine. As we were discussing whether or not to open another, someone put on a song that Manu liked. He stood up and said: This can wait! Right now, we're going to dance. And he took us both by the arm.

When I was a teenager, my mom diagnosed my condition: there was something in me that always wanted more. You just can't get enough, she told me when I got home late because I hadn't known how to choose the right moment to leave a party, and had stayed till the end. Manu and Susana could never get enough either. We stayed even though the party was winding down (the birthday girl had left hours before), talking till it got late, till the alcohol was gone and the speaker's batteries died. The next morning, Manu knocked on my door to ask if I wanted tortitas for breakfast. When I said yes, he told me to invite Susana to join us, she might like some pancakes, too. From then on, we were inseparable.

When we get back to our room after dinner, Mamá tells me she's been seriously considering how much electricity the antenna is wasting. We've been trying to make contact for so many years, perhaps it doesn't make sense anymore, she thinks. Are you going to put it to a vote at the next assembly? I ask, and though she tells me she hasn't decided, I know her well enough to realize she won't be able to get the idea out of her head. She's right that we could use the energy for other things, but the thought of calling off the search chills me to the core.

Though the ranch was ours when the collapse came, our opinion hasn't mattered more than anyone else's for years now. We make decisions as a community. If Papá built this house little by little throughout my childhood and adolescence, Mamá was the one who organized us, the one who united the communities living in our region of the Isthmus of Tehuantepec and offered them an infrastructure, so that together we could all survive.

The world didn't have to end when it did: maybe one or two more generations could have lived under the illusion of normalcy, even in a slow environmental decline. But there's always a breaking point. Was it luck that put Mamá and me on the ranch when the collapse hit? The last communication we had before all our devices went dead was a message from Papá: A new virus, I'll try to get out of Mexico City, it's chaos. Since then, only silence.

I was attracted to Manu from the get-go. He shared so many traits with other men I'd fallen for: a good memory, insatiable curiosity, a desire to explore, to do things, a sense of humor in tune with mine (a blend of biting sarcasm and flights of the imagination that would quickly get away from us). I realized I was attracted to him because I sought out every opportunity I could to talk with him. Sometimes I'd sit down to read or listen to podcasts on my balcony for hours, just waiting for him to come out and find me there. One time, we were both sitting outside enjoying the night air, me with my back against the wall, feet dangling over the edge, he on a bench, drinking a beer. We could've touched one another, hand to elbow, had we reached through the railing.

Do you think you could ever fall back in love with someone you've been in love with before? he asked. Yes, I said, once I love someone, it takes a lot for me to stop loving them. I feel I lose interest quickly, he replied. Not just in people, but in activities too, in places, routines. Once the novelty wears off and I begin to understand how something works, it loses its mystery, its allure. That's what happened when I wanted to learn to play chess. I'm not good at it because I only practiced until I understood what I had to do to improve. I'd figured out the way to study it: I could see the path clearly. I don't know if I'd be capable of following that path, but I had a feeling I already knew the way, which meant I couldn't be bothered to actually go down it. Something similar happens to me with people sometimes. I meet someone new and within a few minutes I can almost always picture where things are heading, what the relationship would be like, who they are. I don't mean to say I'm always right: I've gotten into trouble by judging too quickly, sometimes I'm wrong. The thing is, once I think I can see it clearly, I lose interest. The people who catch my attention are few and far between, the ones who give me vertigo. Vertigo? I asked. Yes, when everything about a person seems so unexpected that I feel vertigo. Like there's no sure path.

I could see it so clearly: how meeting someone could be like standing on the edge of a cliff. I wanted to be one of those people for him. I had a feeling that beneath his words there was an implicit *I'm telling you this because it's what you make me feel*. Now I wonder if that subtext ever actually existed.

If my attraction to Manu came easily, almost naturally, with Susana it took me by surprise. I can perfectly remember the moment when I knew I wanted her. Susana's shift had ended early that day, so at nine she closed out her part of the register, threw on a sweater and sat down next to me at the bar to eat something for dinner. We have to toast, she said. One toast led to another, which led to another, which ended with us walking toward Lavapiés to find a place to dance. We jumped into a club on Calle Cabeza and danced until six in the morning. We danced, drank, twisted and twirled. The place had been half empty when we arrived, but as the hours went by, it got packed. And though we could hardly move for the crowd, even when we jumped up onto the stage, it was like no one else existed. Everything felt possible with her.

When they turned the lights on we took off, hand in hand. I followed her home through the streets of Madrid, taking a route that was longer and more convoluted than necessary. She guiding me and me guiding her. Spinning around half drunk, talking and laughing and then shushing ourselves so as not to make noise. At some point we had to pee, so we took turns squatting between two parked cars. Then we sped away on the off-chance that someone might have seen us. I told her between giggles that I'd never peed in the street before, which gave her another attack of laughter. When I'm drunk, I pee wherever I feel like it, she declared before grabbing my hand again.

I'm not exactly sure what I was feeling. Something was tickling under my skin that I couldn't put a name to, which intensified every time our eyes met. I wish I were back there again, when I realized that Susana would take my hand and lead me all over Madrid without letting go, but that she wouldn't dare take it a step further. And when I realized that, understood it, my reaction was to resist, to stop her mid-giggle, take that step myself, kiss her. Is this OK? I said, like I was asking permission, though she'd kissed me back. She nodded. I was curious what it would feel like, I said. So how does it feel? she returned. I shrugged, smiled, lowered my eyes, may have blushed. You were there too, I said. She laughed at that, kissed me on the cheek and hooked her arm through mine. Homeward, she said.

That was the only time it happened.

When I heard them having sex, I wasn't sure if it was their first time, or if it had happened before. I never asked. We'd come home drunk from bar-hopping that night (Susana leaning on me, Manu walking behind), and I went to my studio and straight to the bathroom, dizzy. I'm not sure why I ended up sitting in the bathtub: it might have seemed more stable than my bed, or I just wanted to be closer to the toilet. That's when I heard them. I wasn't sure at first. I thought I was imagining their voices, but at some point, I heard Susana say Manu's name (actually, she said *Manuel*) loudly, and I knew it wasn't my imagination: the muffled sound was the bed. She was the higher-pitched voice, in a tone I'd never heard her use before, and him . . . Yes, I was listening to him, too. In fact, he was the louder of the two: or rather, his voice was constant, while hers came and went.

I probably would've been embarrassed had I not been so drunk: I would've left the bathroom, closed the door and put on some music. But instead, I sat staring at the wall of white tiles separating us, listening intently. Or maybe I was only halfway paying attention, because something stirred in me as I listened to them. I don't recall picturing them, so I'm sure it was just the sound that turned me on. All my body heat nested in my stomach, and I lost consciousness of my legs, my torso, my head: I forgot how to breathe. Listening to them, only my fingers were left, plus that warmth . . . I thought: If only the wall would disappear. Them over there. Me here.

The next morning, I woke feeling self-conscious about what I'd done. (Why was I embarrassed? For overhearing them, for touching myself, or because I'd burst in on an intimate moment between two people I loved? Would it have bothered them if they knew what had happened? I never told them.) I had to accept that I wanted each one not only on their own, and not only as friends, but together, close, just as I'd heard them.

I was plunged into a deep sadness when I realized I wanted something, but wasn't sure how to ask for it, or if I could even have it. And the feeling only intensified when neither of them invited me to join them for breakfast. Later I realized they'd slept past midday, and by the time they went to knock on my door, I was long gone, in search of who knows what. I walked to the river and sat on the grass to read, pretending I wasn't hungover. I used those hours to convince myself it wasn't worth trying to change things. It's fine, I told myself, it's enough. Let the relationship be what it is. Just the way it already is.

Thinking about it now, I'm sure I didn't want to face being rejected by them. Not then, or any of the other, many occasions I knew they were together without me. At the time, knowing I was going back to Mexico, I figured I didn't have the right to say anything, to change what was between us, though actually I think I was clinging to the hope that not saying anything meant everything was still possible.

I wonder whether they started dating seriously after I left, whether they're still together now, if they've survived the collapse. If they remember me.

I can't sleep. I don't know if it's over these memories, or because of Mamá's proposition that we turn off the antenna. I think about the scientists who waited for a response from space that never came, that time of the Great Silence extending out, confirming our loneliness as a species. I think about the signal we sent. They're called sky waves because they reflect off the atmosphere and return to Earth beyond the horizon. Using them, we could reach Europe. It's unlikely we're the only ones left, but if we can't communicate with anyone else, it's as good as being alone.

To distract myself from my insomnia, I go over every hour of that day in the bar, the last day I would spend alone with them. Of course, we hadn't experienced it that way: even though I was about to leave Spain, it was a day like so many others. Still, I reconstruct every moment and put my memories in order. First, we ate breakfast, then we read, took a nap, watched movies, talked, drank wine: the day went by.

After breakfast, we moved the bar tables aside to make space and took turns blowing up an air mattress. We decided to read awhile before we watched a movie. We put on the playlist we'd made during the many weekends we spent with a hangover (*cruda*, I would say, while they said *resaca*). The warmth of their bodies, together with my lack of sleep the night before, and the sun filtering in through the blinds, put me to sleep. I woke up because my foot was full of pins and needles from being underneath Manu, who was curled around Susana. They had nodded off too. Sleeping like that, I thought, all tangled up together, was symptomatic of the intimacy we weren't able to express. I wanted, like that time in my bathroom, to be closer, to dissolve the distance separating us. To wake them up and truly intertwine our bodies. I shook off the urge and repositioned myself instead: my leg between Manu's, my body pressed against Susana's. Her eyes opened when I moved. She reached out and took my hand. I squeezed her fingers and closed my eyes again.

It's hard to get up in the morning and begin my chores. Today, just like every other day, it's my job to check the greenhouse levels, but when I finally manage to check pH, humidity, temperature and all the other variables that can affect the crops, I'm on autopilot. I can imagine myself five years from now doing the exact same thing. What would we have made, that long-ago day in the bar, of the life

I live now? The more time that goes by, the harder it is to hold on to the hope that one day all we've lost will return: airplanes, internet, instantaneous communication. What are we doing? Yearning for the past as we wait for the collapse to reach us? Surviving, that's what my mom would say. Sometimes I tease her by saying it's not enough to survive, we have to *live*. One day at a time, she replies, as she monitors our supply of canned food, or the crops, or the solar cells, or the water purifier.

Trying to put this thought aside, I return to the night in the bar. It was late, I'm not sure exactly what time, maybe already the early hours. I remember we were drinking wine, waffling over whether to play a game of some kind, when Susana asked:

'Who would you want to spend the end of the world with?'

'It's not *the* end of the world,' I answered, putting my book down. 'It's *an* end of the world. Each day is the end of the world right now.'

'I know, but let's say it was the end of the world. Who would you spend it with?'

'Do you have an answer?' Manu asked her. 'I guess I'd have to think about it.'

'Well,' she said, 'I'm not totally sure, but I'd like to be with people I love, people I feel comfortable with, you know? Maybe my parents, maybe friends . . . The two of you, for instance.'

'For that we'd need Angélica to quit messing around and decide to stay in Madrid,' Manu said.

They looked at me, waiting for a response. I'd assumed it was just another hypothetical question, the kind we asked each other all the time. But now I wonder whether in fact they were asking me to stay, I wonder whether I just didn't catch it, didn't want to hear it.

Maybe if I'd caught the true intention in their words, I would have set my glass of wine down, taken them both by the hand, and told them that if what they were really asking me to do was to stay, I would: I'd spend the end of the world with them. But I kept quiet. I didn't know I'd never have another chance, that the collapse would hit a few months later, and that I was deluding myself every time

I thought I'd go back there, that we'd have time in the future to do everything we wanted. I'd never felt such fear, or such affection, as I did then.

And so I said: 'I'm not sure *who* I'd spend it with, but I do know *where*.'

'Oh, of course! I forgot your dad built one of those bunkers for surviving the end of the world,' Susana said, and didn't press me further.

I'd like to go back to that moment and explore its possibilities. Now everything (the world, time itself) feels small. Having kept quiet means I now must carry the weight of that silence, of everything that might have been.

The buzzing of the generators welcomes us when we return to the antenna in the afternoon. We check the equipment carefully in search of a transmission, and like every time before, there's nothing. I stare at my reflection on the screen, the wavy green line going up and down. I could be looking at any number of measurements: maybe an electrocardiogram, the pulse of one body searching for another, but it's nothing more than another failed attempt, a sky wave with no response.

I think again of Manu and Susana. I let myself imagine them one last time.

I turn the antenna off and the wave on the screen disappears. All that's left is my reflection. I need to believe that beyond the horizon other worlds exist. When Mamá proposes we stop using the antenna, I'll vote against it. ∎

AESTHETICA
CREATIVE WRITING AWARD 2021

SUBMIT
YOUR WRITING TODAY

POETRY
FICTION

WIN £5000
& PUBLICATION

DEADLINE 31 AUGUST 2021   AESTHETICAMAGAZINE.COM

ANDREA ABREU

1995

Andrea Abreu was born in Tenerife, Spain. She is author of the poetry collection *Mujer sin párpados*. Her first novel, *Panza de burro*, will be translated into various languages and adapted for the screen by El Estudio.

THE NEW ME

Andrea Abreu

TRANSLATED BY JULIA SANCHES

The new me is patient and calm. Not even a little deranged or hysterical. Gone is the woman who'd scream Toni-I'm-gonna-crack-your-head-on-the-floor when my husband left the handles of the dessert spoons unwashed. Before, way before, I was the kind of person who didn't understand the importance of doshas, who ate white flour, had destructive thoughts and drank coffee.

My life changed when I worked up the courage to leave Toni and joined the Biodanza class where I met Ruymán. It was being publicized on the bulletin board of the cultural center. That morning I knocked back a barraquito and started walking frantically around town, totally unhinged, more washed-out than a land crab. I felt tired and alone. My son had just moved to Madrid and stuck me with Miqui, a mutt he'd recently adopted from a shelter for senior dogs. His fur was white and shaggy, curly and dotted all over with burrs. Two days earlier, Toni and I had signed the divorce papers. My thoughts kept cycling between fear and euphoria. One second I thought I shouldn't have gotten separated, that nobody would love me because I was bitter and ugly and had ugly hair with split ends that looked like they'd been gnawed on by a goat. The next it was like

I'd lifted a dead weight I'd been carrying right in the middle of my back, like a kestrel perched on my spine.

I started Biodanza the next day. In the mirrored room of Mayte's house – she was the woman who ran the class – that smelled of rust and saltpeter, people smiled all the time, talked slowly and made you feel like you were part of something bigger. There weren't any gross men ripping farts or spitting on street corners. We started with a round of introductions and everyone shared how Biodanza had changed their lives. I didn't say anything because my mind and body were still attached to my previous life. Before I started this practice, I had all these ideas in my head, said a woman of around sixty with grayish, waist-length hair. Love yourself, respect yourself, live in the moment. But it was only in my brain and once I started coming to classes, I felt it in my heart. Biodanza is a game changer when you're ready to take charge of your life, said a younger woman in response. People even noticed at work, explained another woman with glazed eyes. My colleagues say, you've changed, it's like you're happier. Your eyes seem brighter, she finished and let her hand rest on her chest while a man who must have been her husband stroked the nape of her neck. I was scared and a little intimidated. The people in that class knew how to sit on the floor without looking like lumps of meat and to use words in a way that gave them deeper meaning. They talked about themselves as if they knew who they were, when all I knew was that I was on my own after being married for almost twenty years.

After the first Biodanza session there was the macrobiotic cooking class Marina had recommended, followed by workshops on how to shop sustainably, on self-acceptance and family constellations, then there was the one where we designed and built our own compost bin and the one on healthy family dynamics that I tried to get Toni and my son to attend but in the end went to on my own, followed by workshops in African dance, mindfulness, reiki, green fertilizers, contact improv and tantra. After two years of transition and learning, I had unlocked the new me. People trusted me. I had earned a reputation as a woman who was peaceful and knowledgeable about things like growing moringa and Bach flower remedies. That's when Ruymán showed up. Before he came along, the only men in the group had really long hairs growing out of their ears and their noses.

Some of them smelled of cheap lavender cologne from Mercadona, and there's no scent in the world I hate more. But then Ruymán showed up. He was chummy with me from the get-go, kept looking my way and giggling. He was tall and skinny, skinnier than a beanpole, except with a broad back. He was more or less the same age as me, forty-three to my forty-five. Big, dark hands covered in veins and hairs thick as prickles. I found him handsome, even though his head was as bald as a scorched field.

We started sleeping together after our Biodanza meetups even though I knew he was married and had two girls. Our classmates, especially Mayte, suspected there was something going on, but no one said a thing. Nearly everyone enrolled in the course practiced some form of polyamory. Well, not me, really. I only started sleeping with Ruymán after I'd given Toni the boot. Still, I believed in the freedom to love many souls at once.

When I got home after our session that day, I was tired and my stomach was in knots. It was Thursday and on Thursdays Ruymán usually came home with me. We'd practice holistic reflexology and, afterward, sleep together. Except he told me he wasn't in the mood, that he wanted to spend time with his wife and kids. I didn't often get jealous or resentful. I'd achieved a high degree of self-love, especially after I wrote *Being beautiful means being yourself* on the bathroom mirror. This time I was seized by an acid-hot rage I hadn't experienced since I'd stopped living with Toni, who used to stay out until all hours of the night with the girl from the arepa shop. I took a Scottish shower, a technique I'd learned from Nubia, the woman who ran the herbal store. The combination of hot water and cold water makes your veins dilate and relaxes the muscles. I sent my son a message on WhatsApp and stared at my phone for a while, but he didn't answer. I went to the kitchen to whip up some dinner. I prepared a piece of wholewheat spelt toast with hummus and kimchi I'd made myself. I was super proud of my kimchi. I started eating the toast in slow, very slow bites. Since leaving Toni I've chewed every mouthful of food thirty-three times, no more and no less. This helps control gas and eases digestion. When I was on chew number seventeen of my second mouthful, a chunk of bread fell on the floor and I noticed a huge pee stain on the kitchen rug. Miqui must have gotten in somehow, and taken a nice long piss on my precious Lebanese rug. I was always telling the girls from class I'd bought it second-hand for peanuts, but the truth was I'd ordered it on Amazon and it had wiped out my bank account halfway through the month. It was the first time Miqui had peed inside. I cleaned the massive stain with a dish towel soaked in vinegar, the only cleaning product I've used since discovering the new me. I rushed to the back door and walked into the yard. There he was, lying on a bed of old patchwork quilts, quilts I'd made in that workshop Lunita had led at Tacoronte's country house. At first I didn't give a damn about Miqui. I don't really like animals, though I tend to keep that to myself. So when my son left, I laid out a bed of quilts for him under the back porch and didn't let him in the house. I let him have my precious quilts because I figured if I was going to keep a sentient being from living in the house and sleeping in my bed, the least I could do was give him a real treat.

When Miqui saw me at the back door, he looked up at me with those hazy old dog eyes of his, those eyes like mountain fog. I said: Miqui-Miqui-Miquito, that was very bad of you. You're a bad boy. You're a bad boy who doesn't behave. But you deserve to live and to feel. We all deserve to live and be loved. That's why I'm not going to whack you upside the head, even though I really want to. Instead, I'll give you a second chance. We all make mistakes and we all want to be forgiven, isn't that right? I shut the door. Halfway down the hall, I felt a stitch in my chest and turned back. I peeked through the small window of the metal door and checked that Miqui wasn't dead. Ever since discovering the new me, I've been convinced that negative thoughts have devastating powers. I was afraid I'd destroyed him, squashed him like a rabbit on the highway. When I looked through the glass, I was shocked: Miqui was fine, better than fine, even. He was humping the pile of quilts like a billy goat. As his body shuddered over the colorful blankets, it looked like a metal spring. Wiki-wiki-wiki. His movements were electric, unstoppable. There was something magnetic about his penis. It was sharp and red like a tube of old lipstick, and poked out from his belly like a tuberose bud. Miqui was already an old boy by the time they'd neutered him, and he had the libido of a teenager. I watched him for a few seconds, took a breath, then went to my room.

That night Ruymán didn't text me before he went to sleep like he usually did on the days we saw each other. I thought of sending him a WhatsApp but quickly realized that an independent woman wouldn't behave that way, that it'd look like I didn't know how to be on my own. Needy text messages did not mesh with my new personality. I sat at my computer and watched a couple of lectures on holistic health and natural diets that I'd started a few days ago. Though I made an effort to concentrate, this persistent sound kept boring into my ear – the sound of sandpaper. I tried to focus on the screen for a few minutes, then realized Miqui was clawing at the back door. Miqui had never clawed at the door before. He didn't usually make much noise, and the only time I ever communicated with him was to give him Friskies and water. I got up and walked down the hall. I looked through the door window and saw him standing on his hind legs, crying and crying the way little kids do when they're sad. I watched him for a second, then turned around. As I made my way down the hall, anguish split my body like an axe. I wasn't being compassionate, and the new me was supposed to. Since leaving Toni I've understood the importance of vibrations. After all, the world is made up of vibrational energy that transmits information. The vibrations you send out with your thoughts and feelings attract the same kind of energy from the universe back into your life. Like attracts like, Maya, the girl from Pilates, was always saying. I turned around and opened the back door a little fearfully, real slow, like I was trying to keep out something bad – bad and invisible. I'd never had a dog in the house before. My mom couldn't stand animals either, even though her parents kept goats, ferrets, rabbits and chickens black as night. When I was a little girl, she taught me to be scared of dogs. So when my son brought Miqui home, I thought something bad was bound to happen to me, which is why I kept him outside, in the backyard, with the owls and wall geckos.

I let Miqui in the house for the first time. I picked him up by the front paws and tried to lug him to the rug next to my bed. For ages I'd been telling people I slept on the floor with nothing but a yoga mat and a pillow, but it wasn't true, though I planned to start any minute. Most of the time I slept on a memory foam mattress on the floor. Miqui sank his teeth into my arm and I dropped him. I realized that our lack of contact had turned him pretty feral; it was like he'd never lived in a house before. I wasn't much of a caregiver either. I left him in the hall and went to my room. I put on the red viscose herringbone nightie I'd bought on sale at Natura. I put a guided meditation CD on the stereo. I dripped some almond oil onto my hands and started massaging my neck while attempting to concentrate on the words: *Let's begin today by finding a comfortable, calm and peaceful position. Close your eyes and take a deep breath in. Remember you are safe, that in this moment and place you are well. You have nothing to fear. Repeat the following with me, either in your head or aloud: I am ready to forgive myself and to give myself this beautiful gift because I love my* – MIQUIIIII I screamed like I was possessed. While my eyes were closed, he'd snuck into the bedroom and peed. This time, on a corner of the mattress. I dashed out, still slippery with almond oil, and grabbed the vinegar-soaked dish towel. When I got back to the room, Miqui was lying on the shag rug next to my bed. Chop-chop, I started scrubbing at the piss before it could seep through the bottom sheet. I scrubbed so long that my arms hurt like hell, almost as much as they had when I'd held Ruymán's head for an hour the day of his first Biodanza class, while he whispered: I need a woman who will love me and cradle me and suckle me. When I finished, one part of the bed was sopping wet and stank of vinegar. I was overcome with a sudden and overwhelming exhaustion, and

lay down on a corner of the mattress. Miqui was curled up on the
rug and I figured it'd be all right if he spent the night in my room.
I woke up at five in the morning burning hot and covered in sweat. I
was having one of those episodes that had started a few months ago
where I'd wake up gasping for breath and feeling like I was on fire.
There was Miqui. Lying on the rug. Breathing like an old man who's
let himself nod off during a documentary about lions. He reminded
me a little of my father before he'd died, of my father lying on the
sofa in an unbuttoned shirt grimy with cow muck. I took off my red
herringbone nightie and kicked the sheets onto the floor. My legs
were wide open. My skin smelled of almonds and was soft, as soft as a
peach. I circled my belly button with my fingers and touched myself.
Miqui's breathing grew louder and louder, so loud he sounded like
a hog scarfing down leftovers and banana peels. I didn't manage to
come so I stopped for a bit. The image of Miqui shuddering over a
pile of quilts flitted back into my head. His clearly defined red penis
budding like a flower, practically budding inside me. I came without
having to touch myself. It was the first time that had happened to me,
and it wouldn't be the last.

Starting the next morning, Miqui lived with me inside the house.
From the very first day, whenever I got home from the lectures I gave
on Ayurvedic medicine to help pay the bills, he'd be waiting for me
at the door. The house was covered in piss, the cushions, rugs and
corners of every piece of furniture eaten away by urine. I started to
find beauty in cleaning it up. The mix of urine and vinegar whets my
appetite. When my friends from Biodanza call me these days to talk
about their boyfriends, Miqui flops down at my feet. His ear hairs
tickle the skin under my toenails.

He still doesn't like it when I grab him by the paws and lug him
from one place to another. I respect his priorities, but he treats me
like his servant. He tears up every dress he finds outside the closet. He
even shattered the set of Chinese teacups my friend Estrella gave me.
Once, after a phenomenal workshop on how to make vegan cheese
out of nuts and dried fruit, he filled the house with spoiled trash. He'd

pulled out rotten scraps from the compost bin in the backyard and strewn them around every room while I was out. During the day, living with Miqui is dreadful. But the nights make up for it. Every night, like an obedient monk, a doting monk, he falls asleep on the rug. First, he humps it for a quarter-hour while I watch. Then he circles three times and lies down. Every night, like a self-sacrificing nun, I devote myself to masturbating. Around five in the morning I get the usual hot flash. I turn toward the door and watch him breathe. I play with my nipples. I watch his red, curved penis. I don't need much. All I have to do is picture him shuddering like a car about to tear across the asphalt. It's enough just to draw his boiled-crab penis in my head. His penis slipping through the jawbone-shaped holes he's made in the rugs, the quilts and the red herringbone nightgown. ∎

CAMILA FABBRI

1989

Camila Fabbri was born in Buenos Aires,
Argentina. She is a writer, director and
actor. Her first work of fiction was *Los
accidentes*, and her second was the novel *El
día que apagaron la luz*.

NOBODY KNOWS WHAT
THEY'RE DOING

Camila Fabbri

TRANSLATED BY JENNIFER CROFT

Before we broke up, Juan shared a folder with me in Google Drive. It was called 'Quotes' and was an archive of all the things he found intriguing. He'd spent a year compiling quotes from artists, celebrities, and people he overheard on the street or on a bus or somewhere. A place you could go for ideas when it seemed like there weren't going to be any more, ever. He knew perfectly well that it was a treasure, and he gave it to me. I was twenty-eight years old when Juan moved out, and I thought a lot about my family, maybe more than I did about him. Our empty kitchen brought back my dad's clandestine crying, hidden partly under Enrique Macaya Márquez's voice as the football match unfolded on Channel 11, my mom's agitated attempts to argue in a whisper, destroying her vocal cords. I thought a lot every day about how sorry I felt for people who could live like that, with high blood pressure, screaming at each other, as if it were something I would eventually have to get used to. I thought about myself, about those first years of my life, shut in the closet in my grandmother's room so no one could see me gradually constructing my personality.

After Juan left, I started going into the Quotes file on a daily basis. I think I sensed that this wellspring of images had to do with the shattering of something stable. Night after night I went into the infinite archive until I landed on an article from a Spanish paper that specialized in hard-to-believe facts. It was about the *Argentavis magnificens*, a giant relative of the buzzard. A six-million-year-old bird with black and blue feathers that was eight meters wide, same as a school bus. A creature that laid less than one egg per year, one of the lowest fertility rates in natural history. The article came with a picture for scale. A man was looking into the camera from beside the fossil of the *Argentavis*, which was spreading its wings behind him in an Argentine museum. Possibly the largest bird ever to fly the skies. It was amazing and it looked like the shadow of the man who was looking at the camera not really sure of what he was doing. He was alone and well dressed. He seemed to be trying to glean his future by looking ahead, with that thing, like some historical nightmare, perched monstrously behind his back.

So I called Juan. I broke our pact to give each other space, and I said thank you. That he'd made me think about the past. And that the past was family, and family was that bird.

They were both teenagers, both in makeshift pajamas – no patterned pants with bows for them. Instead, they wore T-shirts with rock bands on them and panties. I was there, too. Watching in silence. Distance and obsession. The same feeling I get when I watch high-risk sport competitions, so removed from my quiet urban daily life, yet there it is: the beauty of a ski jumper soaring, who could perfectly well shatter their jaw into a thousand pieces if they fell. I watch, and I admire, almost always from a distance.

It was very early in the morning, and I was very small. I'd just turned five. My sisters' eyes were puffy from sleep and from the disruptions of their hormones. It all started when one told the other she wanted to read, and the other responded with early-morning grumpiness that she could care less, she wanted to listen to music. A long while of this back-and-forth that led nowhere, with me glimpsing now and then their growing bodies, girls who were sisters to each other and half-sisters to me. And me? I hated that idea of *half* so much, I hated not being something fully, that those girls in their underwear were my family, but at the same time, not. 'I want to listen to music,' Ana was saying, and Cecilia wasn't saying anything back anymore, she was just biting her lips because there were no words for something so not fair. The having to share a room when they were practically adults, with their own complete ideas, posters of the Frente País Solidario – FREPASO – the first political party that had excited them as much as Indio Solari moving his neck around in the middle of a stage on the outskirts of Buenos Aires. 'I want to listen to music,' Ana was saying, and she picked me up and started moving around the room with me to the rhythm of an Argentine pop song while her sister Cecilia told her to cut it out, it wasn't funny anymore, Mom was sleeping, and she was going to wake her up. Ana said she didn't care, let her wake up, and let Troy burn. She kept saying that, 'Let Troy Burn', 'Troy is ablaze', and I like didn't have the faintest idea of what ablaze meant.

The first blow came then, out of nowhere. I can still hear the sound Ana's skin made because it was in my foreground. I could feel the movement of her springing back, like a breeze on my cheek. She put me down on the floor so she could bring her hands up to her face. I crawled onto the bed so I could see better. Same as ever: always wanting the best seats for the catastrophe. 'I want to read,' Cecilia said and lay down on the bed. In that instant my sisters were two animals about to work some shit out. Ana leaped on Cecilia and did something to her face, I don't know exactly what, but she did it well, it was like a burst of inspiration. Then they were scratching each other and pulling each other's long hair – both of them had the same hair: long, black, thick, no bangs. All their genes in a hairstyle. They kept saying the same thing, it was like there was no way to revise the script, one of them wanted one thing and the other wanted something else, and they were hurting each other. Watching them do that work was like watching a room fall into disorder. They forgot I was there. They kept screaming at each other for a few minutes until my dad came running in, wearing his own makeshift pajamas, which were also a T-shirt and underwear. All of them exceedingly exposed, clawing at each other in their underwear. The man who barged into the room without knocking and tried to separate the sisters was my father, but not theirs. He could still get angry, though, and snap into action, because this was his house, and that girl sitting on the bed was his daughter, and he was already on familiar terms with these teenagers. He grabbed Ana by the arms and trapped her in an embrace meant to immobilize her. Cecilia sat up on her bed and combed her fingers through her hair. Her face was as red as if all her blood had concentrated there. Ana kept yelling, now in the living room, while my dad kept telling her she was a fucking brat.

I stayed quiet. I was trying to figure out which one of them had won. Cecilia looked me in the eyes, suddenly remembering I was there. 'These things happen when people love each other,' she said – something like that. And that's what I would have believed then. That loving each other is letting Troy go up in flames. That to love is to burn up and burn down.

My mom was asleep in their room. Oblivious to everything. Two hours later we were having breakfast in the kitchen. The teenagers were still in their underwear, and the grown-ups had assembled outfits. We were listening to a football match on the radio. He made comments about miscalled fouls and Rafael Maceratesi, the striker for Rosario Central. No one responded. Cecilia was dabbing a big scratch on her forehead with a cotton ball with alcohol on it. Ana was eating biscuits.

A year after that, my mom told my sisters she could no longer support them, so they found jobs as errand runners for an oil company in town. With their tiny salary they decided to rent an apartment to live in together. Ana and Cecilia were eighteen and nineteen years old, they were radical activists, and they had a group of friends who played witty, unique pranks. When my half-sisters went to live somewhere else, I was left alone with the adults and no other option than to start growing up.

From then on, I started losing my obsessions, and thus came the breaking down. Malfunctioning. The ski jumper's broken jaw.

The moving truck came on a morning I couldn't wake up. I was burning with a fever caused by some loathsome bacteria the doctors ended up finding a number of days later, an illness born in Wales in 1900, which I killed with antibiotics. I was seven: the age of plagues. We moved as soon as it started to get light out. They carted me off, along with the rest of the furniture. We were going to live for an unspecified amount of time with Elsa, my mom's mom. We'd run out of money, and my dad was tired of selling virtual encyclopedias. We had to leave the apartment with the terrace we'd been renting for more than five years. My mom was starting to study psychoanalysis and applied its terminology in our conversations. No one played along. My dad answered with things that were too concrete, having long since shrugged off the mystique of trying to conquer her with sweet-sounding words. Armed with a purebred dog and three electric heaters, we fled.

Sarandí 944 was the new address I had to learn by heart, for things like filling out the entry forms for the contests at the grocery store. Sarandí 944 was an old building, with high ceilings and freezing floors. Sarandí 944 was dark and smelled like an era that preceded my existence on Earth. Opposite was a Chinese temple that was mostly open on the weekends, and next to it, a center for the workers' mutual. Nobody visited us at Sarandí 944 because it was too far away. I wasn't allowed to have friends over, boys or girls. We never talked about how ashamed we'd be to have someone over.

My grandmother was seventy-five years old and had a room of her own. She sold the double bed she'd shared with her husband and now slept in a twin. In widowhood, she felt more comfortable in cozy spaces. A meter-long wooden rosary hung beside the bed. A portable radio with most of the buttons stuck. A bedspread with ordinary flowers, its colors faded. A telephone set, black, with the gigantic Telecom insignia. She slathered on rejuvenating cream every morning because she believed blindly in the powers of any science that smelled good. She took ten full turns around her room because it activated her circulation, according to that radio program at 7 a.m., the one that played an ad every ten minutes with a jingle that went: 'A perfume on your skin, you'll look great, you'll hold up even better, the magic of Biocom.' I was given the living room to sleep in. There weren't any more bedrooms in our borrowed home. I liked it because all things that make no sense enthuse you when you're seven. With us lived her female dog and our male dog. They got into it at least once a day at the end of the hallway that linked the kitchen with the rest of the house, snarling at each other, fur flying. The male dog was three times the size of the female dog and always wanted to mount her because he was always in heat. The sound of a dogfight could be a constant, too, like the argument over the end-of-year bonus and the end of the month, which always ended in a concerted slam of the door. I had to listen from behind the door, I wanted to know the details, what deals were struck, how close exactly we were to the end of their relationship. I stood guard like a huntress, my arms resting on the door frame – that way I could know when one of them was on top of the other or if there was still time to separate them. My sisters were living on the ground floor of an old building with floors so ruined and worm-eaten it looked like a cemetery. I stopped seeing them. We only talked on the phone. They spoke to me in the high-pitched voices of people who feel guilty about something they haven't really come to terms with yet, and I made do with listening to that condescending tone of theirs. The poor little abandoned sister without means was a comfortable enough role for me. Hi Cami, how are you doing, how are you doing, how are you doing.

Sunday nights were for broadcast television. Elsa was a fan of the blonde hostess who wore Silvana stockings and kept brushing the bangs off her face and shrieking in astonishment. One of those nights my grandmother was massaging her chest at the location of her heart. She had heard, also on the radio, that it was good for her valves. I know because she told me so repeatedly – she tried to make health advice stick with me. A man from the countryside had won the million pesos and the albino-haired hostess was exhorting him to tell the viewers all about how he was going to spend it. I think that was one of the first times I ever heard someone talk so devotedly about having children. The man was so happy it seemed like he was ridden with angst. He talked about all the things he wanted to buy his children, all the countries he wanted to take them to. It was an emotional moment in the show and my grandmother narrowed her watery eyes and asked me if I was ever going to have kids. I was eight years old the night she asked and I thought that having kids was just letting them spend hours on end locked in a closet because that, and only that, could seem exciting to them.

At Sarandí 944 I became mute. I started listening behind doors and walls. I stopped sleeping because I had to watch over the couple sleeping in the next room. I abandoned my own ideas and started having theirs. I didn't talk at the table, or at family birthdays, or on Christmas or New Year's. Somebody else always did it for me. I made my calculations, I offered up my savings, I hugged the woman who was my mother while she dried her hair and held back tears, I went for drives with my dad on Sundays once they separated, I went into the bouncy castle and pretended to enjoy it, every time anybody asked me how I was doing I always said fine, I covered the dark circles under my eyes from my insomnia with a liquid foundation of my grandmother's, Elsa, the woman who would wake me up shouting in the middle of the night so I could help her walk to the bathroom, I locked myself in that closet more and more, spending more and more hours of the day shut in. When no one else was around, I would open the door to this piece of furniture that took up an entire wall and dive in among the fur coats and gabardine suits. It smelled like mothballs. Like that famous pianist with the dark glasses and the Afro who moves his shoulders around wildly when he gets really into a song, as if he were giving himself a deep massage. That thing he does, which is so ugly, which makes it look like he's about to fall off his bench. That thing he does, which is so deformed and disfiguring, bears a strong resemblance to how I grew up.

The cat throws up three times on the living room floor. I don't know what's wrong with her. I clean it up with a napkin with animal cartoons on it. I'm never disgusted by what comes out of this animal. I clean and think about other things, anything: respiratory illnesses, statistics, viruses, body temperature, bacteria, minimum wage. I feel like a mother who wipes snot and eats crumbs up off the floor. Someone who has lost their ability to feel disgust. I throw away the vomit wadded up into a ball over Mickey Mouse and drop onto the sofa. The phone rings again and it's Marcos. He's as in touch as he can be with the reception he gets in the Patagonian wind. He asks me if I got my period, and I say not yet. He's anxious, and there's nothing he can do. There's nothing I can do, either. We are facing an infinite and merciless historical event. He asks me what we'd do if the delay turned out to be a child. I tell him I'm not sure yet.

On the final link in the Quotes file on Google Drive I find this video. A baby discovers sounds after they put a hearing aid on him for the first time. Never in my life had I seen an astonished baby before, but that's what happens in these shots. The baby opens his eyes, laughs like crazy, nonstop. He can't believe this appearance of a sense, this good ghost that had been hidden away from the day he was born up till now. You can hear his mother, even though you don't see her in the video. She doesn't stay quiet, quite the opposite, in fact, she shrieks, full of emotion. She lets her nerves escape through her mouth. Hers is a maternal joy, something I haven't experienced, but it seems right to me. The baby laughs, the mother cries. This child with the hearing aid is their family and their future now. The baby's astonishment persists, he's looking at the camera now. He stays still there. He has no idea what he's doing. ■

DAINERYS
MACHADO VENTO

1986

Dainerys Machado Vento was born in Havana, Cuba, and is co-founder of the publisher Sualos/ Swallows. She is the author of *Las noventa Habanas*. 'The Color of Balloons' is part of a new project, *El álbum de las treintañeras*.

THE COLOR OF BALLOONS

Dainerys Machado Vento

TRANSLATED BY WILL VANDERHYDEN

Rogelio saw me take my phone out of my purse and was about to start complaining that I was always on Instagram, so I shot him the first question that came into my head:

'So how are they going to do the gender reveal?'

'What?'

Neutralized. He's always hated talking about babies, especially in those days, when we'd spent more than six months fucking day and night, trying any way we could to get me pregnant or for me to get him pregnant, if that's what it came to.

'I asked if you know how my *prima* is going to reveal the sex of her little blessing.'

'Leydi isn't your *prima*.' Clearly he was itching to change the subject, since he knows full well that Miami is the city of *primos*, and that here a *primo* isn't a 'cousin' so much as the first – *el primer* – human being who lets you into their life, especially when you're as poor as we had been for so many years.

'*Oye*, why are you being so lame,' I defended myself with

conviction. Something told me it was a good day to win any fight I felt like picking. 'Do you or do you not know how their baby's sex is going to be revealed? I mean, Google says we're going to an event that could put our lives at serious risk: November 2019, gender reveal in Texas, a plane crashed carrying 350 liters of pink water minutes before letting the parents know they were bringing a little female worker, potentially a Republican, into the world.'

'Female worker? What's the matter with you? All I'm asking is that you don't say anything at the party about us trying to have a baby, be it boy or girl.'

'Or non-binary, Rogelio, I don't want our baby to be put into some heteronormative straitjacket at such a tender age.'

'Will you please put your phone down?' Dream on – he was trying to distract me from my social convictions and my desire to mess with him.

'Why? You're the one driving. Oh look, here's another example: a year earlier, April 2018, 47,000 acres set alight in Arizona when a couple tried to use colored fireworks to reveal the sex of their little worker, another potential Republican. It says here that their worker-girl was born healthy a few months later, but that the firefighters spent eight million dollars putting out the flames caused by the parents' stunt. Can you even wrap your head around how much eight million dollars is? No, no. You can't. These kinds of parties are known as "*Cultura de blancos heteronormativos*" hashtag #straightwhiteculture.'

'With balloons, mijita, with balloons. Por favor, don't be such a drama queen.'

'What'd you say, you fucking dipshit?' I only thought the vocative, I didn't actually vocalize it, I cut my question off at 'what'd you say', retaining a modicum of decency.

'Leydi is going to do her gender reveal with helium-filled balloons that they'll let out of a box: if the balloons are pink, they're going to have a girl; if they're blue, they're going to have a boy.' My husband was feigning patience.

'You're telling me this total *hija de puta* is going to kill off three or four endangered birds who are going to mistake the balloons for food and choke on the plastic?'

Rogelio gave me a withering look. I tasted potential victory and returned to the attack:

'Either way, *mi amor*, they already passed on the idea of having an abortion; she's been carrying her little blessing around for seven months now, who'll probably vote Republican too, and get breastfed exclusively for Instagram posts. Look: hashtag #nursinginpublicisaright, #breastfeedingnomatterwhat, #titsweatandall, #fuckedbuthappy.'

'*Ño*, wow, gender-reveal parties really get you wound up, mija. Please, I'm begging you, put your phone away.'

'No.' I summoned my best human-rights-defender tone. 'I'm checking my ovulation calendar, and looks like tonight we have to fuck again, these are my good days.'

'Don't start with that, *coño*, it makes me not want to go to the party.'

'What can I say, with my degree in biology and my master's in gender politics' – and my impulse to mess with people, I should've added – 'I have zero desire to go to this fucking ode to capitalist binarism. None of these people give a shit that a flock of birds is going to choke to death on those balloons, be they pink or blue. And let me ask you, Rogelio: what if the baby isn't a boy or a girl, what color should the balloons be then?'

Silent, defeated, Rogelio drove on till we reached the last corner separating us from the debacle. As we turned the corner, a street lined with new cars parked almost on top of each other opened out in front of us. Miraculously, we found a spot on an old lady's lawn who – oh-so accommodating – greeted us kindly by flipping a right-hand bird.

I got out of the car, shot the old lady a look, put my phone back in my purse and scanned the sky in search of killer airplanes. We were safe. For now. I grabbed the expensive – very expensive and unnecessary – gift we'd bought two days before; a gift that Leydi's baby boy or baby girl (or non-binary baby, though the balloons wouldn't admit such a possibility) would probably outgrow within three months of being born. Rogelio went on ahead so he could enter the house by himself, hands in his pockets. It's not like it was cold outside, just the opposite, the dog-day Miami heat had my makeup running and the back of his shirt damp; it was just his way of indicating he wanted to get away from me, that I'd won the first round. This party was shaping up to be a blast, especially when it came to my desire to mess with people and my six months as a failed vagina.

'Greetings Kendall people,' my *tío* Esteban shouted when Rogelio and I walked through the door. 'I'm wondering when I'm gonna get my invitation to your *yendereveal*, you're up next.'

'Hola *tío*, how have you been?' I call him *tío*, but Esteban isn't actually my uncle, either, which is why I always address him with the formal *usted* and never let him hug me, because his hands tend to wander.

'Fine, *sobrina*, fine, waiting for you and Rogelio to decide to have a *beibi*.'

I hadn't told anyone about my failures. And to tell the truth, we weren't really sure we wanted to bring another little worker (boy, girl or enby) into the world, but we'd been told a thousand times that a child born in the United States tended to expedite the citizenship process. So I smiled at my uncle, who is not my uncle, and gave him a pat on the shoulder, not offering any kisses or details, or a chance to surreptitiously grope my ass.

'Leydi is out back, come in, come in, she's expecting you guys.'

Leydi was doing her gender reveal in her backyard, hashtag #lowerclass god level. I took a moment to imagine how the pictures of the party would look on Instagram.

'*Amiga de mi alma!*' she shrieked when she saw us walk out into the backyard, and her belly began bouncing up and down like a yo-yo that was trying to pop out of her throat. 'I'm so glad you guys are here! If you brought a gift, put it on the surprise table, I don't want to see it. I hope you bought yellow or white, because we won't know this baby's sex for a few hours.'

'Hours?' I couldn't help myself.

'Ay, chica, I mean the party is going to last a while. I don't know if it'll be hours or minutes, I'm so excited. But this *angelito* in my belly will be a blessing no matter what,' Leydi said, so predictable, so basic, so unphotogenic, and she wrapped her arms around her belly as if they were a boa constrictor ready to squeeze the life out of its prey.

'Sure, sure, *prima*, no problem, it was just a question, hashtag #soexcited.' I took cover behind any justification I could, while setting my expensive gift down on a table with a nylon (!) tablecloth.

'Speaking of crazy questions, *amiga de mi alma*, when are you and Rogelio going to invite us to your gender-reveal party? You're running out of time, right? I mean, you're already getting up there in your thirties.'

'Haha,' my husband grumbled, not actually a laugh, but a 'here we go again'. I grabbed his sweaty hand with feigned passion, all to take revenge for the fact that he'd left me behind when walking into the house. I kept quiet for a few seconds. I savored the panic in his eyes when he thought I was going to reveal that we'd been screwing day and night for six months, to the point where we were disgusted with each other. But no, Leydi had ruined the party all by herself with her bad taste, she didn't need my help:

'Who knows, Leydi? We haven't made up our minds yet. There's still time.' I heard Rogelio let out a sigh of relief.

'Time? No, no, you're using up all your time deciding, you've been in Miami for four years now, you both have stable jobs, good credit –' Here, having credit is more important than health when it comes to procreation. 'I would say that time . . . time . . . you don't have so much, I mean, look at Julita, waiting around for Mr Perfect, she's gonna end up a nun, poor thing . . .'

As if summoned by her name, Julita's shrill voice interrupted the pathetic scene that was promising to drag on and on:

'Hola, hola, *mi gente*!' – never more apropos the idea of being 'saved by the bell', the bell-like voice of Julita. 'So good to see you guys. How are you, Rogelio? How are you, girlfriend? It feels like

I never see you two anymore! We run into each other at a gender reveal, but then I won't see you till there's a funeral, if at Easter then not until the Fourth of July, if at Christmas not until New Year's . . . oh no, wait, that last one doesn't work,' Julita burst out laughing like a ringing bell at her own joke. 'Oh, it's so good to see you.'

'Likewise, Julita, good to see you. Mario didn't come?' My question followed the natural course of a conversation in a twenty-first-century household. Julita isn't going to become a nun. Julita has been with Mario for years, but Mario is one of the leaders of the Democratic Party in Florida, and a Republican family would never accept a guy like him.

'No, no.' Julita's cheeks reddened. 'Papi is here, so it's better for Mario to stay home. I don't want people talking politics or messing with him. But tell me, amiga, when is your gender reveal? When will it be you and your husband throwing the party?'

'Who knows, Julita?' The answer had worked the last time, ten seconds before. 'We haven't made up our minds yet.' Maybe it'll work again . . . Or not.

'What do you mean you haven't decided? Don't give me that, I mean, you guys are already pushing thirty-five, almost closer to forty.'

'Well, for now we don't want to have kids,' Rogelio interrupted and I was a little surprised by his embarrassed tone of voice. I felt a little bad for him – even pretending to be a dipshit, he couldn't cope with the harassment. Welcome to the world of a childless woman in her thirties.

'Time for the gender reveal. We're going to release the balloons!' someone shouted from across the yard. There was always shouting in that house. Julita and Leydi ran, one after the other, encumbered by Leydi's belly. Rogelio left me behind again while his embarrassed 'for now we don't want to' ran like a loop in my head, which, to be fair, could really have been an 'apparently she can't'.

Guillermo, Leydi's husband, stood in the middle of the yard, beside his mother and twin brother. The three of them were carrying a meter-and-a-half-long box, covered with storks and bruise-colored hearts. The box has had a fucking heart attack! I thought.

'Hola, Rogelio; hola, amiga,' Guillermo let go of a smile and also of his hold on the giant box in order to give me a kiss. He hadn't bothered to warn his mother and twin, who were suddenly forced to compensate for the lopsided weight of the box they were holding, and staggered as if they were standing in front of a broken mirror. Faces drawing expressions of panic, they scrambled to rebalance the box, which wasn't only ugly, but now orphaned by the pair of arms that had been providing stability.

'Hola Guillermito,' I returned his greeting, attempting a cordial tone.

'*Puta,* my name is William.'

'Your name is Guillermo, Guillermo Pérez, and people call you William, so don't give me that crap. My name is Elena and nobody's said my name once since I walked through the door. That's life, get used to it.'

'What's up with you, Elena? Is it your time of the month? Or are you just jealous the party isn't for you?'

'More like menopausal, she's been cranky since she got here' – though it may be hard to believe, Leydi's interruption had a conciliatory tone. 'Enough already, let's do the gender reveal, I'm so excited!'

Guillermo Pérez has always listened to his wife. So he smiled again and, as an offering of friendship and peace, said:

'Elena, I wonder when you guys will be inviting us to your gender reveal, you're running out of time, you better get on it.'

But, alas, no friendship, no peace. The plane endangering the party came careening down for a triumphant crash landing.

'Look, Guillermo Pérez, give me a fucking break with the whole gender-reveal thing, I don't want to have kids and I definitely don't want to throw a gender-reveal party in my own backyard to let three ridiculous balloons go that'll just end up killing a flock of defenseless birds.'

'Amiga, calm down, this is not the time,' Julita intervened.

'*Coño*, amiga . . . Elena, you're being so rude. Are you on your period?'

'I don't have my fucking period for fuck's sake. I've been here ten fucking minutes and you've already asked me five fucking times when I'm going to throw a gender-reveal party for my hypothetical baby. And what if the baby comes out trans? Does that make it any less my baby? And, like I said, not one, not the other: I'm not going to fuck over four birds with three balloons and I'm not going to destroy a forest with disposable diapers for a little brat that can't even wipe its own ass.'

'How can you be so insensitive,' Leydi muttered, her serpent hands now freely slithering out to strangle her belly.

Guillermo Pérez and his twin brother were looking at me with the same offended expression, like photocopies of their mother. Behind me I heard a growing murmur, until from among the wreckage of voices I could pick out once again the grunt of a 'haha' from Rogelio. I don't know if it was on purpose or if he was just nervous, but what the fuck was he laughing at, was he laughing at me?

'What a bunch of narcissists, you know that fossil fuels are running out, that water is running out, that the poles are melting, and yet you keep on breeding and using up the world. We were better off in Cuba without gender reveals or colored balloons.'

'Communist, go back to Cuba!' the shout came from Esteban.

'You know that Mario Rodríguez is Julita's partner, right? Hashtag *#elcomunistamásgrandedeMiami*!' I screamed back at the top of my lungs, crossing my fingers to make the sign of the hashtag. He didn't move a muscle.

'Too far,' the bell in Julita's throat briefly rang.

'Calm down, mija, let's just drop it, okay?' Leydi was sobbing, tears falling even from her ears. And seeing her in the role of sensitive mother was the cherry that had been missing from the top of my cake, the last little light on the runway as I came in for the landing.

'My name is Elena, Elena like *Elena de Troya*, Elena for fuck's sake.'

My screech was so shrill that it startled Guillermo Pérez's mother and she dropped the box covered in storks and bruised hearts. The brown-paper seal broke. Six balloons flew out: three pink and three blue. The small group of guests stood there, mute, for a few seconds. They watched the balloons float up and away. What – beyond reprieve from my sudden silence – was that celebration of colors supposed to mean? Everyone turned to look at Guillermo Pérez's brother, who started jumping up and down, hands in the air.

'Twins! Twins! Leydi is having twins! *Jimaguas* man! A little pair! *Ay dios mío!*'

'*Felicidades*, Leydi, *felicidades*, William.' 'Oh my God, congrats!' The murmur of the party slowly began to swell again. I grabbed Rogelio's sweaty hand, he was still flashing his dipshit grin, and dragged him across the yard and into the kitchen; from there into the living room. 'Hashtag *#hijosdeputa*, #motherfuckingbirdmurderers.' To be honest, I don't think anybody heard my parting shots. They went on celebrating loudly even after the six colorful balloons had disappeared, probably stuck in the throat of some poor animal.

'You know I don't want to have kids, right?' Rogelio said as we got in the car.

'Me neither, we're good the way we are. Free, happy, with plenty of money. If we made it past thirty without ever wanting kids, we're not going to have them now just to get a green card faster.'

'I don't know what we were thinking.' His reproach was a blow.

And yet, it was already too late. Eight months later, our little blessing was born. Hashtag #highriskmother. Neither Leydi nor Guillermo Pérez came to the gender-reveal party we threw in our backyard. They didn't get to see the video of the pink balloon popping in my face. Lame bastards blocked me on Instagram. ■

ALEJANDRO MORELLÓN

1985

Alejandro Morellón was born in Madrid, Spain. He is the author of *La noche en que caemos*, which won the 2013 MonteLeón Foundation Award, *El estado natural de las cosas*, which won the 2017 Gabriel García Márquez Hispano-American Short Story Prize and, most recently, *Caballo sea la noche*.

THE ANIMAL GESTURE

Alejandro Morellón

TRANSLATED BY ESTHER ALLEN

First a glow at the very center of the screen grows into a radiance without circumference, then an image appears, clarifies and resolves into human form: a man or woman under the night sky. It's a fake night, projected onto a blue screen at the back of the studio, moonless, but with a few recognizable constellations. Among them, to the right of Orion's Belt, between Betelgeuse and Canis Major, the face appears. The irises of its green eyes are flecked with dark spots, and the heavy eyeliner and Roman nose give it an almost pharaonic look. On the eyelids, ultra-long lashes rise and fall as if a butterfly were struggling to take flight.

'I've heard the cry of the nymph Salmacis, and I have drunk from the same waters as the son of Hermes and Aphrodite. From the transfusion of their bodies I, Avalovara, too, have emerged, to channel the voices of the spirits of the Algonquin, O my daughters, and the absolute voice of old Baba Yaga, and the voices of Hatshepsut and of Hathor, the cosmic goddess with the ears of a cow, and the voice of the Cathars and their Lady of Thought, and of the mystic Beguine Hadewijch of Brabant and St Mary of Egypt, and the voices of Marguerite Porete and Fra Dolcino, and the voice of Tertullian with his famous phrase: "I believe in these things because they are unbelievable." '

In what is clearly intended as a dramatic pause, Avalovara's eyes turn toward the audience, lips opening to reveal a tongue tinted blue by a lollipop. The camera recedes to reveal a dark mahogany table; at its center, next to the lollipop, is a desk plate engraved with the name Avalovara and a phone number for viewers seeking advice. Nearby, arrayed on a black cloth, are candles, effigies, tarot cards, crystals, feathers, a rosary with beads of imitation ivory, the skull of a horse or some horse-like animal, and other unidentifiable objects. The camera pans across an arm muscle, a broad back, a graceful neck and a black tulle dress that crosses the torso diagonally leaving one breast bare, the left one, crowned by a metal pasty.

'And I speak to you now, my daughters, in all of these voices, in this world that seems so brutally divided. But has there ever been a time when the world was not brutally divided? Between men and women, believers and unbelievers, orthodox and infidel, polytheist and monotheist, between the little children and those who control them, the oppressor and the oppressed, those who prostitute others and those who prostitute themselves, between victim and torturer, witch and inquisitor, bourgeoisie and proletariat, delusional and sane, healthy and diseased, the world above and the world below, in an endless parade of antitheses, an infinite and uneven struggle of opposites. And now? What is happening now with the new Papesse? Why such visceral hatred of Micaela Andreína? Hear me well: despite all the deliberations of all the conclaves, the world seems indignant that someone who does not happen to be a man, someone who is a WOMAN, now holds papal authority, wields the miter and crozier, has become Holy Mother and *summum pontificem* and vicar of Christ and servant of the servants of God, and furthermore that this same WOMAN is so young and has a gaze that is so decisive, and especially – or so say the gerontocrats, the ancient Apostolics and Romans of the Vatican – that she once had the arrogance to approach the edge of the stage, kiss her fingertips and raise them toward the devout multitude like a mother bidding her children goodnight.'

Avalovara kisses her own fingertips in turn, and bows to underscore the gesture. The cascade of pure white hair catches the light as the head tilts in profile, listening to instructions from the hidden earpiece.

'. . . and it seems we now have a live feed direct from St Peter's Square, the long-anticipated moment when the new sovereign of the state is named . . . Let's go to video.'

The cardinal protodeacon fills the screen. From the balcony, Michelangelo Bernufoni clears his throat and begins intoning the *Habemus papam* as the faithful join together in hymns and victory chants, holding up tapers, crucifixes and the flags of every country while shouting words of glory and blessing. For at last, after many days of media tension and electoral sequestration, the white smoke has billowed up and dissipated across the sky over the square, and now the sacred words ring out across the basilica's facade. To the cardinal's right is an illuminated space where at last Micaela Andreína makes her appearance. There's a light of incomprehensible origin in her face, and her features express determination and great calm, hair falling in a smooth cascade over her shoulders. Before her a sepulchral silence falls which, from the balcony, she breaks.

'The only human flaw that exists is this: to lack the capacity to be nourished by the light. By the flame of understanding that is radiance emerging from confusion, the light that emanates from the face of Our Lady of Magdala, an image that came to me one night and cleared my vision; the curtains were stilled, the ecstatic flame now burned unflickering. Then Her sweet breath washed over my face and eyes and She said: I have no wounds but I feel them. Then I understood the defects in my thinking, the ancestral uncertainty, the world's atavistic fears though my own fears, and She knew I knew, and I knew this knowing was unpronounceable and that this faith and this light could not leave me to be transferred to others. And likewise, I knew that both were part of my task, to help others find it – find faith – and be nourished by it – by light. To be scout or bulwark, guide for the blind or counselor, a stronghold, an interlocutor's voice, to be a rent in the veil of lies, allowing truth to penetrate further into the shadows so we can understand all the certainty there is in the word of the Goddess, in the extension of Her love, in the magnitude of the heroic but humble acts that flow from Her strength. For She has poured Herself into Her creation, has given Her Being to me and to all women so we may give it back to Her, so we may redistribute it for and through other women, those who do not yet hear us today but will hear us tomorrow. The past and future are the sole treasure of the woman who champions herself, waves the flag of herself, no longer clinging to spiritual dependency but renouncing it to flee the consolations of religion and of man, denying the immortality or utility of sin or final absolution, remaining all the while a creature of grace, not as promise but as fact, my sisters, participating in the divine transmutation, obedient to the order of the world, to amor fati, to the splendor of negation and renunciation, aspiring, as in St Augustine's apophatic theology, not to knowledge of the divine but to the renunciation of such knowledge, for faith ceases to be faith if it is sustained by knowledge alone. The light that can be understood is not the true light but can only be fictitious, explicable, transcribable and therefore limiting and limited. For the true light, the absolute clarity, cannot be contained, the pure truth exists only in the infinite, unending image, in the image and the memory of the image. For the truth is one and many, and the one truth is in no way distinct from all the others, the truth is repetition and multiplication, it is that which pours forth from the ruptured seal, an embrace of the air, an idea attained by releasing the mind into dreams, and also by the word, for thought gives the word, and thought is given to us by the word, and thus we must become our actions in imagination, and our imagination in our actions . . .'

The camera slowly closes in on Micaela Andreína's mouth and eyes as she looks steadily out at the crowd. For a few seconds, the faces of the Papesse and Avalovara are superimposed. They bear little resemblance to each other, though they might be said to share a certain authority of expression, both inscrutable and self-assured, and an eloquent, theatrical solemnity. Then, as the image of the saint slowly dissolves and disappears, Avalovara alone occupies the screen, hands folded in a gesture both pious and pensive, to address the audience.

'You've heard the words of our new Papesse. What is it about her, I wonder, what is it that stirs up such veneration and hatred, in equal measure? Are her actions the fruit of saintliness or delirium, dementia or beatitude? There are those who say her accession to the papacy is a clear omen of the final collapse, and others who believe, on the contrary, that this woman is come to offer us absolute redemption and the definitive communion with the celestial realms. The beginning of the end? Or the end of the beginning? We'll know very soon, no doubt, but for now, my daughters, don't forget to say your prayers to the saint of understanding. Do that for me.'

The silhouette fades out behind a veil of mist and the set's floodlights come on. The director gives the signal to cut, gives a brief thumbs up to let everyone know the take came out well, and leaves. Avalovara sits at the dressing-room mirror and squeezes a barely perceptible blackhead below one nostril. When the time comes, the requisite kisses are distributed among the girls who work in the same unit, and hours after midnight Avalovara leaves by the studio's back entrance, to keep admirers at bay, and takes a taxi to the slums.

The house is old but grand, with high ceilings and a spacious central room, its walls covered almost entirely in oriental motifs, Japanese engravings, photos of Asian men and women. A large folding screen with a print of Mount Fuji stands between the bed and the desk, dividing the room. In the smaller half, next to the window, daybreak slowly illuminates a bust of Ezra Pound.

Avalovara heats up a packet of noodle soup and lies down next to the cat on a futon on the floor, in front of a screen that covers most of the wall, where *Madame Butterfly* is being projected.

'Look at her.'

'. . .'

'Isn't she adorable when she's downcast like that?'

'. . .'

'She gazes out past the edge of the stage, searching for something.'

'. . .'

The cat to whom Avalovara addresses these observations half-opens its eyes, throws its head back and yawns, tip of the tongue curling upwards, sharp puppy teeth clearly visible in the newly luminous room, then buries its head between two cushions again.

'Cio-Cio-San knows very well that her anguish is unique to her and isn't experienced by anyone else. It's her way of identifying herself, locating her status of inequality with everything else, differentiating herself through small expressions of emotion.'

'. . .'

'Look how the singer rises in ecstasy.'

'. . .'

'See how her eyes are half-closed?'

'. . .'

'See how she smiles through her pain?'

'. . .'

'Speaking of the love that may never return.'

'. . .'

'I will wait and hide.'

'. . .'

'A little to tease him, a little so as not to die.'

'. . .'

'Waiting for the boat that doesn't come, for the officer who's the cause of her despair, gazing sadly out at the horizon, disconsolate. And then, a sudden hope: perhaps the ship now arriving is *the* ship and her wait is coming to an end.'

'. . .'

'See how she lifts her arms and holds them outstretched?'

'. . .'

'As if offering them for the audience to take in?'

'. . .'

'As if she wanted to convey all her sorrow in this one gesture?'

'. . .'

'*E un po' per non morire.*'

'. . .'

'See how she walks to the farthest, darkest corner of the room where the little boy sleeps on his side with his legs folded? And now she understands that this one isn't going to be *the* ship either, and perhaps also that *the* ship doesn't exist and never did?'

'. . .'

Avalovara lifts hands to face, as if trying to hold her cheekbones in place. There are still traces of mascara on her lashes and makeup residue around her eyes. The white wig is gone and black curls fall across her forehead. Two of the fake nails fell or were tossed on the bed. The cat batted them around a bit but then went back to sleep and is purring.

'See how she's opening and closing her fists?'

'. . .'

'As if she were gripping some invisible thing?'

'. . .'

'She moves like a ballerina to stand before the audience at the most visible point of the stage. Then, after Suzuki exits, she takes another step forward.'

'. . .'

'Until she lets herself collapse, exhausted.'

'. . .'

'And chokes back her tears.'

'. . .'

'Only a little longer.'

'. . .'

'And now releases them.'

'. . .'

'She weeps, turning her head to one side.'

'. . .'

'So the audience can see that she's weeping.'

'. . .'

'She gives the world a glimpse of her pain.'

'. . .'

Avalovara falls asleep and then the clamor of street sweepers awakens her and she gazes up at the distant, inexpressive sky made familiar by habitual insomnia, a sky still without form or substance. The morning clarity finally spreads out to light up the surfaces of puddles, then the buildings, turning gray mist to blue and washing over the house like illuminated water, bathing all the furniture in the room, the dresser, the desk, the Hokusai screen, and progressively filtering across the other objects. On-screen, in the final scene, Cio-Cio-San takes her own life, plunging the tanto into her throat and collapsing, in a gesture halfway between despair and renunciation, the final comprehension of the inevitability of circumstances. Still lying on the futon with the cat, Avalovara, body undone by Cio-Cio-San's helplessness, falls back asleep, *un po' per non morire*, until late afternoon. ■

JOSÉ ADIAK MONTOYA

1987

José Adiak Montoya was born in Managua, Nicaragua. His most recent novels are *Lennon bajo el sol* and *Aunque nada perdure*. In 2016, the Guadalajara International Book Fair featured him on their list of noteworthy Latin American writers born in the 1980s.

LEVERT'S APPEARANCE

José Adiak Montoya

TRANSLATED BY SAMANTHA SCHNEE

First came beauty. Let me tell you what happened. Levert was born one spring day when the sun, king of stars, radiant sphere of spheres, illuminated the verdure of life on Earth, and the world raised its voice in song, and all creatures rejoiced. It was the day of the eclipse. For a moment the sun was dispossessed of its strength and every citizen, I tell you here and now, was mesmerized – they all thought, *what a glorious sight!* – by the darkness that fell on this side of the planet. Levert left his mother's womb, where he had spent nine months dreaming peacefully, floating in warm liquid, safe from the world. His cry from out of the darkness was one of helplessness. All eyes awaited the moment when the sun would be revealed so as to contemplate the newborn in all his splendor. A perfect child. A fallen cherub. The very picture of joy. Like the sun, he illuminated the hut in which he had been born and the stunned faces of everyone in the room. The residents of that slum, where no one could remember the last time the electricity had worked, swore that the light on the post over Didiane's house flickered on that night, and shone brightly, illuminating the rickety shack like a sole candle in the darkness, while inside she was still captivated by the child in her arms. Her seventh son.

They say that, as we all witnessed, the neighbors stood in a weaving line along the length of the dirt alley that led to Didiane's door. There were babes in arms, eager children holding their parents' hands, women and old folks. The news had spread that a child so beautiful he must have been heaven-sent was born in the barrio, and everyone wanted to see him. For some it had been weeks, others months or years, since they had spoken with Didiane, but today they would all say, *Hello, Didiane, we've come to congratulate you on the birth of your son, to wish you all the best. How's your family? How's Julien? How's life?* The whole neighborhood made the pilgrimage on foot that night, the sun hidden, their arms laden with gifts: chickens, platters of food, children's clothing.

At the door of the house, Julien, the proud father, received everyone, saying, *Welcome, thanks for coming*, and the old ladies, the kids, the men and the women entered, depositing their gifts and crossing the tiny, decrepit room to Didiane's bed, where in the half-light they regarded the little god in her arms. His brothers stood next to the bed, three on each side, standing erect as if they would have to guard him for the rest of their lives. But as everyone will surely know, that's not what came to pass.

The family watched over him all night long. And as the small hours of the morning approached, Didiane didn't tire; she felt strong in a way she hadn't felt since childhood, when she would go out after the rain to splash in mud puddles in the street for hours on end. Bit by bit the line of people shrank, and the hours passed. The pilgrimage was over, everyone in the neighborhood had seen with their own eyes that it was true, an angel had been born among them. The boy was radiant, he gave off the scent of fresh almonds, he was beautiful, perfect. Levert's six brothers were nodding off in exhaustion when their mother finally sent them to bed, in the one decent-sized room they had always shared. Her six children before Levert, all boys, born one after the other.

D idiane had spent half her life pregnant, she looked decades older than she was, but all those births hadn't aged her as much as poverty had . . . Back when she was a girl jumping in puddles, poverty was something that belonged to her parents. Hunger was normal, she didn't know anything else. Once she was a grown adult, carrying her first child, she came to realize that she was poor, that it was a base condition and that she didn't know anything. For the first time it pained her to be illiterate, to not understand how her own country worked, to not be able to find it on a map. It was then that Julien became like a piece of driftwood in a shipwreck. A man to care for so that he would never leave her side, so that they could share their poverty, so that the viscid waters of their misfortune would not rise to the height of her mouth and drown her. As far as he was concerned, he had saved that innocent creature whose hips appeared to him like succulent fruits . . . saved her like a guardian angel flapping his wings, holding her by the arms to prevent her from drowning in the tide. They fell deeply in love; night was for merging their bodies on the pallet they shared, unable to separate from one another, trusting that each day fate would provide for them, that they needed nothing more than to love each other to survive. And so, I say to you all and as everyone knows, the poet once said fertility is the curse of the poor, and so it came to pass that the curse fell on Didiane. Over and over again. As had befallen her mother before her, until Didiane herself had been born, the seventh and final birth that had been the cause of her death. So Didiane had no one to tell her about the curse of love, she had six older brothers who muddled through life, each stepping over the bodies of the others. And like her mother, she chose what she thought was love but turned out to be misery and the pain of labor. She became old before her time, with rotten teeth, her mouth fixed in a hard line.

With Julien at her side, she had had to bear the weight of many children in order for this child to arrive. And now the house was brimming with food. In the streets of the barrio people addressed her as if she were royalty, as though they had awoken from a deep stupor and realized that she, Didiane, was a woman who deserved respect. Her graying hair grew darker and her wrinkles disappeared in the light; for the first time in a long while the unchanging rictus of her mouth turned into a smile as she graciously received gifts from her neighbors, who told her *for the child, for you, you need strength to raise this gorgeous piece of heaven, so healthy, a little cherub,* while they came close to pinch his little cheeks after which they discreetly touched their own, as if with a special balm.

She wanted for nothing.

Now I'm going to tell you exactly what we were told. There were three Ministers, all elderly and nearly blind, though they say they had once been young, back when the Comandante was young, too. Some said they were his brothers, because no one knew anything about the Comandante's family; he was an institution who had always been there, since before time began. It was said that sometime before recorded Memory they had betrayed him and that later they were pardoned, holding no rancor in their hearts, and that the Comandante bestowed them with glory, making them Ministers. Or so they said; there were no sworn witnesses. Others said that the four were inseparable childhood friends, that they had roamed the streets together, before Time. The country was full of stories like this.

The truth is that they were three dour old men, and it had been a long time since they had attended meetings, assemblies or political parades. They knew they were alive only because their deaths had never been announced.

We knew of their whereabouts up until they accepted the mission to visit Levert, to follow the trail of his light, when they said, *Si mi Comandante, we'll go and see him and bring him gifts so that everyone throughout the land can see the kindness with which you rule the nation.*

Then they left in a convoy of black vehicles, one for each Minister, crossing the city through downtrodden, sleepy barrios, between squat buildings bogged down by age. They spent the night skirting the foul-smelling market on the outskirts of the city, the fortress that poisoned the beach waters, whose stalls the waves barely touched before turning foul. And they did not pass without trepidation; as was known, and as we all know, at night the market was haunted by deformed beings, people with two heads, thirty fingers, fish eyes – beings whose monstrosity offended human sight – poor souls rejected by the city, who sought refuge in those filthy alleys.

They were seen passing through slum after slum. In the north and the south, three shadowy old men. In the east and the west, three dark ghosts.

The Ministers spent days searching for Levert, getting lost and finding their way again, returning to their path and their mission. Eventually they couldn't afford to waste any more time, and no more time did they waste. Soon thereafter they arrived in the barrio where Didiane emanated joy.

It wasn't hard for them to identify.

This barrio wasn't gray like the others, poverty wasn't rampant. The land had become fertile, full of orchards and glades, there were no black streams of garbage where dogs and pigs went to drink. The water ran clear as crystal and children frolicked.

We've come to see the newborn babe, bearing gifts, they said as they arrived. And when the people saw them, they gave way and let them pass, the same people who had been standing in the sun for days, waiting in line to see the child, Levert.

And the Ministers entered like a single shadow split into thirds by shafts of light. Julien and Didiane welcomed them. And the couple's children, fierce guards of their little brother, stepped aside to let them pass. There, in the pale light, they saw Levert. The Ministers fell into deep silence, their feet nailed to the earth, while inside each of them a storm raged, a tidal wave uprooting the trees of evil within. Laying eyes upon that most beautiful of children swept away everything inside them, leaving naught but traces of their wickedness. The Ministers had been purified. In Levert's eyes they saw Time, and they saw themselves observing Time in Levert's eyes. I tell you here and now, it's said that they experienced perfect knowledge. They understood that the Comandante feared the child and envied him because the people adored Levert as they had never adored their leader. They realized that he wanted to do away with Levert, take his life, and that they were spies, instruments of his far-reaching talons. They turned around, kissed Didiane and Julien on the lips, handed over their offerings, and departed without a word, in the opposite direction of the National Palace, away from the Comandante. Nothing more was heard of them. And that, they say, is what happened. The fragile flower of benevolence arose from the ashes of their evil.

S ometimes dreams can be overwhelming, places where you walk on clouds or sand, where nothing is what it seems, full of omens . . . So many omens originate in ancient dawns, birds soar in our dreams, they want to communicate more than just the beating of their wings, much more . . . But dreams themselves are seldom clear omens, without birds as messengers, they're just simple announcements without shadows, lucid monologues, direct warnings.

And so it came to pass:

Once the three Ministers, erstwhile henchmen of the Comandante, now masters of their own virtuous souls, embarked on a road that was not the one they had agreed upon with the leader of the nation, and once the place of Levert's birth was revealed, Julien had a dream, and this is what he saw:

He saw himself dozing, slumped in a chair, his body enveloped in sticky heat, when a dusty wind delivered a vision: he saw something approaching from a distance, but its size didn't change as it got closer, then a dwarf-like creature stopped just in front of him, part human, part duende, bent nearly double by the weight of a coarse hump, his skin taut and leathery, mud-splattered, like one of the creatures from the night market . . . He settled his huge eyes on Julien: I come . . . I come from the bowels of the National Palace; I followed the three Ministers here without their knowledge, silent as a shadow I have traced their steps through barrios and slums until I got here to tell you what I must tell you, that the Ministers in their black suits came here on a different mission, one of death, which they did not fulfil, but the boy . . . The boy is in mortal danger, the boy must leave at once, I tell you . . .

His booming voice faded into the harsh wind and the heaviness of the dream. When Julien awoke, his pasty mouth needed water and his eyes still beheld the eyes of his apparition, and the warning resounded in his ears. In the darkness Julien recognized Didiane's labored breathing. He shook her awake and told her about his dream in great detail. When he finished his story he said, *Tomorrow we're leaving this place.*

That night neither of them slept another wink. That's what we were told, and that's what we're telling you.

The morning after the ominous dream they were surprised to find dozens of people outside their home, some of the women who had come from nearby villages to bring gifts for Levert had even spent the night there, all they wanted was to return home with a bit of his scent, his healing essence, because the whole barrio had blossomed thanks to him and his unique aroma, the sight of him alone could make homes flourish, too.

All day long Didiane and Julien received visitors. They exchanged frightened glances, but there was nothing they could do, they had to wait for nightfall to depart. All afternoon they attended to old folks, men with broken souls, mothers with babes in arms who said their children were fortunate to grow up alongside Levert, lucky that they would play ball together one day, it would be a barrio where the children grew up in abundance and splendor. Levert's six brothers watching over them.

In the early hours of morning, the same hour in which Julien had had his dream, while the following day's visitors slept soundly outside their home, Didiane explained to her children that they had to take a nighttime walk, and they needed to be completely silent to do it, so as not to awaken the people lying about the patio. The boys, bleary-eyed but excited by the proposed adventure, nodded their six heads.

Silently, Didiane and her husband stashed the most valuable gifts Levert had received during the past fortnight into large bags along with provisions and clothing. In the half-light Julien noted that for the first time since the boy had arrived, his wife looked drawn and haggard, as if their life prior to Levert had stretched out a finger and left a mark on her forehead.

They slipped out into the night, a silent procession amid the snores of the patio-sleepers. Didiane carried Levert in her arms, wrapped in blankets that completely shrouded the light from his body. Something told her not to turn around, but she disobeyed, looking back at her home, and saw the light bulb above the house fade and die, plunging the barrio into shadows. As she strode off, the wrinkles on her face seemed to blossom again.

It's said they crossed mountains and valleys, wandering day and night, and that their feet were covered with sores, but they forged ahead, running from the dangers foretold by the dream. Wherever they went, with Levert in their arms, there was abundant fruit and water.

Days passed, then weeks, and the anger of the Comandantísimo grew, like a cloud of smoke rising from the earth. No one in the entire governmental apparatus had the slightest clue as to the whereabouts of the Ministers. They had disappeared, along with their mission.

Three of his most important men were dead, no doubt about it. Clearly, the Comandante thought, the child was more dangerous than his black heart had surmised. He was a fool, he had been mistaken to send elderly functionaries to locate such a major threat to his authority, it was the biggest error of his entire tenure. The child threatened his hold on power. The stories about him that were making their way around the country were eclipsing the reputation of the Comandante, which had frightened him, and his fear had made him act rashly, causing the death of his three Ministers, the three agents that were the cornerstones of his power. Now he needed to act boldly.

And he did. As it is known.

Heretofore he had never had reason to be riddled with anger, fear and desperation like leprosy. He gathered as many government officers together as he could, their uniforms creating a murderous, green tide. Young men accustomed to sowing horror and reaping terror, men whose hearts had been replaced with the blackest coal of fury and hatred for life. They had become one with the steel of their weapons. There was nothing left within them but anger, the same anger that inspired the Comandantísimo's orders.

Sirens wailed in every street throughout the city, and from the highest tower of the National Palace the head of state watched his army of wrath march off to enact his orders.

And the soldiers flowed through the streets like the unstoppable current of a churning river. Their weapons homing in on the innocents who slept in the barrios, the people calm and unsuspecting of the death that was marching closer, unaware that a rain of bullets was about to fall on the undernourished bodies of their children.

Without warning, zealous boots began kicking down doors.

S ome didn't have life enough to hear the bullets that killed them, only to glimpse the faces of the soldiers firing. Other, luckier children never knew a thing, the slugs hit while they were kicking balls, scoring goals they'd never celebrate.

The night filled with screams, so they told us, and so we saw; and so it will be told forevermore. Screams that rose into the black sky, along with the sobs of mothers that turned into screams.

The soldiers hunted every child, searched the nooks and crannies of every home in the slums, and such was their offense: it was known that where innocence is a crime, only death can reign.

Mothers, hanging like dead weight from the uniforms of the officers, begged and pleaded without understanding why . . . But the green plague swallowed all. Each weapon was the arm of the Comandante, reaching down into the stinking barrios, places he would never set foot himself, but no matter how far that arm stretched, it could not find Levert's tender, beautiful body, wrapped in Didiane's blankets, fleeing, becoming one with the mountains. Didiane, Julien and their procession of offspring.

The Comandantísimo lay in his bed that night in a state of profound peace, thinking that nothing could now threaten his ascent to glory. Believing that the danger was gone, he fell into a deep sleep of still waters, the sleep of a man with a clear conscience and no debts. Meanwhile, far from his might, escaping through valleys in the arms of his mother, Levert let out a heart-rending cry, perhaps a cry of hunger or perhaps the dawning awareness of his cruel fate, which had been decided far, far away that night.

The sun shone brighter than ever the following day, and the blood dried. It shone on the pavement, on the little corpses still warm from their parents' embraces. The streets were deserted, because everyone knows that a city without children is doomed to silence.

And in the barrio people were asking about Didiane and the savior-child who had also been the cause of their condemnation. Very few people knew what had happened to them, because this part of the story went untold, but there are some who said they found respite, while others said that they went hungry, no one knows for sure; no one knew a thing about them after they ran away from home, slipping out among the pilgrims sleeping on their patio.

People imagined the family had settled somewhere, since Levert was still a babe in arms; others said that in their new home they planted a garden where tomatoes grew as large as melons, all Levert needed to do was to plunge a tiny finger into the earth – with the help of his mother or one of his brothers – and anything would grow. No one actually witnessed this. Others said the family wandered from city to city, a ragged old couple followed by a procession of malnourished boys, begging for shelter and bread, the youngest shielded from human eyes, because to see him was to give him away, signing their death warrant.

No one knows what became of them during this time.

What is known is that months later, tired of being on the lam, when the blood had dried in the barrios but tears still flowed, they appeared in the distance. Eight figures silhouetted by the sunset. Perhaps a mirage in the merciless heat, perhaps the hallucination of the damaged minds that filled the streets of the nation. But no, it was ·

them, returning; that's what we saw, what became part of the story, what I'm telling you.

Now, in this land of silence, all that remained of the children were the traces of dried blood beneath their parents' fingernails. Everything else had returned to the earth. People wandered about aimlessly, some carrying the balls of the uncelebrated goals. And so it was that, orphaned of their children, they first heard the approaching cries of the child they had once adored, unaware that he was no longer one of them. That he no longer belonged anywhere, because his birth had brought about the death of so many innocents. And they laid eyes on him, no longer radiant, just a common creature.

They entered the barrio that had once been theirs. People stared at them in shock, at first avoiding them like hungry cannibals who don't believe their eyes. The six boys, alive and healthy, walked fearfully. All eyes were on them.

This procession of ghosts stood still for a long time. All was motionless. The wind took another route so as not to disturb the meeting of these two worlds that had once been one. Levert's family was frightened by the watery, amphibian eyes staring right through them. One of the boys' bladders released its liquid as he trembled, a warm puddle forming at his feet. When she saw this, Didiane broke the spell, grabbing him by the arm and heading toward what had once been their home. The stares of the villagers slithered after them as the family disappeared behind the door.

Inside was a complete disaster, nothing remained of what little they had left behind. What was there had been destroyed. The gifts, everything they had received due to Levert's beauty, were gone; there was nothing but a trail of destruction. The smell was unbearable, like garbage.

Didiane and Julien looked at each other, realizing they had returned to a graveyard. Their faces trembled, trembled in a way that shook Levert's composure; the boy launched into a loud, painful wail and so did his broken parents, their sobs resounding throughout the barrio. Everyone outside was chilled to the core by the baleful sobs, their mortal wailing, an evil omen. And for the first time they were afraid of the one they had formerly adored. So they told us, and so it was told.

For many days the family lived in fear, knowing They were outside – what was left of their neighbors – wandering aimlessly through the streets. Didiane and Julien knew that if they set foot outside, those eyes would nail them with accusatory stares, burning their skin. But soon the boys got hungry, and Levert continued wailing. They'd consumed what little they'd brought with them. It was time to go out and face the desolate landscape, to confront those dead souls.

Julien crossed the threshold, sinking into the silence of the barrio. The streets were still. Even the wind avoided the place. The silence was bathed in a hateful, coppery light, like a never-ending sunset.

Then Julien saw someone approaching. So they told us, and so it was told. The figure wore rags, making Julien think it was an old woman. But when she got closer, when she was right in front of him, he realized it was a girl of about fifteen: gaunt, dirty, frail. She held her arms out to Julien, two fragile twigs, a gray, moldy tomato in each palm. Julien watched the scene fearfully, the gaze of this apparition locking with his. Then she opened her gaping mouth and said that the gardens were dying, that everything that grew was blighted. She clenched her fists tightly, forcing worm-ridden mush between her fingers.

The first bulge appeared around Levert's first birthday. At the same time that the well water began to turn black. It was a lump at the base of the boy's neck, the size of an adult's thumb, smooth and soft, so full of liquid that it eventually burst, creating blisters around it, and so Levert became a fussy child covered in bulges surrounded by watery little blisters. And it became known, because we all witnessed it: as the little one's ills multiplied, the earth in the barrio became drier and more infertile. Everything was born dead. And the little that remained on the trees and bushes, which had previously borne an abundance of fruit, shriveled up due to rampant disease. There was hunger, and more hunger. The only children in the barrio – Didiane's alone remained – looked like little grotesque skeletons tasked with protecting their now grotesque brother, covered in sores. They were to protect him from the others, the souls in mourning outside their home, whose children had been torn away because Levert, the star-child, had been born among them.

When Levert's wailing escaped the walls of the shack the whole barrio covered their ears, because that was the wail that had wrested their children from them.

Very early one morning, so they say, Julien awoke shaken by torturous dreams; he looked at his aging wife, her clothes in tatters, their stinking children, and in the half moonlight he looked at Levert, listened to his snores, like the croaking of an army of frogs, his deformed bones merging into the coarse flesh of his back, his nose hardly visible among the bulges on his face. That's how he saw his son, he saw him as a monster. So he walked out the door and didn't look back. He was never seen again. So they say.

Awakening was like being stabbed. Even before she opened her eyes, Didiane could feel Julien's absence in the bed. She knew what it meant; it was something she had feared so much. A few shafts of light began filtering inside the house. Levert's snoring ceased. She lay alone in the bed she had shared with Julien for so many years. A second's sadness was all she felt, then came desperation, a stab of desperation that made her jump up and scream at her children to get up and go find their father.

And so they were seen leaving, following their mother and then dispersing into the streets, moving among the walking cadavers who inhabited that place. They left Levert at home by himself; he had never been alone before, as is known. Bewildered, for the first time he experienced the embrace of abandonment, an embrace that would not release its grip on him for many years to come. The house had become a dungeon. And in the silence and the stillness he began to wail, it was a wail that paralyzed the barrio like a siren announcing the arrival of death. And so it was that, wailing, he took his first clumsy steps – the first of his life – toward the door.

When she heard him, Didiane, who had ventured quite far from home, beat a quick path back. She cut her bare feet on the thorny, uneven ground. As she ran, she saw everyone turning their eyes in the direction of the wailing. Transfixed. In terror.

When the house came into view, Didiane realized she was too late. She remained standing, but her life fell to its knees: using the doorframe for support, barely upright like some wobbly, newborn animal, was the monstrous fruit of her womb. His stretch-marked skin and bulky muscles, covered in bumps and pustules, his misshapen bones, his nose lost among the tumors on his face, exuding a stench of rotting almonds that reached every nose. Everyone in the barrio stared. This is how they saw him, and how we saw him.

And all their fury and misery was unleashed on the beast.

A hail of stones.

This, as is known, is what happened next:

And they were banished from the barrio, and for many years during her banishment, Didiane would wonder, in a cloud of uncertainty, if she had really experienced the ephemeral happiness that now seemed so unreal. Everything became vague, even Julien – that energetic face which had promised so much love to her, an illiterate, hungry young woman – seemed woven from unrealities, an invented memory; and that hungry, illiterate young woman now seemed blissfully happy compared to what she had become. She'd been full of pluck, which was impossible for the toothless old woman she was now to imagine. Her loving kindness was dead, and her fleeting dignity had become a shadow that wandered the streets begging for alms, holding the hand of Levert, whose hideousness was concealed by a blanket that had once been white, a single hole cut out for his eyes. Ugliness destined to shock and repulse, to inspire sorrow or compassion when it was unveiled by shabby Didiane, following a painful monologue in front of a group of strangers in a plaza or on a bus, her palm extended for coins.

Levert wasn't allowed to speak, only to move his eyes, two greasy little drops lost in the topography of his face, staring at the strangers who appeared before him, different creatures, beings who shook when they saw him because he reminded them of their own fragility. Every time his mother lifted that blanket, he was bared to a world where he would never belong, never have a place. A single flash of light before the return to darkness.

Didiane would get off those buses pulling him furiously by the arm, because at day's end she inevitably recalled her former happiness and felt the weight of the certainty that this monster had ruined everything, infecting what had once been beautiful. He had created joy, so that she would know what it meant to lose it.

And that's how Levert came to understand that the day Didiane died they would be coming for him, six shadows would fall on him in the night, showing no mercy on his lumpen flesh, breaking every one of his bones till he was naught but a puddle of black blood left to dry in the sun without anyone so much as caring. All six of them belonged to the world Levert had ruined when the innocents were slaughtered on his account. And that world was dangerous.

And so it came to pass, and so it was told. Like his father, who fled from the sight of monstrosity fifteen years earlier, Levert fled from the sight of monstrosity too. He snuck out without awakening his mother or brothers, fleeing something more diabolical than his own reflection in the mirror.

All he brought was his blanket, his shield from the stones of which he was born to be the target. And so it was known, and as everyone knows, he wandered alone for a time, traveling at night and hiding by day. Until, with neither family nor Comandante concerned with him, he came upon the doors of the city's huge market. It was waiting for him like the mouth of a dark animal, the place where by night he could blend in with the rest of the plague-infested outcasts, where he could fearlessly remove the blanket that covered him, because no one there would take notice of his misshapen body. One with the monsters. Levert gazed again at the doors of that world he had heard so much about, and without hesitation he stepped into his new life. ∎

© Gala Phenia

ANIELA RODRÍGUEZ

1992

Aniela Rodríguez was born in Chihuahua, Mexico. She received the 2016 Comala National Prize for Short Fiction by Young Writers for the story collection *El problema de los tres cuerpos* and she is also the author of the poetry collection *Insurgencia*.

DAYS OF RUIN

Aniela Rodríguez

TRANSLATED BY SOPHIE HUGHES

'Things changed, see? They don't sleep any more on
the beach.'
– Murray Ostril

It wasn't your son's pale skin or his gaping eyes that made you race, Carmelo, to the shoreline; a little body that barely fit in the cradle of your arms and that you had learned to love the way one loves a plant that's been rooted in the garden for a long, long time. It wasn't that, but something you had never thought about, and which hit you like a rush of cold water the second you spotted him in the distance, in the dead of night, his lungs drowned in salt water and helpless to survive because he was too fragile, too small, and you, Carmelo, had left him there to drown. It was the fierce dread of losing Marina. Because, although no one ever explained this to us, however brutish we might be, we're still capable of feeling something more than rage and fury.

So, with your balls shrunk from terror, you kicked off your huaraches and started to walk, you walked until you wore your mind out imagining what would happen next, because when you're drunk things happen that you don't expect will happen, especially not to your own child. Especially not when you decided to take him out in the middle of the night, to feel the blackened sand under his feet; feet still too young to understand that none of it made any sense, Carmelo. You lifted him out of his crib, making the most of Marina having gone to visit her mother, who had caught a fright and fallen ill. She had left him with you in an act of faith, because in spite of everything, she believed in you, she expected you to take good care of the child. And so, contorted and with the thick night air sticky on the nape of your neck, you walked, and looked all about you. The boy was over there, face up, foaming at the mouth like an animal left to his fate; as if the real animal wasn't you, Carmelo, who had just left the little boy there to die. And not any boy but *your own*, the seed you'd sown in Marina when, all that time ago, she'd hitched up her skirt on one of the old wooden pallets from the feria to show you some of that good stuff, and from there to the home stretch came months of touch and go: for some your wife still loved you, and for others she no longer looked at you tenderly and surrendered to soul sadness, to *tirisia*. How were you going to tell her Carmelo? How were you going to tell her you'd lost everything down the bottom of the bottle? That the one good thing she had left in that place had simply disappeared like foam.

You wandered lost on the beach for some time, not knowing who to turn to. You could no longer feel your arms: by the time you bumped into Jacinto you were exhausted and before you knew it you were asking him, help me, compadre, and at first he heard you out but then he realised that the lump in your arms was your son, and that he'd soon be dust. Help me get him to Doña Pancha, you begged him, believing she could cure your son; believing, against all evidence, that this mess was just a bad dream and it would turn out the baby was bloated or in shock from spending the night out in the open.

You walked and you walked, Carmelo, muttering the same futile words over and over: the boy'll be better soon, the boy'll come out crawling any minute now, Marina'll come back and I'll never drink like that again, ain't that right, Jesusito? Because you were incapable of looking death in the eyes. You stood and took it when your feet sank into the cool, windswept sand. Ain't that right, señor? You took it, too, when Doña Pancha opened her reed door only to shout in your face: What the fuck is wrong with you, Carmelo, the only thing this boy needs is his last rites and a decent burial.

You walked down the narrow streets that led from the seafront into town. You put your son on your back wrapped in one of Marina's rebozos, and people noticed you staggering around street corners wearing it. They talked; it was a small town. They could judge you all they liked. Your senses had been dulled anyway, although you could still remember certain things, like the last mouthful of black beans with epazote you scarfed down earlier and which was now repeating on you, as if to tell you what a moron you'd been to crack for a shitty hip flask of cheap liquor that hadn't given you even a moment of glory. A dog snapped at your trouser leg and you stumbled, almost falling flat onto your humpback, the lump that had once borne your son's face, but you struggled to your feet and crossed the threshold you would come to wish you never had, Carmelo.

You sat for a while with your hands clasped in a knot. You looked up at that man with blood running down his forearms and withered feet, nailed to a splintered post, and you cried even harder: you didn't even have the fucking consolation of a wound. You sucked up your snotty tears and then he appeared in the middle of the altar. I came looking for you, Father, you snivelled, but he didn't reply. The sour stench of your bender reached all the way over to where he was. I came to confess 'cause no one'll hear me, you finished, and he understood that, though drunk, you still had a modicum of decency. He opened the confessional door and sat you down as best he could. What have you got there, Carmelo? he asked, and you said nothing. Tears fell down your face into your moustache. My boy, *padrecito*, or what's left of my boy, and you unwrapped the shawl to reveal a swollen little body still dotted with patches of sand. I came for you to cure my fucking sadness, and you fell to your knees. You could no longer hold down the hot bile building up in your throat and you confessed everything to him: how the night was cold but just the same you'd taken him out for a walk to show him the sea. How, a few drinks down, you went back to bed and forgot to take him with you. How, by the time you woke up it was early morning, and that's why you were there in that state, weak-kneed and reeking of cantina, desperate for someone to tell you what it was you were supposed to do now. That was all you needed: the false sensation that someone was guiding your steps and there was no chance you'd mess up again. You were sick of always messing up.

The priest buried his face in the grubby weave of the rebozo. Inside, a tiny thing with salt still dusting his forehead and stiffened lips which in life had never spoken a word. You were sitting now on the pew, Carmelo, wondering whether your wife was home yet, whether she'd found the empty crib, noticed the absence of your usual ranting and the boy's babbling. The priest took a deep breath. He noticed that sourness hanging in the air around him, that smell of belch and urine and salt water pervading his church. And what do you expect from me, Carmelo? he said. This child doesn't have so much as a face to mourn.

You didn't want to go home now that the sun had come up, Carmelo. Father let you stay. In the end, you didn't really know why you'd gone to see him. He took that lump in his arms, revulsion surging through him, and carefully carried the boy to the sacristy; a place where you could no longer do him any harm, even if there was no more harm to be done. Boy's dead, you repeated to yourself. We're alone, no more boy. Nobody could have understood you, much though you wanted them to. The priest, you noticed, anointed his forehead with holy oil, even though the poor thing had already passed over. He dressed him in a white robe, someone's cast-off, and cleaned his little face, wiping away the spots of sand from his cheeks.

Carmelo, pass me that taper, he said, and you fumbled, as if you'd never seen a damned taper in your life. As if, suddenly, something had erased your memory of all those Sundays in that church, where you once took Marina to carve your names into the tree just outside. Now you couldn't remember if time had worn away those names or if you yourself had scratched out the letters in a fit of rage. Nothing made sense. You took the taper and lit it, wondering if the most sensible thing would be to let the memory of your son burn out, and with it, the pain you'd been shouldering since last night.

You felt that man's eyes on you. You understood: to him you were dirty. He said a couple of things: wash your teeth, son, put this blanket around you. You accepted a piece of bread and a warm tea, to calm your nerves. He told you not to worry, that soon the Lord would be closer to you. Would he, Carmelo? you wondered: the only thing you felt close to was the nausea clawing at the walls of your stomach. But he insisted, and dressed the boy with a tenderness you hadn't seen in such a long time. Gradually your body relaxed. Let the poor child rest in peace now, you heard him say, followed by more words. You didn't understand them all, but you knew he was praying for the boy's soul; some of the prayers, intoned in perfect Latin, you didn't even bother trying to make sense of. All you wanted was for them to bless him, and beyond that, whatever was in store for you didn't matter. The deed was done, Carmelo, and there was no way for you to scratch out the letters of your sin.

The smell of burning incense woke you. You'd never been too good at telling smells apart. With fish, for some reason, it was another story; you could tell the difference between a sea bass and a hake. They even moved differently when you manoeuvred the nets to catch them together in one haul. You made your living – like so many others in that godforsaken town – from fishing: thankless but honest work that put food on the table and also filled your lungs with an air the likes of which you'd never breathed before, nor would you again. An old-hander, you knew the sea's whims by heart; you understood it in some strange way, the way one understands a person they have loved their whole life. Even when it snatched from you the thing you loved the most, forcing you to ask yourself: was it not the boy, Carmelo, the thing you loved the most?

Half asleep still, you tried to move. You wanted to see his little body, if only to remind yourself that yes: it was you who swallowed him and not the sea, by leaving him there to be smothered in sea salt and the cold night air. Waiting for someone who was never going to come, Carmelo. Was it really you your son waited for? Now you wanted to see him and give him one last kiss: wrap him up warm, even though he no longer felt the cold; tell Marina that everything was going to be okay, that now they had an angel to look after them and guide the boat in bad weather, and that nothing bad would happen from then on. What else could possibly go wrong, Carmelo, when you had already stirred the very depths of hell? Move, Carmelo, you told yourself, the alcohol still weighing your body down like a stone.

Lord, you have come to the seashore, you heard them sing in chorus, the same people who up until yesterday had been your people: tough, hard-faced, but always your people. Get up, you mumbled, get up and go find the boy and give him the burial he deserves.

You didn't move, *You, fisherman of other shores*. You couldn't tell if it was exhaustion or grief rooting you to the spot. A moron you've always been, but at least you used to be nimble enough to run and run without your feet sinking into the wet sand. You were no longer that man, Carmelo, what happened to you? You would never understand it, no matter how tightly you squeezed your eyelids together and willed something inside of you to click. A moron perhaps, but still you noticed the rope tying your ankles together, and another at your wrists. You looked all about you. The priest had disappeared and the boy's body was nowhere to be seen. What could you do, Carmelo? Shout, cry, laugh? You heard a growl in your belly, that growl that had so often been hunger, and just as often rage.

That's when you realised you wouldn't be alone for much longer. *O, Lord, with your eyes set upon me.* You heard voices reverberating off the stained-glass windows and something inside you clicked. A mass of legs and voices came pounding over the pews and across the altar. It was the mob, who had come looking for you to cleanse your spirit of its sin. They could smell your fear and came running to find you. And as much as you wanted to take the past and crush it in your hands, there it was in front of you, right under your nose.

The first thing you spotted was the priest's crisp, clean vestment. Behind him, the horde: a pack of hounds with their jaws wide open, ready to sink their fangs into your rotten flesh. Drunk with joy, some of them, others disappointed to see you unmoving and unsure what to do, they closed in on you. They could smell your fear, Carmelo. All you wanted was to see the boy one last time, to be allowed to run your finger over his eyelids, bruised and dry from all the salt. To be allowed to feel that ache in your body, the kind of heartache only a man who has left his own son out to die could know. Tugging and slashing at the rope, they untied you from the chair. You closed your eyes: who could you plead to for mercy now, if the only one who could save you was yourself? It was the people, the townsfolk, against your word: the faithful people who were coming for you, who pulled you by the arms and legs and spat in your face when they could, and who ripped the clothes off your back to make you feel the same cold that your son would have felt at the break of dawn. You screamed, Carmelo, when you felt those shunts and scratches, because you knew there was only one way for this to end.

Pushing and shoving, they charged you out of the church and made you walk down streets that seemed to have no beginning or end; a labyrinth, Goddammit, the kind that only appears in dreams. The sound of the lapping waves that night came back to you. You could hear them so clearly: the boy lying face up, waiting for you to hold and rock him in your arms. But you didn't, Carmelo; and now they were the ones holding you, under a shower of punches and bloody saliva. They were the ones, armed with sticks and rocks, who used their bodies to trap you so you couldn't get away. The townswomen trailed the procession, praying the rosary for the soul of the drowned child, that son of yours who was now just a tiny bundle. He wasn't yours any more, Carmelo. He never would be again.

Your bare feet touched the wet sand. You could hardly see any more; your eyes were so swollen every punch hurt a little less. What's the difference between a hug and a shove, Carmelo? You were no longer sure you could tell them apart. You stumbled along amid the men's shouting and the women's peaceful praying. Your legs had stopped responding. Instead, they dragged you to your feet and made you walk the length of the shoreline as the scratches on your flesh became knife wounds and the harshest blows broke your ribs into pieces. You thought about your days at sea: how you used to cast the nets and sit and wait. You would wait and wait to feel the fish move, the tremor that told you everything was all right, and the sea, like you, was following its course. You thought about your own little fish, the one you'd left gasping in the tide in the same spot where the mob had now brought you to a halt. You listened to their hymns, the sacred songs sounding in your ears. The blows and insults rained down and the procession rued the day you were born. It left you crippled, made you walk along the shore, pierced your hands and mouth to let the salt water sink into every cut, every laceration. It cleansed you, Carmelo, even though you couldn't begin to imagine the amount of water and blows it would take to wash a sin of that magnitude. Remembering you had been left without the solace of a wife or a child at your side didn't hurt you now. From the sea you came, and into the sea you were condemned to disappear.

Sometimes, Carmelo, you just have to surrender and beg for time to do what it will; that's why you clenched your fists with what little strength you had left and waited, you waited for the last of all those wounds: the one that would come like a limestone rock to the back of your neck and stain the sand a red you'd never seen before. You sensed the dying heartbeats in your chest with a peace you didn't fully understand. And that's why you surrendered to the consolation of that wound and unclenched your fists, Carmelo, as the townswomen finished singing and praying for your festering soul, *At your side, I will seek other shores*. ■

ESTANISLAO MEDINA HUESCA

1990

Estanislao Medina Huesca was born in Malabo, Equatorial Guinea. He is a teacher, writer, scriptwriter and audiovisual producer. He is the author of *Barlock: Los hijos del gran búho*, *El albino Micó* and *Suspéh: Memorias de un expandillero*.

WANJALA

Estanislao Medina Huesca

TRANSLATED BY MARA FAYE LETHEM

It was a little after three in the morning when Heriberto Ebula shut off the engine in his old Toyota Corolla. They'd found the perfect spot to carry out the verbal agreement they'd reached, all hot and bothered, at a private table in Morena's pub, or *paff* as they're called in Malabo. Their agreement was none other than to find a dark, isolated place and have sex, once and for all, as they should have done since forever. Heriberto suggested this place because, according to him and his drinking buddies, it was the darkest and least traveled spot in the neighborhood of Elá Nguema, a witness to this story. Clearly, this was the best way to keep out of the sight line of prying eyes in a place where *congosá*, that malicious, hyperbolic form of gossip, had come of age, where it had learned to smoke and snort.

His headlights off for several meters already, Heriberto parked halfway between the María Auxiliadora school run by Salesian nuns and the Elá Nguema municipal cemetery. In that sinister spot, avoided by children and skittish adults alike, the night was dark as the armpits of a man dressed in a suit coat, and christened with sprinkles of bass that blared from countless loudspeakers in the distance, and the honking of solitary cars rolling along the asphalt on Calle José Sí Esono, perpendicular to where he'd parked.

It was December, when the customary tolerance for noise was more conspicuous than during any other month of the year. Music played everywhere, at all hours of the day and night, including, obviously, the outer edges of the capital city's graveyard, whose inhabitants had to put up with both the joy of the living and night-time visits from guys like Heriberto, disrespecting the souls of the faithful departed.

Heriberto was pure poetry, an excellent cabbie who liked to hit the bottle to dilute his outrage and then pontificate, calling into question how the Republic's government and its cronies were being managed, which, thanks to his own hybrid experience, he considered collateral damage, byproducts of poor Spanish management and its brutish, excessive colonization. Someone had to pay the piper. His Guinea wasn't a country, it was a project, an 'aborted' project, like all the other projects started here. According to Heriberto, every initiative in his native land ended up aborted. That was why the roads were never finished, or the building projects, or the benevolent work, the decrees in support of the most vulnerable layers of society, the cinemas, the Nzalang national football team, educational programs, laws of inclusion, the arcades and recreation centers for kids and teenagers (though there were a considerable number for adults), not even agreements with companies, embassies and countries, to give just a few examples. All of these, each and every one, had been halted for reasons that defied logic. Some initiatives never even got off the ground. Money flows like manna, but always in the wrong direction. Instead of falling from the heavens, it burbles up from the ground in the form of crude oil, yet another incentive to disrupt, slightly more, the nation-building project, especially when all involved were looking to line their pockets.

Heriberto blamed Spain. He always did. There was no way to make him budge on that. Stubborn as a royal mule. It didn't matter that Spain had been his refuge when members of the MAIB, the Bioko Island independence movement, were forced to flee via Cameroon, thanks to the persecution of that government 'project'. His father had been a hyper-proactive member of that organization for self-determination, known in those days as the 'group of rebels'.

More than twenty years in Spain had taught Heriberto to hate the Spaniards as much as the Fang people, despite the fact that he had several Fang friends who weren't like those other Fang, and he always told them this, because they didn't do Fang-like things. More than twenty years in Spain getting shaken up and down by people intolerant of tolerance; by racists, supremacists, xenophobes and all sorts of individuals with 'problems' acquired in childhood, who had free rein. Spanish institutions themselves belonged to the ranks of those who exploded with mental orgasms when recalling how the sun used to never set on their country. Delusions of grandeur. Ignorance of the laws of physics, especially the ones governing the rotation of Mother Earth.

Heri came back to Malabo when he was twenty-seven, and despite having two degrees it took him a thousand and one nights to find work. The old-boy network also worked in reverse. Instead of opening up doors for him, they were all slammed in his face. That's normal in a country so small that everybody knows one another. And his father's shadow stretched long in the sun. A year after moving in with his older sister, he managed to land a somewhat decent job. Being banned from entering Spain for his association with the 'rebels' finally started to weigh less on him. But as they say, 'Happiness is fleeting in a rebel's house.' He was fired for requesting a pay rise, and for relentlessly putting bugs in his coworkers' ears about 'bad practices' like striking, demanding contracts, seniority and 'suchlike things', of which the bosses in his hometown were not the least bit fond.

Heriberto never beat around the bush about things, never backed down, saw things through to the end. That was the legacy his father had left him, and he was willing, if need be, to abandon this bleak, inequitable world the same way his father had. But let's not forget our saying: 'Happiness is fleeting in a rebel's house.'

Heriberto was already pleasantly lit that 27 December, and so was she. Maite, she of the nice ass that had slayed him forever, well-shaped and bouncy. Their sexual tension had remained unresolved since they'd met in high school, in Fuenlabrada outside of Madrid. About ten years had passed since they'd last seen each other. Being the only black guy in class had given him a clear advantage with her, but in those days he was a tangle of raging, rebellious hormones.

Hurriedly they reclined Heriberto's seat and resumed the kissing and petting they'd started in Morena's *paff*. For a while now his erection had been in a constant state of charged tension.

Regrettably, neither of them had anticipated this encounter, so they had a struggle of coordination while removing her ripped jeans and his camouflage Bermuda shorts. If that weren't enough, Maite had been living in Bata for a while now, so Heriberto had to endure, in her every movement, every lick, the unmistakable aroma of a woman from the continental capital. That briny smell of the sea that bathes the coastline and a kind of corporal dankness, the result of Bata's unbearable sun. It put a little pressure on his mind, though he didn't complain the way he might have years ago.

They laughed at their clumsiness, but ended up in a position that worked for them both. Taking advantage of the car's relatively spacious interior, and the outstanding maneuverability of the driver's seat, Maite was able to straddle him, her rear end sharing its personal space with the steering wheel, which was never quite far enough away.

They shared passionate kisses, letting out gasps of pleasure that muffled the nearest party's music, which now somehow seemed a little farther away. And so, Heriberto's heart galloped frantically in his chest, craving this contact, this triumphant entrance into her garden of delight.

He wanted to be careful, though, to enjoy every second, every lick, every bite, but at the same time be quick enough to reduce the likelihood of a passerby recognizing his license plate and running off to tell his wife, whom he'd married traditionally three and a half years ago. His mother had begged him to marry, hoped it would quell the rebellious streak that might land him in Black Beach prison or six feet under like his father. It goes without saying it was his mother who arranged the marriage to the daughter of one of her closest childhood friends. The whole idea had gone entirely against the grain of the youngest of the Ebula family's way of thinking.

Maite, lost in the heat of arousal, anointed his member softly with her sex in little up and down movements, sending his blood-sugar levels spiking, compelling him to tear his lips away and remove her white top. And suddenly he found himself face to face with her dangling, defiant breasts.

He exhaled in jagged breaths, licked his lips.

Not a second did he intend to waste. He fastened lusciously onto her nipples, killing an obsession that had danced around in his mind for a long, long time. She took hold of his member and introduced it slowly into her moist depths, still charmingly coy despite the barrage of nibbling. They both held still for a moment, aware they'd reached the point of no return. Heriberto's mind raced in all directions, but each one carried him down to the pleasures of that precise instant.

Before they could set themselves into motion, a familiar light appeared in the darkness. His heart committed suicide the second he caught the reflection in the rear-view mirror, a thunderous drowning sensation took over his chest. He knew those headlights well. She had a better view of the scene, and immediately pulled away to recover her jeans and white top.

Before Heri had a chance to cover up the situation, a police officer was banging brazenly on the windows of his car.

'*Muf!*' he shouted angrily in Pichi – Move it! 'Open up! Get out! Open up! Open up!'

Heri lowered the window timidly and greeted him, his voice faltering.

'Good . . . good evening, brother!'

'Don't you good evening me, who do you think you're kidding? Get out of the car! What the hell is going on here!'

They didn't give him a chance to hitch up his Bermudas. Classic tantrum, completely by the book. By the time the first cop had finished speaking, another had come out of the rapid intervention vehicle and flanked them, an angry look on his face, disgusted by what he saw, even though it's exactly what they all did in the streets of Malabo when they weren't on duty, even sometimes when they were. If they got caught, they just flashed their ID and case closed. You know, the old guard.

'Hey, *wä*, get the fuck outta there!' the new arrival said to Maite, who had managed to pull up her underpants, but not the rest of her clothing. 'Open up or I'll break this glass, *einñ*!'

They both stepped out into the glare of the *cangrejo*'s headlights. All Heri had on was a Hawaiian shirt. Maite, her underpants and now the top, which she'd put on as she was getting out of the Toyota Corolla.

'Brother, there's no need to shout. We know we've done wrong.'

The soldier seemed confused by those last words and the tone he used to speak them.

'Oh, so you know more than I do, huh?'

'I didn't say that my brother. Can I speak with whoever's in command, please?' asked Heri cautiously.

'What do you mean in *command*? What the fuck kind of talk is that?' the other officer replied, annoyed, working himself up even more. 'You're breaking the law.'

No shit, Sherlock, thought Heriberto.

'I know brother,' he said in a near whisper. 'We had nowhere else to go, brother. You know how it is.'

Keep it up, Heriberto, his consciousness murmured again, while the cop decided whether or not to answer him, circling the car as if searching for a dangerous suspect. *Call him brother as many times as it takes to calm him down. They say it relaxes them. Don't cave in. Keep cool. Don't show signs of anger. Lower your head. Speak calmly. They like you to kiss their asses. You're moving in the right direction.*

'No, I don't know how it is,' the policeman said finally, walking over to Maite.

A few centimeters away from her, he pulled out a flashlight and slid its beam from Maite's feet up to her face, which was bowed from the unresolved sexual tension with Heriberto. He lingered a while on her crotch, on her cleavage, where he drew little circles of light around her breasts.

'You two come from Spain, you have studies,' he spoke again, briefly moving away from Maite, though keeping the beam of his flashlight pointed at her. 'You think you know more than us, is that it?'

Shit. My accent gave me away again.

'That's not it brother,' Heriberto said. 'You know, we were just partying, brother. We've had a bit to drink and . . .'

The end of Heriberto's sentence was irrelevant to the young officer. He wasn't listening, his attention was back on Maite.

'You!' he shouted at her. 'Lift your face! Little late to be acting the saint. LIFT YOUR FACE!'

Maite immediately obeyed, blinking like someone who'd just woken up in an operating room. Just then, the cop who'd banged on the car window reemerged on the scene and quelled his impatience by grabbing her by the arm.

'*Muf*! Go on! Get in, get in!' he shouted as he waved them both into the rapid intervention vehicle.

'Give me the keys to this car,' said the one with the flashlight.

'Wait a second brother. We can work it out, right?'

That's it Heri, set the bait.

'You can talk all about it up there. You know they're going to lock you up and you're gonna have to pay. This your wife, right?'

'No brother. She's a friend.'

The soldier, or policeman, hard to tell, grinned, and sought out the complicity of his colleagues for a good laugh at the situation at hand.

'How come you having friends like this?' he asked, then took advantage of Maite's movements to illuminate her rear end. 'I want a friend like this too.'

'Brother, let's talk. How much for us to get back to our little party?'

Well done. Now that wasn't so hard. Wait and see what happens.

After a quick silence and a half, the aforementioned answered with a question.

'You see how many we are?' he said, turning his torso toward the vehicle, out of which hung, like bats, officers hungrily watching the scene.

'I do. How much can I slip you?' he said in a paper-thin voice. 'She's married and so am I. We can't go up there, you know what would happen, brother.'

'Don't look at me, I didn't tell you to come here and do these things.'

Agree with him Heri, tell him he's right, that will puff up his ego and he'll lower his guard.

'I know, brother. All my fault. All my fault. She had nothing to do with it. That's why I'm asking, please.'

There was another pithy silence, interrupted by recriminations in Fang from the rest of the policemen, or soldiers, he had no idea how to tell the difference. Their jurisdictions almost always overlapped.

'Fine. Don't got all night. You cough up a hundred grand and make it quick. All you out there drinking and doing your stuff, and it's us looking out for you.'

'Can you lower it a little, please? I don't have that much.'

'Friend? You trying to screw around with us?'

Careful now. Careful. Negotiate well. Negotiate wisely. Remember what Reyes told you. Learn to lie to them. Learn to lie to them. In the end they'll take whatever you give.

'No, officer. How could I be? I just don't have that kind of money on me.'

He made a disapproving gesture and then spoke.

'How much you have?'

'Around twenty grand, I think.'

'You think?' he asked with a marked change in his tone of voice. 'Yo, Lucio, put 'em in the vehicle! They can go talk to the commissioner directly, let's see if they get off with less than two hundred grand.'

So stupid. Fix it! Quick!

'Okay, okay, hold up,' Heriberto said in desperation. 'I have another fifty grand at home. We can fetch it there, no need to go anywhere else.'

Silence. Then the one holding Maite by the shoulder finally spoke. 'Where you live?'

'Close by, over behind the church.'

Idiot. Fucking idiot. So pathetic! Who are you even?

After a brief exchange of words in Fang with his colleagues, who by now were champing at the bit, the guy holding the flashlight said, 'All right, let's go. It's Christmas, we don't want to ruin it for you.'

Of course not, you son of a bitch.

Heriberto and Maite were allowed to get dressed, the soldier or cop, he couldn't tell which, hustling them on. They headed over to Heriberto's home like a posse, him driving the Toyota Corolla with that same policeman, Maite in the vehicle with the other soldiers to make sure he didn't hightail.

Heriberto parked along the square in Elá Nguema at a prudent distance from his home, just in front of the church run by the Salesians. He got out of the car with the keys in his hand and trotted over to the door of his house. He opened it deftly and went inside, heading straight to the room where his wife was sleeping. She was hogging the entire bed to underscore how she resented her husband staying out late yet again.

'Consuelo! Consuelo!' He woke her up with subtle but effective little pats.

'What?'

'Where's the money for Junior's school registration?'

'Why? What's going on? What time is it?'

'Those bastard soldiers seized my car. They say I'm missing some document.'

'What document is it this time?'

'The waybill.'

'What?'

'The waybill.'

'Again?'

'Again. They don't even bother to change their strategy anymore. Please, give me the money. I don't want them to impound the car because then I'll have to cough up three hundred thousand, which you know we don't have. I'll work it off tomorrow and pay it back. You know I can.'

'What?'

'The money, Consuelo.'

'What money?'

'The money I gave you yesterday to pay Junior's school tomorrow.'

'Oh, *that* fifty thou.'

'Yeah.'

'I don't have it. I lent it to Papá yesterday so he could see the doctor.'

'You what?'

'I lent it to Papá yesterday. He said he'd pay it back day after tomorrow, when he gets paid.'

'You gotta be kidding me.'

'I don't have it, *main*. Let me sleep now! I'm tired.'

'Fuck! So, you pressure me for the money, then go and give it to your papá so he can see the doctor for drinking, when he's not supposed to be drinking?'

'What?'

'Shit! Shit! Shit!'

Heriberto walked out of the house, scratching the nape of his neck. He had to find a solution before it all blew up in his face, before his inner peace turned into inner war, and outer war too, because Maite's husband was an influential second lieutenant in the air force and he'd just been assigned to the capital.

But when he got to the plaza, to his horror, his distress, they'd all vanished: the policemen, the *cangrejo*, Maite. ∎

Edinburgh International Book Festival

14—30 August 2021

The World, in Words
An online celebration of books,
stories and ideas featuring some
of the finest writers, poets, thinkers,
artists and activists from the UK
and around the world, broadcast
live from Edinburgh.

Programme launch:
End of June

Sign up for news &
event announcements:
edbookfest.co.uk
@edbookfest

MUNIR HACHEMI

1989

Munir Hachemi was born in Madrid, Spain. His first stories appeared in fanzines, published by the collective Los Escritores Bárbaros. He is the author of *Los pistoleros del eclipse*, 廢墟 and most recently, *Cosas vivas*.

VITAL SIGNS

Munir Hachemi

TRANSLATED BY NICK CAISTOR

For Sifan Zhao

1

As he made his way down the lower floors, G was thinking of the body's materiality, its weight, the mass it was meant to lose at death, the air lodged between its joints, the effort it was costing him to carry it, and that none of this seemed plausible to him. By the second floor he was no longer thinking of anything, or at least anything of the sort.

The workmen were surprised when they saw him appear. An ambulance's dipped headlights languished at the far end of the parking lot. The driver was leaning against the side of the vehicle; even at that hour of the night the heat was almost unbearable, but it didn't seem to bother him. G didn't feel able to make it the thirty metres between him and the double doors to accident and emergency, so he asked for help. The two technicians took several steps back; the ambulance guy was looking at his phone and didn't seem to hear.

'How did you get here?' the younger one asked.

'I live five or six blocks away,' G replied, and realised he was panting.

For a few seconds, the men didn't know what to do or say. G doubled over to retch, and lost his balance. The older workman jumped forward, managing to catch the body before it fell.

'So sorry,' G said absurdly.

The younger one was visibly scared. He walked three or four metres away and looked over at the ambulance operator, who was still unaware of what had happened. The other technician was holding the body under the armpits and staring at it as if it were a completely strange object, as if he himself didn't also have a body. G thought momentarily of the fear a body can instil, and then about why the man had put himself at risk, had decided to hold it up rather than let it fall, as if that body could matter to him, as if hitting the hot asphalt would make a difference for the body and hold some meaning for it.

The man placed two fingers on the dead body's jugular.

'It's dead,' he said, then immediately corrected himself, 'I mean, she is.'

G made no answer. He took a cloth bag out of his pocket and a paper, and began to roll a cigarette. The young technician had moved even further away, until he disappeared behind the sliding doors of A & E. The older man said:

'Will you roll me one?'

Without a word, G took another pinch of tobacco and another paper. The technician looked down at his hands, remembering another not-so-distant time when everything was different. The humidity was suffocating. He thought he could see the asphalt breathing, the steam or mist rising from it. Then he thought he was probably mistaken, and that this vapour must correspond to another phenomenon he was unable to explain. There wasn't a soul on the other side of the parking lot, apart from the ambulance driver. He could hear the street lamps buzzing.

G finished rolling the cigarettes and passed one to the technician. They shared the weight of the body so that they could smoke; G laid it against his right shoulder, the other man over his left. That way they both had a free hand.

'I don't have a light,' the man said, searching in his pocket.

G felt in his back pocket for a lighter. He tried to remember if he had put one there before he left his house, but couldn't. He jerked his head, as if towards the body. He muttered something.

'What?'

G stopped digging in his pockets for a moment, took the cigarette from his mouth.

'I said she was my grandmother.'

'Ah.'

Before G could renew his search, the hospital doors creaked and two men came out into the tranquil night. One was the young technician. The other was wearing a pale yellow uniform and was pulling on a pair of latex gloves as he walked. He wasn't much older than G or the young man beside him, and was unsuccessfully trying to look angry or annoyed. Two drops of sweat slid down his forehead.

'Are you crazy?' he whispered, glancing at the far end of the lot and the ambulance driver. The older technician cupped the cigarette between his fingers with a practised swivel of his free hand.

'We have to take her to her village,' G said, adding its name.

The newcomer asked the older technician to bear the whole weight of the body, and bent over to listen to the chest. G took the chance to renew his search, pulled out the lighter, and began smoking. With every lungful he blew up into the air the mosquitoes swarming round the street lamp flew away, only to regroup a second later.

'This woman is dead; she isn't going anywhere. We only transport live bodies. Nobody saw you bringing her here?'

G shrugged.

'I live five or six blocks away.' The tip of his cigarette glowed between his index and middle fingers when G pointed in the direction of his house. 'The village is about sixty kilometres from here.'

G fell silent. For an instant the only sound came from the disjointed voices on a video the ambulance driver was smiling at on his phone.

'Please,' G said eventually.

The man in yellow hesitated or seemed to hesitate for a moment, and finally said something to the technicians that G couldn't hear. Without waiting for G to take the cigarette out of his mouth, the older man passed him the body, and the three of them walked a few metres away. The young one was complaining about something, and stood apart from the other two. They began arguing. G thought that only a few hours earlier he had been playing cards and drinking spirits with his grandmother. His daughter and wife were asleep on the sofa in front of the TV, while the two of them bet quietly. He thought how lucky his grandmother had been to get to know her great-granddaughter, and an instant later how empty that idea was, how absurd it was, even though he didn't know why. He heard some phrases from the men's disagreement, with words such as 'tradition', 'burial' or 'last wish'. G recalled that when his daughter was born, a friend had dedicated a poem to her. 'An opening breath,' it read, predictably enough, 'a change in the atmosphere, a frontier.' Something like that. He had used the adjective 'labile', in reference to a private joke between the two of them. G thought of how long it had been since the last time he saw his friend, and what he would be doing now. If he were doing anything.

The argument between the three men became more heated, pulling him out of his daydreaming.

'The problem is that people of your generation think you're better than everybody.' The older technician had hold of the younger man's lapels, and the youngster was peering terrified at his hands, his knuckles, then at the man in yellow, back to the hands, then at G and his lit cigarette and the other man's that had gone out, thinking he understood something, though he was not sure exactly what.

The ambulance man came over.

'What's up?'

'This woman,' the man in yellow said, as though surprised at what he was saying, 'is alive. You have to take her to her native village.'

He said its name. G nodded. The ambulance driver looked at them, puzzled.

'I'll go and fill in the proper form,' said the man in yellow. 'You get her into the ambulance.'

He left without waiting for a response. The others exchanged glances and set to work. They wouldn't let G help them. The older technician lifted the body onto the trolley, then the three of them pushed her up the ramp into the ambulance. G finished his cigarette, reflecting on the weight he had freed himself from, in that he wasn't sure if this was what he really wanted, in that he wouldn't have to wash her any more, that one day he would be that too, a body, not something similar but exactly that, his grandmother's body, because even though we pretend that's not how it is, there is only one body, a suffering, hard-working body, his grandmother's, his own, his daughter's, the ambulance driver's, the calf's whose veal they had eaten tonight, before they had begun playing cards. When he handed her over to the technician, G caught one final whiff of his grandmother's breath. She smelled of liquor, and death, and veal.

2

A few months later, G thought back on all this while having breakfast in a restaurant. He had his daughter on his lap while she was playing – despite her being profoundly serious about it (at least so thought G) – at looking at herself in a mirror and banging her nose against the surface. She almost touched it with her tongue once, but G managed to stop her just in time. They had permission to be in there for another seven minutes and a few seconds. G smiled at his wife, staring at her protruding cheekbones, then looked down at his bacon and egg toast.

'She's alive,' the man in yellow had repeated that night, handing the ambulance driver a form.

The driver glanced at it.

'Whatever you say.'

G was in the back with the body. It was still warm, although that was perhaps because it was summer and everything was hot.

They didn't pass a soul for several kilometres; only ambulances and other special vehicles were allowed on the highways. At the first two checkpoints the officials didn't open the back doors of the ambulance. They did at the third: two men in uniforms pointed a torch at the body, then immediately shut the doors, covering their mouths with the tops of their shirts. It wasn't until then that G realised there was a smell inside the ambulance. The heat made everything worse. Outside the men were shouting at the driver, but the words only reached him muffled through the metal sides. They were speaking very quickly in the local dialect, so G only caught a few words: 'gas', 'corpse', 'grandmother'. He wanted to get out, but couldn't: he had to keep his hand under the pillow because the vital signs device was secretly connected to his right index finger, so that the figures on the screen were in fact his. He began making sentences out of the words he heard: 'You need a permit to transport grandmother gases.' 'At night we are all hospital people.' 'Current regulations do not authorise death.' Suddenly he wanted to write a poem or a song. He felt as if he didn't know his own tongue, as if he were thinking in a foreign language.

Soon afterwards they set off again. G didn't ask anything, and the driver didn't give any explanations. G wanted to carry on creating poems or at least phrases, but couldn't. He thought he missed the sound of words, and then that maybe they were still echoing round the metal walls of the ambulance but he was unable to make them out. He wondered if it wasn't the same with starlight: if in thousands of years on another planet someone would hear things like 'intubated', 'stench' or 'vital signs'. He was almost certain the answer was no, but couldn't have explained why.

Four or five kilometres further on, the driver pulled up on the hard shoulder. G heard the sound of the driver's door and the night air hit him in the face when the back door was opened. Then and there the air came in cool. Dozens of tiny insects were fluttering round the ambulance's rear lights. The driver pulled up his T-shirt to cover his nose, then turned round and put on a surgical mask. He climbed into the container. That was the word that went through G's mind to describe where he and his grandmother were: a 'container'. The driver looked him straight in the eyes, intently, for a few seconds. He seemed frightened, but the mask made it hard to make out his precise emotions.

'She's swelling up,' he said, pointing to the body.

Several images flashed through G's mind: images of his grandmother in the fields; of the day her only daughter (G's mother) was born; of the way she rubbed a balm on her calloused hands after a hard day's work; of those same hands weaving a wicker basket or pulling up weeds; and then strangely, of the face she would have pulled decades earlier, when she was the same age as G now, if she had been told her body was swelling up. The images were so clear and new to G that he thought perhaps they were reaching him through the vital signs device, that maybe the clip gripping his finger and hers was acting as an antenna. Instinctively, G pulled his hand from under the pillow. He realised that several minutes had gone by, and that the ambulance driver was removing his grandmother's rings. Only one was left. G tried to remember how many she had been wearing when she collapsed across the card table, but it eluded him. All at once he felt infinitely weary.

'What are you doing?'

'She's swelling up.'

G didn't move. The other man slowly removed the last ring. G smelled an aroma of menthol in the air, and thought the driver must be using ointment to grease his grandmother's fingers. He couldn't resist falling asleep any longer, and closed his eyes. He opened them again when he felt the man's arm brush against him as he took the necklace off her neck. G had no idea how much time had passed. He had the impression it had been many hours, although it was still night-time. The ambulance driver seemed to be smiling behind the mask, and G thought he was telling him everything was all right. The next time he opened his eyes, the man's pupils were fixed on his and he was poking at something inside his grandmother's mouth.

'If my grandmother could see that, hey . . . see really . . . not a corpse . . .' G muttered.

The man's hands froze for an instant in mid-air. The heat, humidity and hunger made G feel nauseous. Crickets were chirruping in the distance. All of a sudden there was a bleep from the G's trouser pocket, and then what sounded like a woman's voice:

'Sorry, I didn't get that. You say you want to get rid of a body?'

His phone assistant had been activated by mistake, and in a tone somewhere between robotic and jocular, the voice had responded with what had once been considered a joke. G wanted to laugh but found it impossible. Staring at the other man, he said:

'Siri, call the police.'

'Calling the police. Your whereabouts will be automatically transferred to their switchboard.'

The ambulance driver quickly pulled his hand out of her mouth, as if G's grandmother had bitten him (G even thought he could see her teeth marks), and rushed out of the container. He waited until the driver had started the engine before silencing the confused voice questioning him on the far end of the line. It was only after he had switched off the phone – and without knowing why – that he guffawed and began slowly to slide down on the stretcher next to his grandmother. He put his arm round her, rested his head on the pillow, and wondered what their two bodies would look like from up in the sky if the ambulance, the stretcher, the vital signs machine and the driver . . . if everything were transparent except for the two of them, if there were only their two naked bodies floating at a hundred kilometres per hour over the asphalt, how they would look to an extraterrestrial if the light they emitted were to reach him some day. 'Identical,' he thought, 'that's how he would see us,' and decided they would have to wait another week before they buried his grandmother. 'Seven days,' he thought. 'Seven is a good number for remembering the dead.' Then he fell asleep. ■

IRENE REYES-NOGUEROL

1997

Irene Reyes-Noguerol was born in Seville, Spain. She is the recipient of the Tigre Juan Young Writers' Award, the Brocense Award and the Camilo José Cela Award. She is the author of two collections of stories, *Caleidoscopios* and *De Homero y otros dioses*.

LOST CHILDREN

Irene Reyes-Noguerol

TRANSLATED BY LUCY GREAVES

'Because I could not stop for Death –
He kindly stopped for me –'
– Emily Dickinson

For the lost children. And their mothers.

That's what Grandma always said. See, hear and say nothing.
Awake, in the small hours, eyes open in the middle of the
night, the Girl wonders. In the cold March darkness – a sweet, dirty
smell – she stares at the ceiling, tosses and turns, changes position,
tries to edge closer to the other side of the room, out of reach of the
Brother's trusting sighs, over where the walls listen to the insomniac
breathing of the Mother, who at last lets slip her scales, her masks, her
differently textured skins, outlines that the Girl learns to distinguish.
She watches the Mother and studies her. She compares her with
the princesses in her stories, with the witches who terrify her. She
would like to know more but can't, there's no way to catalogue that
ButterflyMother's metamorphoses, impossible to retain the beauty of
her wings between her fingers, to guess when to hug, flee or stay silent.

Outside, the cats yowl. Dressed in the moon, they arch their backs. Their waving tails draw question marks that only she understands.

On weekdays, Mamá holds her hand as they walk to school. They hum the same old rhymes – *an elephant stood on a spider's web* – and Mamá asks if today her tummy hurts, or her throat or her ear; sometimes she swings her and lifts her up above the pavement of this old southern city. The Girl feels like she's flying, poised mid-air; she strokes her mother's arm and loses count of its constellations of moles. Mamá clasps the palm that finds shelter in the heat of her hand, infusing tenderness with the rhythm of each beat, holding the Girl's fingers as if love could break them, singing *lovely lovely, lovely, little hands*. They walk together, their strides matching, two tin soldiers, two hearts in time. The Girl looks up and recognises curved eyebrows, a nose, a soft mouth, those ocean eyes that sometimes laugh, sometimes fill with water or sink into longings no one understands, on shores thirsting for shipwrecks. In class, the Girl will write *mymamálovesme* in her best handwriting and the teacher, for once, won't insist she stick to the lines in her exercise book. The Girl writes correctly what she believes to be correct. She'll think: this is Me. She'll think: this is Mamá.

Later, Mamá picks her up from school, wraps her arms with their fragrance of flowers around her, takes her home. Mamá left food ready for her Brother, it's still steaming; she gives it to him slowly, as if following a ritual: soft blow to cool it, mouth wide open, hangar for the little aeroplane that comes flying in, skilful little spoon between plump lips, napkin mopping the bit left at the corner of his mouth, ceremony repeated until the bowl is empty. The Girl asks why he doesn't eat on his own. Mamá replies: *he's only Little*. But she's not convinced. She's Little too and she's grown used to the *other* days that can't be named and which the Mother seems not to remember. Because the Mother wilfully forgets them, like you might hide a box in the attic, and pretends nothing is happening when the *Other* appears with her gas-scented perfume, when there are no more walks to school or songs or lukewarm jars of baby food for the Brother.

The Girls sees. The Girl hears. The Girl says nothing.

With no warning or sign, the Mother disappears or hides and

then – *two elephants stood* . . . – what to do with so much on your shoulders, when Mamá suddenly stops being there because she turns into a motionless lump on the bed, there's nothing left but a mute body that doesn't respond or turn or react. At first, the Girl tries to entertain her by being silly, regales her with improvised gifts, paper aeroplanes that she folds and folds so they're perfect, not a pleat out of place, not a wrinkle. Nothing works. The *Other* takes over everything, supplants the face, which the Girl scrutinises from afar. And the Girl rocks the Brother and sings nursery rhymes to him softly but stays alert, her senses are upright while she observes those still, glassy eyes. She puts the Brother down far away from the *Other* and closes her eyes so she can't see that LizardMother any more. But then there's the weight of silence on the house, one side of which never sleeps, while she hugs or clings to the baby and assures him that tomorrow will be a new day, that it can all change at any moment. You never know.

And the thing is Grandma went to heaven. No more low bun or bottle-bottom glasses, no more brown headscarf. Goodbye to the noisy kisses, to the tight hugs that squeezed and warmed her from the inside. Before that, a bald doctor talking to Mamá because a nasty creature, something like a crab, had bit Grandma and was making her ill, and the Girl there peeking round the door of that sad room which smelt of medicine, hearing ancient cries and prayers, a black rosary in Grandma's gnarled root-fingers. Mamá cried in secret – *be good you two, don't make a sound.* But some days Grandma called to her like before – *come here and comb my hair, my Girl* – and the Girl unwound her grey bun, the soft comb stroking her long, fine mermaid's hair. By then Grandma didn't talk much, her voice worn out and hoarse: *do you know your mamá loves you more than anyone? – More than you? – Yes, more than me – except that sometimes she's not herself, you must have noticed.* And so the Girl learned: *you have to look after Mamá, watch over your Brother and hide until it all passes – because everything passes –* and then Grandma said: *get your notebook with the cats on it,* and the Girl, in neat handwriting: *make sure Mamá takes the tablets, shut the windows properly, turn off the gas, see, hear and say nothing*, and a list of important things she must *nevernevernever* forget. Grandma's white eyes in the Girl's memory. Alwaysalwaysalways.

Before that, long before, Papá – shouts and slammed doors – ran away from the round belly which foretold the Brother, from the Girl who would cry, maybe because of him, from that MillipedeMother and her lock-and-key faces: she tries to hide those faces from the world, protect them from the sun, shower the dark side of her moon with shadows.

Sometimes Mamá wakes up waxing; at other times, waning. The Girl follows and dances around her when she seems full, brimming, swollen with light. In a second she seems to stretch or shrug off a bad dream and there are moments of relief from the heavy weight pressing on the roof of that insomniac house. Happiness returns, the chance of levitating by simply wishing it, the joy of an instant that stretches out and persists in the Girl's memory during silent hours, crouches on her lips, in her gap-toothed smile – *Mamá, I lost another one!* – and in her little voice, terrified of confessing untold truths, and the omens of an unwanted adulthood, her lost voice that sees, that hears, but says nothing, that shouts in a whisper *don't leave me, I'm Wendy, I don't want to grow up.*

But everyone grows up, even Wendy, even the Girl, though there are still days when she jumps into the bath with the Brother and they play with the rubber ducks and splash and roar with laughter, clean and unafraid. A distracted Girl who didn't notice that today the *Other* – the cold eyes   had turned up unannounced: the *Other* who opens her deep, yawning mouth, her oven-mouth that scorches and says ugly words, bad words, her angry gestures that shout and make the baby cry, her face like a mask that barks *shut up, shut up, the two of you are going to be the death of me, I can't take it any more*, her vicious hands holding the Brother's head submerged for one, two, three, seven seconds, his anxiety bubbling under the water, the Girl cries, *please, Mami, no, he's only Little*, she gets up to fend off the claw-hands that shove her now, hard slap, stinging cuff, the thunder of the wall in her ears, her eyes cloud over and it aches but it doesn't matter, it doesn't matter because the Brother is out, he's finally out, he got his little blonde head out and watery tears are running down his face, there's distress in his pale eyes, staring at the red string at the corner of the Girl's mouth, the blood tastes salty but not to worry, not to worry, because VampireMamá soothes her, strokes her, kisses her, *oh, myprettygirl, oneIlovethemost, what happened to you?* and the *Other* retreats little by little. There are smells – the sweet, dirty smell of gas, the rusty smell of blood – that calm the *Other* so she lets Mamá come back to her children.

Outside, the cats yowl. Soaked in the night, they caress the windowsill. The dawn has split in two and their irises stain it green.

In summer, Mamá takes them to the swimming pool. The Girl loves swimming; she feels like a nymph in the water. When she dives in, she imagines wearing coral hair clips and a tail of precious stones. She does somersaults and stays underwater until her chest burns, enduring a noseful of chlorine and pruney, wrinkled thumbs and a trail of haphazard bubbles behind her. She takes it all gladly just to hear Mamá's praise, to see her open, sincere smile, the rewards of a fractured happiness. But, playing chase through the water, she catches a hint of that expression – inert pupils, that savage absence – which she can recognise by now, and tries to camouflage her panic that Mamá might catch her, so she laughs or attempts a nervous giggle, her heart beating wildly, and when the adrenaline seems ready to force out a sob, she suddenly stretches her body out on the surface of the water. She plays dead. She floats on her back, closes her eyes and the light floods her with orange, allows her a blinking warmth, a peace that twinkles and flickers. No more fear. Afterwards, she goes back to Mamá or to the *Other*, to the uneasiness of the new moon. She makes an effort to kiss her, to love her unreservedly, to hug her without fear. She replies that no, nothing's wrong, her tummy and throat and ear don't hurt. It's her mamá that hurts.

Some days, the house smells of gas. The odour makes its way from the kitchen and colours the siesta with sweetish tones. An invisible sleepiness falls on the furniture and the Girl's head spins like on a merry-go-round, clutching the Brother, she feels as if at any moment she could fall and knock everything down, abandon herself to a kind of peace that carries her off without resistance, hand herself over to that swinging Ferris wheel, like rats to the piper; but the certainty of knowing she's being tricked and the questioning look on the Brother's face overcome that stupor. In the kitchen, Mamá in front of the oven's yawning promise, absorbed in a landscape of gas, contemplates the open valve, the house awash, a nursery rhyme that comes at the wrong time, the lullaby of an unspeakable desire. The Girl shakes her – *come back, come back* – or dreams that she does; at some point everything stops and the Mother sighs back into the bedroom. Mamá says: *Let me go.* She says: *Not a single star will be left in the night. The night will not be left.* The Girl doesn't see, doesn't hear, only hushes the tides that propel her, the waves that drag her, protects from the scourge that suffocates her, the noose that at once saves and condemns her, woman slave to the fate of the moon. The Girl doesn't ask, doesn't want to know but knows, watches her sinking, *girl, blind in your soul,* plummeting into nameless, boundless chasms, barely balancing between two razors' edges, her exhaustion teetering on a cable that's about to break. She calls her and there's no one, hugs her and there's no one. There are no warning signs.

The Brother and his half-language – *donlikeitdonlikeit* – when back to school means the return of DragonMamá: fiery eyes, claws that pinch, that scratch, that hurt, to then caress, kiss the wound, *whoops-a-daisy, silly boy, let's kiss it better, all gone now?* And the Brother smiles, all bruises and snot. With sweet lullabies he'll fall asleep in the claw-arms, cradle-arms, little puppy in love, no memory.

Hiding under the bed, the Girl doesn't smile. Dread, anxiety, guilt at not being able to save him, not this time, drum in her temples. Her tears sharpen on their way down to her neck, back come questions that had stolen away since the absence of the Father, since Grandma's passing, since the weight of another elephant the spiderweb can't withstand. For how long the uncertainty, the secret that grinds at her hope, day by day grating it, debilitates her with its hardness, its severe, rough-edged strength, its fragility of needles and thorns. It grates, grates, grates and the Girl learns – she sees, hears, says nothing – and the softness of her age hardens, becomes armed with edges, with sharp angles. A crown of silence.

Outside, the cats yowl. They complain, whisper, drag themselves along. They look like little children, lost children who are crying.

The Girl says: *mymamálovesme*. She says: *shesthebestintheworld*. In the golden days of autumn, Mamá bursts into leaf again, bears fruit, she's full to the brim with spring. She kisses the Girl on her forehead, on her cheeks, on her belly button – that little cord is what linked us – she strokes her back, sings to her of hope, pupils shining with measureless joy, as if someone had pulled her string like a toy; her body is taken over by some prefabricated happiness, a hysterical pleasure, so close to a cry for help. But the Girl doesn't care. She enjoys it and knows that everything ends, that sooner or later she'll be left at the school gate and not picked up, her classmates' parents will ask her and she'll put on her best smile and say well, down with a cold or an earache or a headache. Wearing her best smile she'll convince them that nothing's wrong, she can get a lift with her neighbour, never mind the empty chair at her performance or what other mothers might say in the cafeteria. She'll stand her ground and say *shesthebestintheworld* and that sometimes she disappears or disconnects herself like a toy whose batteries have run out only because she gets tired; it's normal, she works a lot, the Girl knows how to entertain the Brother too, and can help when needed, she's big now, she forgot about Wendy, she knows and prefers not to know because she follows her Grandma's advice – she sees, hears and says nothing.

When she gets home, she learns to change nappies and hold her breath so she won't be sick – it smells like gas – sometimes she eats, sometimes she doesn't, but she goes into the pantry and tries to get food ready for the Brother, she reaches up for the bottle of milk and can almost touch it, she's almost there, she stands on tiptoe till she can't any more and the bottle spills all over her, but it doesn't matter, it doesn't matter, the warm liquid gets in her eyes, she imagines the taut udder being milked, milk from CowMamá that runs down her body and – someone left the gas on – she starts to retch, the pictures on her favourite T-shirt start distorting but never mind, never mind, she tries to find a cloth as her feet are getting wet, the baby is frightened so she conjures a smile for him, gets him to dance in the pools of white worry, *splat, splat,* she claps for him and comforts him with cuddles, she combs his hair, it's blonde and soft and shiny, Goldilocks, sometimes the porridge gets mixed in with his dirty nappies but never mind, never mind, the Girl handles it and changes the Brother again and tells him *it'll all be fine, don't be scared,* though she can still smell gas and this time Mamá has shut herself in the kitchen – how much weight can the spiderweb bear – and there's no time, her masks blur together through the glass, her outline is translucent before the oven – *why is she bending down, why isn't she moving away* – she turns her face towards the shouts – *I am looking on the last sunset, I am hearing the last bird* – towards the voice covered in milk and piss and horror, she doesn't say anything because there's no need, the Girl sees and the Girl hears and the Girl says nothing. Clever Girl who always knows what's going on but today doesn't get there on time. Doesn't turn off the gas. Doesn't get there on time.

Outside, the street and the rain. November rears its head in the puddles. The smell of wet earth. ■

© Arien Chang

CARLOS MANUEL ÁLVAREZ

1989

Carlos Manuel Álvarez was born in Matanzas, Cuba. He is the editor of *El Estornudo* and has written for *El País*, the *New York Times* and the *Washington Post*. He has published a collection of essays, *La tribu*, and two novels, *Los caídos* and *Falsa Guerra*.

BITTER CHERRIES

Carlos Manuel Álvarez

TRANSLATED BY FRANK WYNNE

Years after all the things that mattered, I would buy supermarket cherries to eat in front of the television. Huge, juicy, red cherries; real cherries that had nothing in common with the ones I ate as a child, from the cherry tree that, for some unknown reason, stood in the backyard of my grandmother's house. It was a puny thing; you can't plant a cherry tree in a town consumed by heat, or subject a cherry tree to the roiling commotion of a city and expect it to produce healthy fruit. But this incongruous, gnarled and twisted tree remains the archetypal cherry tree for me. It was stunted, with a trunk and branches that were emaciated, a trunk and branches that were piteous, but a trunk and branches that I could climb. The cherry tree produced tiny fruits, some yellow, but mostly green and sour, with a minimal layer of acrid flesh and worthless stones that I chewed and instantly spat out again. Cherries that I crammed into my mouth by the fistful, whose intense acidity caused my face to contort, brought me out in a sweat, as if I were transforming into something else, and even brought tears to my eyes. The pleasure of eating backyard cherries masquerading as punishment and torture.

This carried on until the first hurricane ripped the consumptive cherry tree out by the roots – how could it be otherwise, what was a cherry tree doing in that backyard in the first place? The wind carried it away, leaving its seeds planted in the desolate backyard of my memory. A cherry tree unlike any other, whose astringent fruit was nothing like the supermarket cherries that demand to be eaten one by one and that ooze a dark, highly addictive juice. One single word describes two different things, because the cherries from the backyard in Colón were not cherries; I was the only person who had eaten them, so I was the only person who could give them a name. It's pointless to look for a word to describe something that no longer exists, something non-transferable, that belongs only to an individual language, that is, to silence. No one else would know what the word means, and if I were to persist in this futile exercise, to give it a name, people would imagine a mediocre version of a supermarket cherry, or a cherry from a bad harvest.

So, far from everything but the supermarket, I would eat cherries familiar to more or less everyone, cherries eaten by more or less everyone, and as the intensely satisfying taste filled my mouth, it erased – or I thought it erased – the pugnacious taste of those bitter green cherries.

After the cherry tree had been ripped up by the roots we moved house, and, eventually, my grandmother died. Grandparents should never be forgotten or neglected. Parents, on the other hand, are best forgotten, and the sooner the better. With grandparents, there is no need to engage in acrimonious quarrels, they're not so relevant, they can be treated like people we know vaguely, people we've seen around from time to time and greet politely. The culture of deception begins with relationships like this, where you claim, and believe, that you know more about the other person than you actually do, and have to negotiate a love equal to that absolute. In contrast, the only thing your parents do from the moment you are born is hide truths from you, including present truths. You're an instrument of their pettiest vices. You're a testament to their basest passions, their marital squabbles, to all the things from their past they strive to hide. Can anyone honestly say they know about their parents' childhood? It's as though they had never existed before we were born, as though we were overwhelmingly wanted, when in fact most children are not wanted, they arrive by mistake. There is no right time to have a child, and parents cannot be blamed for that, a child is a detour on the road to freedom, a road that is always open, as roads not taken invariably are. A child is a tailback on the road that is never going to clear up, a detour to something else, to mistrust, half-truths and insinuations. Meanwhile, children also learn to lie from an early age, and their lying begins with their parents. Later it extends to teachers, but lying is a skill we hone with our parents. We hide bad report cards, we hide offences against our neighbours, we hide our petty thefts and our forays outside the neighbourhood.

As a child, I played marbles; I was probably the best player in three barrios. I'd clean up, then sell the marbles, five for a peso, and start over somewhere else, like a hustler slinking into another neighbourhood in search of new victims. To stray into unfamiliar territory and inveigle myself into a game already under way took some nerve, and I felt a thrill, a shudder of exhilaration whenever I headed out to Pulmón, to Pedrera or Marina, leaving behind Fructuoso or Fundición, the barrios I considered my turf. I have no idea how I was viewed by the other boys, strange interloper that I was, but I remember how remarkable it seemed to me whenever a child from another part of the city showed up in my neighbourhood, a boy no one had ever seen before. They were like magical beings fallen from heaven, they wandered around half dazed and seemed burdened with some ageless loss that left me speechless and my – as yet undamaged – heart crushed. They would ask to join a spur-of-the-moment game. A new boy, a new recruit, was a precious gift, and any initial wariness prompted by the sudden appearance of a stranger would quickly fade. When you're eight or nine, spending five minutes with someone your own age constitutes a tight friendship. Besides, everything worth knowing about a person can be said in five minutes.

These were the first times my heart ever felt crushed, an ache that now feels as if the years, like hands, have scrubbed it over and over to remove some fresh stain (the stains never go away, perhaps because it's the heart's duty to accumulate stains, or perhaps because the heart *is* the stain), or as if a filthy, insubstantial piece of clothing were being carelessly stuffed into the Friday-night laundry basket. For the most part, these boys were poor. They had to look out for themselves from an early age, they had no schedule, no routine, no mother who'd show up to give them a clip round the ear to remind them of the way home, as my mother did. She would stand on the corner like a sentry, not saying a word. Whenever I saw that electrifying presence framed against the smudged cityscape of late afternoon, I was instantly rooted to the spot.

The primal conspiracy is governed by these rules: parents are enemies, jailers from whom we have to hide all the things about ourselves we consider important, all the things we long to tell other people, all the things we think mark us out as unique or individual. A misdemeanour, a sin, anything unseemly. Parents are the incarnation of discipline, the expression of punishment, and this is a notion we'll never be able to shake off, however much we grow up and leave our parents behind.

A grandmother, on the other hand, is the opposite: an outpouring of candour, a trusted and inexhaustible repository of sense, someone who divulges secrets to you, someone with whom, when all is said and done, you forge a relationship that is indefinable. It begins before we are consciously able to wield words and, as such, is neither determined by nor dependent upon language. This, in a nutshell, describes my relationship with my grandmother, a bond unlike any other that has come along in life. We begin life anchored by these strong ties, and everything that comes after is a gradual unmooring, a drifting, and eventually a headlong plunge into the bottomless pit of the self. Until the age of six, in this little town called Colón, it was my grandmother who walked me to school and collected me afterwards, who woke me every morning with a little song I hated, a song about how it was important to arrive at school on the dot, always on the dot, although I can't even bring myself to think about that right now, honestly, I feel like I could cry right now, my grandmother bending over me, shaking me a little, not too much, and, in a voice made hoarse by years of smoking, singing that irritating little song with a gruff tenderness that means I am here today.

To live with your grandmother can be stagnating, kindness breeds stagnation, but it spares you from being uprooted; a grandmother is not going to up sticks and move away, while a parent is still searching, and embroiling you in that search. The option of staying on with my grandmother was not, perhaps, the best start in life, but when I gauge the cost of being uprooted, the heavy price to be paid by those who take their first faltering steps in life and realise that rootlessness is a condition from which there is no return, I'm not sure which is better; I weigh the options, I think about them, and, honestly, I don't know. Not that it matters, since my parents uprooted me from Colón and took me to live in Cárdenas, and my grandmother didn't join us until five years later, and it was there, in Cárdenas, between the ages of eight and thirteen, that the saddest things of my life occurred. I mean, my childhood was happy, extremely happy even; my mother let me play and get dirty in the streets of the barrio, and learn the local lingo, but there were also long moments of introspection, nights when I could perceive the weight of the loneliness I felt then, in real time, and the loneliness I would come to feel later, the essence of the future loaded onto me, the mark of the future invisibly tattooed on my skin, a nostalgia for what was destined to happen, a larval awareness that, no matter how much I struggled from now on, there was no way I could become anything other than what I would inevitably become.

This melancholy stems from things I haven't yet experienced, I thought at the time, since I barely had experiences to draw on, and no memories that could resurface, except perhaps a single moment that encompassed all others, one that, with the years, took on greater relevance and significance. It was a trivial incident, one that happened the afternoon I left Colón. There was a bookshop on the way to the park, near the place where the *colectivos* stopped, and I paused for a moment next to the shop window and stared at my reflection. I perfectly remember the face of that little boy who is not me, the features half blurred, blanched by the afternoon light, but recognisable nonetheless, as my mother calls to me, urging me to hurry up, tells me we're not going far, when every journey, every dislocation represents precisely the same inner distance, the same unfathomable distance. The boy reflected in the window of the bookshop in Colón, a block from the park where the *colectivos* stopped, knows that he is leaving, the penny drops as though until this moment he had not fully realised that he is leaving, that he will no longer be living in the house he has lived in until now, no longer see those people he has seen every day of his life. This is a fact, it will happen, there is nothing that can stop it and nothing to suggest that things should not be this way, and the boy reflected in the window speaks to me, tells me to say goodbye, tells me that, for my own good, I need to learn to say goodbye, but, sadly, in that defining moment, I didn't listen, though the reflection in the window waved desperately, begged me to do it, I didn't say goodbye, I didn't learn how, I simply left, taking everything with me. The gamble I took then was one that would stay with me forever, since few things in life are more important than learning how to say goodbye.

We tend to be what we have been; we don't like that zone of strangeness, the idea of transforming into something else, of looking at ourselves and no longer recognising what we see. This is the point of abject sadness no one ever wants to reach: the point where you no longer have the faintest idea who you are, or why you are where you are, just as I later felt so many times while eating supermarket cherries. I can't tell if there was a time when I felt otherwise, not knowing who I was, or why I was where I was. In the long run, staying or leaving both lead to the same absurd condition. Looked at carefully, neither action is innate, neither expresses normality; you settle into running away or you escape by settling down. When you are left with only these two wretched and profoundly melancholic options, it means a rift has opened inside of you, one that will brutally tear you apart in a slow, impassive double-helix motion, like some stately wrecking machine. And this is how my mother, my father and I came to board the *colectivo* and in the space of forty-five minutes – God, in the blink of an eye – we found ourselves catapulted into the future, settled in another place.

I foresaw my grandmother's death with utter clarity. We don't foresee the deaths of those we don't love, nor do we see death approaching even when it comes to those we do love, so while this is something I will probably never experience again, still I experienced it in this case. I stepped through the front door and without hesitating, without knowing why, walked straight through the house, skirting every obstacle, not stopping anywhere, not in the living room or the bathroom or the kitchen, and when I reached the backyard I shrugged off my school bag and knelt at the feet of my grandmother, who was not expecting to see me and gave a little start of surprise, just as she always started whenever I came back from somewhere and we met again; I took her hands and kissed them, two hands almost disembodied but intact, two hands that had come to the end of their life, my grandmother sitting in the armchair where she always sunned herself, her discreet queen's throne, and I studied her through the magnifying glass of devotion and reverence, her arms, her skirt, her blouse, and we gazed at each other, her eyes, by now deeply sunken, seemed to have lost something, her smile a sombre farewell rictus, her toothless mouth told me not to cry.

She seemed to understand the significance of my gesture, my unexpected closeness. She took off her glasses, pressed her face to mine and said what's all this then, but we both knew perfectly well what all this was, and knowing, we both knew that 'all this' meant we had to be at peace. In fact, what she was saying was: yes, I am going to die, but it is what it is, and I gave a little sob, little suspecting that later, many years and thousands of kilometres from that moment, in some foreign land, I would be haunted by nightmares in which my grandmother was still alive or half-dead, in which she would run towards me so I could save her from something, and, not knowing how to save the dead, I would stand there, motionless, and still I didn't know how to save the dead or what they needed to be saved from; but that would come much later, eating the juicy supermarket cherries.

In that moment, I cried my fill and said nothing more, the death of an eighty-year-old woman is not easily shared with others, since people assume it's just someone who has lived their life, someone no longer young, someone who hasn't died as the result of a tragedy, and besides, it's not like we're talking about a father, a mother or a brother. The death of an elderly grandmother takes place in an emotional void, it's a non-transferable pain, an inexpressible grief that cannot be quantified, and for which there is no relief; no one will think the loss you've suffered is particularly horrible – or, yes, maybe horrible, but bearable, acceptable – and although this seemed wrong, like flawed reasoning to me, I realised it also had its advantages, because it meant that no one asked me about her death, and no one treated me like someone recently bereaved, no one broached the subject, and since no one knew what there was to know, I figured it was high time to make an escape.

Twenty or twenty-five years before those supermarket cherries, my grandmother was the one who looked after me, bathed me and made me breakfast. My grandmother was dead now, yet not long before she had devoted herself to looking after me, perfectly aware that what she was doing for me wouldn't add more years to her life, that what she was doing would not benefit her at all, yet still she carried on like it was the most important thing in the world. It seemed like an awful lot of responsibility to me; the bath times, the breakfasts and the inexhaustible care lavished on me by my grandmother. In fact, it was a spiritual reserve I brought along with me, I knew not where.

After her death, we drove from Cárdenas to Colón to inter her bones in the family vault, the white limewashed recesses blazing in the pitiless midday sun, the gravedigger dozing at the cemetery gates circled by thirsty flies, the stone crosses and the sarcophagi and the pitiful municipal graves all engulfed in a silence swelled by the mute dialogue between objects, and later, after we drove home, burdened by the weight of these vibrant, devastating images, in the still hours of the evening, someone knocked at the door. That someone was the postman, a pot-bellied *mestizo* who was always smiling, always chatty. He was wheeling a bicycle with a basket full of letters and magazines; I knew precisely what the postman's visit meant and, for a second, I felt a wave of terror. I didn't want the postman to speak, better for him to say nothing, but you don't tell the local postman to shut up, do you? You don't tell someone to shut up when they have no reason to know that it's better to say nothing, and I wondered how I was going to react, how I would respond, whether I would answer solemnly, whether I would make a scene, whether I would be curt, all the while knowing that the greater grief was not mine but that of the poor postman, who, a moment from now, would have to put on a brave face when he discovered what had happened, though he would be devastated, completely devastated, since the postman genuinely loved my grandmother, and whenever he showed up my grandmother would give him a cup of coffee, a glass of water or something, the small gestures that in such towns are priceless and forge friendships.

The postman asked for the lady of the house, the usual question, the genial question, the question he invariably asked when he showed up and which, until now, had always resulted in friendly and affectionate conversation; I said nothing, and the postman asked again, the lady of the house, he repeated, he had brought her pension cheque, the meagre retirement my grandmother received every month, which he seemed to think would be delivered for all eternity, as though my grandmother had worked as many years as God had in his time, and as a result my grandmother was entitled to as many months' pension as God himself, and I said gently, the lady of the house has died, we've just come back from her funeral, and I said it a little self-consciously, as though her death was a moral failing, or as though the postman was my grandmother's true family, and it was then, from the shocked expression on his face as I relayed the news in the middle of this postal delivery, this trivial event, this hackneyed conversation, that I truly understood that my grandmother was never coming back, the postmen knew this, I had had to tell him, it was not a joke, it was not a phase, the postman reacted as someone reacts to a calamity of serious proportions.

My mother cashed that month's cheque, of course, since until that month my grandmother had still been alive, and it was mystifying to see bureaucracy carry on in spite of death; meanwhile, having heard the news, the hard-working postman left the house, he slunk away, he did not want to know any more, there was no need to know much more, what he knew was already more than enough, and it was through him that the good news spread far and wide, delivered from every post office to every letter box, conveyed in almost every gesture, not with grief or pain, but rather with discretion and serenity, and even in the days of supermarkets, while I ate ripe, juicy cherries and entertained myself watching television, they still reached me, through the advertisements, the TV shows and the flickering commercials, the subliminal telegrams of death. ∎

SPANISH LANGUAGE FICTION
IN TRANSLATION FROM GRAYWOLF PRESS

THE TWILIGHT ZONE
by Nona Fernández
*Translated by
Natasha Wimmer*

NERVOUS SYSTEM
by Lina Meruane
*Translated by
Megan McDowell*

THE FALLEN
by Carlos Manuel Álvarez
Translated by Frank Wynne

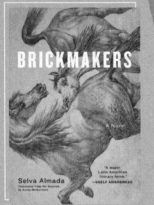

BRICKMAKERS
by Selva Almada
*Translated by
Annie McDermott*
COMING IN NOVEMBER

**BRING ME THE HEAD OF
QUENTIN TARANTINO**
by Julián Herbert
*Translated by
Christina MacSweeney*

GRAYWOLF
PRESS

DIEGO ZÚÑIGA

1987

Diego Zúñiga was born in Iquique, Chile.
He is the author of the novels *Chungungo*,
Camanchaca and *Racimo*, the story collection
Niños héroes and the non-fiction works *Soy
de Católica* and *María Luisa Bombal, el teatro
de los muertos*.

A STORY OF THE SEA

Diego Zúñiga

TRANSLATED BY MEGAN MCDOWELL

It was said in passing, while we were killing time in a bar near the sports center, waiting for someone to drop off our tickets to go see Tani Loayza's grandson. That was the big news: Tani's grandson was debuting. He was a kid who'd grown up in northern Argentina, but who considered himself profoundly Iquiquean – I almost said Chilean, but really that would be imprecise, because Chile has never given the kid anything, while Iquique has: a place, a name, a practice space and all the facilities needed to make him into a boxer of his grandfather's stature; Iquique, land of champions, land of Tani Loayza and Arturo Godoy, men who went off to New York to compete for the world title, who made history in spite of their defeats and showed the world that a city in northern Chile, a salt mine port town slinking away from the Atacama Desert, was the cradle of the best boxers from the end of the world.

So there we were, killing time before going to see Tani Loayza's grandson, a couple of beers in, when someone offhandedly brought up the name Chungungo Martínez, though no one skipped a beat, no one said anything; it happened fast – the name, his story or a piece of his story: they were talking about moral victories, and how Chile was just that, a bunch of defeats hiding behind a couple half-wins, a title here, a championship there, a fleeting joy that would enable an endless harangue about *lo chileno* and our talent for bouncing back from adversity. That was how the name Chungungo Martínez had popped up. Though first someone had to mention, of course, Tani Loayza and his feat in New York that night in July of 1925, when he contended for the middleweight world championship and lost to Jimmy Goodrich because the ref stepped on him, typical Chilean bad luck, an injury pulled him out of the fight and that was it, the dream of becoming world champion ended there, and so the legend began, the moral victory, the *what would have happened if* . . . We've lived a whole life off of that, same as with Arturo Godoy's fight against Joe Louis, in Madison Square Garden in February 1940, when he withstood all fifteen rounds only to lose in an evenly split vote, once again that rotten Chilean luck, that *hair's breadth away* for the guy who had Louis up against the ropes – the Brown Bomber himself, one of the most celebrated boxers of the twentieth century, the greatest heavyweight in history. *¡Viva Chile, mierda!* someone surely cried, and then the subject changed and everything was lost to the background noise and the beers and glasses of *pipeño* wine, and then the name Chungungo Martínez came up and no one wanted to run with it, even though he was the only one – out of all those mentioned earlier – who *had* been a world champion, the first world champion Chile ever had, though not in boxing, no, this is Martínez here, the marine otter, the *chungungo*, that's what they called him, the man who would dive into the ocean and hold his breath underwater for seemingly forever while he slid around the rocky bottom, hunting whatever crossed his path. That's how he moved under the water, they said, like a *chungungo*, a Chilean otter, the 'marine cat' that lives among the rocks, sometimes swimming on its back, letting the currents carry it out to sea. And maybe Chungungo Martínez would be there too, not in the bar, but walking toward the sports center to see Tani Loayza's grandson debut against the Bolivian boxer Churata. It was the event of the year in Iquique and the whole city would be going to the sports center, or else they'd be close by, near Plaza Condell, hoping to hear something of the fight, the shouts, the cheers. The important thing was to be there, to be part of it, spend time with family and friends, buy a chorizo on bread from a street vendor, maybe a few sopaipillas, hang around till the fight began, the debut – and hopefully it'd be a dream debut, the start of a story that would put Iquique back on top and really earn all that talk about the *land of champions*. With any luck Tani's grandson would take the Bolivian out quickly, that was the key.

They were chattering about all that in the bar and no one remembered that the name Chungungo Martínez had even come up, because Chungungo Martínez was cursed. Or so said the rumor that had been going around for decades, after he'd gone missing for several long years because he'd seen what he shouldn't have seen. But things had gone bad even before that.

M aybe it all started that winter morning when a group of men went into Caleta Negra – a small fishing cove about eighty kilometers south of Iquique, just a couple wooden houses and not much more – where Martínez worked as a fisherman. We're talking about the beginning of the seventies here, the last gasps of the Frei Montalva presidency, a Christian Democrat government that the CIA supported in order to keep Salvador Allende from ascending to power. It was during those years when this group of men headed into Caleta Negra to find Martínez and offer him a spot on the Chilean Underwater Spearfishing team. The sport's 1971 world championship was going to be held on the beaches of Iquique, and they needed to put together a competitive team that could hold its own against the Cubans, the Italians and the gringos. Those teams were the cream of the crop. They were the *capos*, the most dangerous. That's why these trainers were traveling around to all the fishing coves in northern Chile, those lost towns between Arica and Coquimbo where a handful of families had settled, looking for a better life, a livelihood. The Chilean trainers knew the only way to face the championship with any dignity was to search out the best, the ones who'd been raised there, in the ocean, those boys who headed out in boats before sunup to hunt the depths with a harpoon or whatever was on hand, holding their breath to descend several meters and spear whatever swam by. No one knew what was down there better than they did, the Pacific's trickery, its seaweed forests, the rock formations and the habits of the fish. They were the men who would lead the Chilean team, and the trainers had already spent several weeks combing the coves when they reached the one where Martínez lived – his name had already been circulating, people said no one could stay underwater as long as him, that he could bring down anything that crossed his path, that no one had stamina like his. Their offer, strictly speaking, was to let him compete with the thirty other boys they had already selected: of that whole lot, only six would remain, the six official members of the Chilean Underwater Spearfishing team, the ones who would go off to seek glory by plunging into the depths of the sea.

'Go on, Chungungo, you'll take 'em all for sure,' said his friends, the other fishermen he'd lived with in Caleta Negra for several years by then. They were his family, they'd known him since he came there as a child uprooted from the desert, a little kid who'd learned to swim in the Loa River and was astounded when he saw the ocean for the first time: he couldn't understand what it was that moved those waves with such force that they crashed onto the shore, didn't understand why that blue stain never ever stopped moving, as if it were a sleeping animal that could turn wild at any moment.

Soon, he learned to distrust the sea. And he quickly understood that you can never let your guard down in the water. A slight distraction and everything could fall apart: life, future, dreams. You never had options in the sea, and Chungungo Martínez knew it.

So, he said yes.

He competed.

He came in second.

The trainers confirmed everything people said about him, and still they couldn't believe the strength that let him stay under for two or three minutes and surface, always, with some hefty, significant catch: a conger eel, an albacore, a sea bass that weighed three, four, five kilos. And then he'd start over again. And on and on, for almost two hours. That was spearfishing, which he had never practiced as a sport, it was simply his everyday work. The only difference here was that whoever speared the largest catch and accumulated the most weight was a winner. In those two hours, he competed against the other thirty boys and managed to bring in a catch of almost fifty fish, mostly sea bass and a couple of conger eels. He didn't come in first only because he wasn't familiar with that area of the Pacific where they competed – one of the beaches where the championship would be held, near Los Verdes – and so he'd gotten lost more than once down there amid the seaweed forests that obscured his view.

The trainers didn't tell him so, but they were already convinced there was no limit to how far Chungungo Martínez could go, and the possibility of winning the world championship was, for the first time, very real.

That was March of 1970. A few months later, Salvador Allende would win the presidential election and read his first speech, his victory speech, that early morning of 5 September 1970, when the Popular Unity government was inaugurated.

Exactly one year later, in the early morning hours of 5 September 1971, Chungungo Martínez and the people of Iquique were celebrating his achievement, his triumph at the World Underwater Spearfishing Championship. His face was plastered across the newspapers, and the city shone in those photos the world over; the port city, the northern Chilean city, a slice of land between ocean and mountains that could up and disappear on any given day if a tsunami decided to make it so, to erase the entire landscape so all that remained would be those tall, gray hills, like an inviolable wall. A little further on was the desert, then the border.

The competition lasted two days, Friday and Saturday, but the city needed months to prepare for the event: they built housing, remodeled the airport, paved streets, and spent weeks spiffing up the Délfico Theater, where the results would be announced.

They say Chungungo Martínez's performance was bestial. How

even on that first day when the team headed out to sea early, he dove in with his frogman suit and became one with the landscape: just slipped on his mask and disappeared into the depths. Two hours of nonstop diving and surfacing, filling his lungs with air and then gliding skillfully around down there, spearing one, two, three fish in a single trip – a beast, said the foreign journalists who had come to cover the championship and who couldn't understand how that man never got tired, how he dove over and over without stopping.

Friday was amazing, but Saturday – according to the reporting at the time – was full-on outrageous. And so, that early morning of 5 September 1971 turned into an endless party, because after so many second places, so many unfair defeats, Chungungo Martínez rose up as the first Chilean ever to be a world champion of a sporting event, the best of them all, the conquering hero, triumphant man of the people, the common, everyday man who had, for the first time, reached the pinnacle, leaving a record there of his name and the name of a city, of a people.

We were already on our fourth or fifth round of beers and the guy still hadn't turned up with our tickets to see Tani Loayza's grandson. By this point, as you can imagine, no way did anyone remember the passing mention of Chungungo Martínez, but his story hovered there among us, disbursed in a handful of torn, faded images that didn't seem to lead anywhere. In the middle of it all, rumors and silence. Because Chungungo Martínez had reached glory, but what came after was an ineffective, mistaken sense of joy. There wasn't time for embraces, because time itself broke down. First came the glory and then the lies and the jostling for position and the back-stabbing, so much shabbiness all around him, and we'd have to trace the end of it all back there, to those days that followed his victory, to the promises no one was going to keep, to the spitefulness of his friends, of the federation, of all those who took advantage of him until the next championship, in Cadaqués, Spain, where Chungungo Martínez arrived as the favorite but didn't even manage to finish the competition. He blacked out down there. Fainted. He had to be rescued by the Cuban team, who saw him lying there at the bottom of the sea. He hadn't calculated well, hadn't understood that the Mediterranean was very different from the Pacific, he completely forgot what one must never forget: never let your guard down in the water, never trust, ever, but he blacked out and his life was miraculously saved and after that nothing was ever the same again, because everyone turned their backs on him, they abandoned him, though he kept at it, it was his life, the ocean, fishing, he knew he could do more, that what happened in Spain was a misstep, and he deserved a comeback. But there was no comeback. There was a *coup d'état* and after some of his friends disappeared, after they arrested several fishermen he used to go out to sea with, he saw what he shouldn't have seen.

They say it was early one October morning when the sun was struggling to filter down into the sea, but still he set off in his boat, hoping to get back to his previous level and prove to everyone he could be the best again – he was convinced, and that's why he went out to sea every morning, a few kilometers from Iquique, he'd leave the city and head north where he knew the currents were unpredictable, because that's what he needed: to push himself to his maximum, to not know what he might find in the depths when he dove down with his harpoon amid the rocks and the seaweed.

They say it was early, one October morning, when the sun struggled to filter down into the sea.

They say there were two bodies, though others will tell you four or five. But what we know is that he was chasing a conger eel hiding in the rocks when he saw them. They hadn't been there more than a couple of days, because the sea hadn't yet done its job. They were intact, so people say, the bodies were still bodies, though they were missing their eyes and their hands. The torsos and legs were a violet shade that contrasted with the white of their faces and arms. He was going to remember that, and not much more. He would talk about that contrast of colors, about the hands and eyes that weren't there.

He would talk about that when he was offered a glass of wine in some tavern, now far from that morning when the sun couldn't filter down into the sea. At first, he would be speechless – days, weeks, months, and no one would really understand what had happened, why he'd gone so quiet, why he didn't want to practice anymore, why he decided to go back to Caleta Negra – but then the wine loosened his tongue, and after that no one could stop him from talking. Until one day he talked to the wrong people, and Chungungo Martínez disappeared.

Here, at this point, the versions shoot off and never quite come together again. They talk about journeys out of Chile, about threats and extortion, about money, a lot of money for his silence. They talk about beatings, about nights in solitary, trips out into the pampa, simulated executions. They talk about a caravan that abandoned him in the middle of the desert, about a town that welcomed him, about a handful of young people who saved his life.

No one knows what happened to Chungungo Martínez, but one day, when the dictatorship was coming to an end, when the military was realizing that the die had been definitively cast, he returned to Iquique. He showed up in Cavancha, crossed the beach and headed over to the cove, to see if he could find his friends. Someone recognized him on the way and spread the word. It was Chungungo Martínez, the very same, just a little older and now with a scar across his chin, a scar that seemed to emulate a restrained, slightly awkward smile.

They say that he went back to the same life as always, that he settled in Cavancha, that he goes out early to fish with the youngest of them, but he no longer goes into the water. That he doesn't dive anymore. That he keeps to the surface, teaching the kids the tricks of the trade while he collects the sea bass, conger eels and frogfish and carries them to the market to sell.

Every now and then you can catch sight of him walking around downtown Iquique. Maybe he's inside the sports center now, ready to watch the debut of Tani Loayza's grandson. And here we are, still holding out for our tickets, though it may be time to accept that we got taken for a ride and we're going to have to listen to the fight on the radio. Might as well order another beer. One more round and we'll go. ∎

CRISTINA MORALES

1985

Cristina Morales is from Granada, Spain, and is the author of *Los combatientes*, *Últimas tardes con Teresa de Jesús*, *Terroristas modernos* and *Lectura fácil*. She works with the contemporary dance company Iniciativa Sexual Femenina and is executive producer of the punk band At-Asko.

ODE TO CRISTINA MORALES

Cristina Morales

TRANSLATED BY KEVIN GERRY DUNN

They are creatures crafted from the finest material and the way they shift between martial honor and showboating is impeccable. Impeccable as their light, shimmering attire, their tightly pulled-back hair, their economy of expression, their demure though impassioned devotions to the Virgin Mary, their glistening sweat. Impeccable as their injuries, which indicate not pain but grandeur: the grandeur of human potential. Neither flaunting nor concealing their wounds, they privilege us with a view of vulnerability as well as strength, as if to say, 'Gaze upon our abundance: the stuff of mythology, all the world's knowledge condensed within us. The divine uses us for its own ends, rewarding or reprimanding us, and that is our academy. Most of all, we are free, and the sea or the mountains or their urban surrogates roar at our backs.'

Their human radicalism makes us naively grateful to belong to their same species. When we see them, we think, 'If you hit us, do we not bleed?' (as in the Shakespeare monologue); 'If you immobilize us with your knees, can we not punch our way free?' How foolish we are, clinging to culture, clutching at straws to feel a connection with these venerable creatures! Wretched, useless, fraudulent humanism! Wretched, useless, fraudulent medicine, obsolete propaganda, coaching, self-help, democracy and the sinister consolation of morality and law! Never will we experience an elbow masterfully smashing our face in, never will we be toppled by the likes of Julia Avila, a 32-year-old Mexican American weighing in at sixty-two kilos, with ten professional MMA fights and eight wins, four by knockout and one by submission, or the likes of Kana Morimoto, 28-year-old Japanese K-1 fighter weighing in at fifty-two kilos, with twenty fights and seventeen wins, seven by KO.

We, mere fans of mixed martial arts, suffer and inflict violence every day; we are undeniably violent and violated as we trudge through life, but the punishments we give and receive pale in comparison to a knockout punch or a loss by submission. She who says knockout, who says tap-out, speaks the words of glory. The word for what you and I suffer and inflict is violence, that cheap natural phenomenon of survival or domination. Not so for the fighters. If violence is the unwilling subjugation of one person by another, then their fights are devoid of violence. In its place, there is longing; longing is all there is. The fighter has come for the express purpose of beating the shit out of her opponent and getting the shit beaten out of herself. Depending on which of the two she longs for more, we can say there are two basic modalities: attack or counter-attack. The attacker is in a rush, she wants to edge in on her opponent, back her against the ropes and devour her, whereas the counter-attacker remains in the center of the ring waiting to be devoured, strategically withdrawing, periodically kicking to keep the attacker at a distance. With the legitimate authority of the devoted fan, I have christened the first modality the Locomotive School: full steam ahead, smack her in the head!

Women of martial arts, I sing of thee. O willful creatures, amassers of strength, vessels of action and silence like polished weapons wrapped in velvet cloth! What do you hold within your elongated deltoids, your robust quadriceps, your bull necks? You hold desire. And in the massif of your biceps, the valley of your latissimi dorsi, the orography of your abdominals? More desire. Your shattered knuckles? Desire there, too, my idols, and desire in your deviated septa and your cauliflower ears swollen from so many hours with your heads rubbing against the gi and the mat. What a crepuscular poet would call 'the threatening air that envelops you' is but the perfume of your plenitude, for your existence belies the false binary of body and mind. You are not threatening, nor are you intimidating: the poets have gone mushy from stewing in their own masculinity so long, they're less precise than an arcade gun, so of course, packing a prop like that, they feel threatened not by the fighter (who utterly stupefies them), but by her serenity, her millimetric grasp of when to rouse herself and how much damage to dole out.

I sing of thee, Joyce Vieira, 28-year-old Brazilian amateur MMA fighter in the 60–80 kilo weight class who, in April 2019, interrupted your photoshoot with a friend on the beach of Rio de Janeiro to brutalize a man who was masturbating while watching you from the bushes.

'Are you kidding me, dude? Put that thing away!' Vieira yelled.

'Why? Don't you like it? Why don't you come on over here,' the voyeur replied. And Vieira, with her monokini and her salon-fresh hair, was happy to oblige.

Blessed be thy name, Joyce Vieira, for venturing confidently wherever you are called and leaving emancipation in your wake! 'After that "come on over here", I went straight for him without even thinking, I was in a state of ecstasy because the whole thing was so surreal. Usually when you catch people doing stuff like that, they deny it, all, "no I wasn't, no I wasn't". But this guy, he just kept jacking off.' With his pants around his ankles and a hard-on, he fended off the battery of low kicks you delivered to his legs with the generosity of a sharpshooter aiming for non-vital body parts. The ingrate managed to land a right hook. 'It just made me angrier when he punched me, I wanted to kill him, I wanted to beat the living shit out of him. When he realized I was about to start hitting him for real, he started screaming. A kid broke us up and the guy got away. In martial arts they teach us not to get into street fights, but I didn't want to stop beating on him, no way.' The victim forcing the sex offender to cry for help and run away! O Vieira, Annihilator of the

Patriarchy's Foundational Concepts, I sing of your unstifled rage and your brilliant interpretation of the martial arts code! You were right to attack, not only because he was violating you, but because he believed he had the right to do so. Your low kicks and jabs didn't just halt his aggression, they struck down the presumption of docility cast over all women. I don't know your aggressor's name. If I did, I would include it in this ode so we could all laugh at him, so the women of Rio could laugh at him and rebuke him wherever he goes, and so the men of Rio wouldn't rush to his defense in the spirit of masculine solidarity, but instead would reprimand him and fear to follow in his footsteps. We don't know his name, but there are photos online.

I sing of thee, Polyana Viana, 28-year-old Brazilian weighing in at fifty-two kilos, with fifteen professional MMA fights and eleven wins, four by way of knockout and seven by submission. In the very same city where Vieira imparted justice, you had already restored the planets to their rightful orbit four months earlier when confronted with a vile miscreant – whose name we know and whose photos can be found online – when he dared cut off your path while you were waiting for an Uber. Is it possible, O Viana, that you were the inspiration for Vieira the Low Kicker? It's the Locomotive School all the way in Rio de Janeiro: full steam ahead, kick him till he's dead!

'Sorry, do you know what time it is?'

'Yeah, lemme check,' Viana responded, pulling out her phone. 'Seven fifty-five.' But instead of leaving, Max Gadelha-Barbosa invaded Viana's space and said:

'Give me the phone. Don't try anything, I've got a gun.'

O Polyana Viana, she who walks unaccompanied wherever she pleases! The turdlike Gadelha-Barbosa reached for his gun, but you, O Lucid Supernova, could see that it was just a little blade at best. 'He was very close, he was practically on top of me. I thought: if he does have a gun, I won't give him time to draw it.' Let us relish every detail, O Polyana. Lead us with your example. 'I threw two punches and a kick. He fell, then I caught him in a rear naked choke.'

'Let me go!' Gadelha-Barbosa pleaded with the tiny thread

of breath Polyana's arithmetical arms allowed. Make them beg, O Human Greatness, O Erector of Due Respect and Overdue Repentance, O Destroyer of Male Privileges! 'I just wanted to know the time.'

'My ass you wanted to know the time!' Polyana responded with the unassailable fury of a fighter whose quiet evening had been disrupted.

'Then call the police,' implored Max the Deflated, who, like all outcasts prostrating themselves before the very hegemony that shuns them, would rather embrace the necropolitics of the State than the life-expanding opportunity Polyana was offering. 'Then I sat him back down.' And you placed him in a Kimura lock.

'Now,' you told him once his face and shirt were covered in blood and his eyes had sunk into his swollen cheeks and brow, 'now we'll wait for the police.'

'After leaving the police station, I went home and made dinner. The next day my hands hurt a little, but nothing serious.' O Polyana, Inimitable Caretaker of Herself, Attentive Minder of Nutrient Intake, what a gift it is to picture you opening the fridge, plucking a bag of ice from the freezer, lighting a burner, peeling a carrot, seasoning a steak, lifting the fork to your mouth at the dining-room table, swigging a beer, tearing off a mouthful of bread, wiping your lips with a napkin, taking little pauses to soothe your hard-working hands with the ice, unhooking your bra with your T-shirt still on and pulling it out a sleeve! O Polyana, Woman Who Eats!

'It's not the first time it's happened to me. When I was living in Belém, two men on a motorcycle drove up to me. One got off, the other stayed on. The guy who got off broke my umbrella and tried to take my phone. I said I wouldn't give it to him and he tried to grab it out of my hand. I punched him in the face and he got scared. And I was scared too that time, maybe because there were two of them. But he was more scared than me. He got back on the bike and they rode off.' We do not know either man's name, and there aren't any photos.

O Polyana of the Healthy Appetite, O Joyce of the Unrestrained

Legs: mediums, mystics, boomerangs who return violence unto the violent themselves! In your struggle, you liberate not only yourselves, but also, in solidarity, your aggressors. How well established the Locomotive School has become in Brazil! It must be the influence of Paulo Freire, who as early as the sixties proclaimed in his pedagogy of the oppressed that 'paradoxical though it may seem, the oppressed punching her oppressor is a gesture of love'.

O lethal and obedient fighters, obedient to none but yourselves! Your fervor to kill your opponent is a sign of respect, as it is, in any case, one of the rules of the fight! That is what distinguishes the ring from the street: in the ring, the octagon, you have no aim but the annihilation of your opponent. The referee is there to make sure no one is killed or gravely injured, halting the fight with the lightest of taps or by simply raising a tensed, gloved hand, thereby awarding victory to the fighter who will immediately, cleanly release her prey with jumps of joy.

The deep hollows of your armpits are but empty spaces where other humans would house their pity, which you want for neither yourself nor your opponent: anything short of injury is humiliating. You are trained to practice the mathematics of pain – that's what you're paid to do, to perform for the public and the cameras, to speak with the commentators and journalists, who are, in most instances, profoundly misogynistic, inept, offensive and garrulous, wantonly ignorant of the sport and the athlete their shitfucker news channel sent them to cover, who shamelessly peacock their ignorance for all to see. In Spain's case, this isn't true in most instances. In Spain, this is systematic. (Below, a few verbatim transcriptions; I have decided to forgo using [*sic*], as it would appear too often.)

'Um, uh. What title fight were you most nervous about? This is the second, right? The uh, the second one you got, right?'

'Right, I'm the defending champion. Last March we won in France. It was us, aaaand . . . my opponent was from France, so we were the away team, you know. And, so, we weren't under so much pressure, it was just us, and . . . and obviously we were happy how it turned out, we won by KO in the third round and got to bring home the belt. So now defending the title we were a little more nervous, but we worked through it. We have a sports psychologist with . . . And I mean, I studied sports psychology too but, er, you need another person, you know, to work on that side of things. So, yeah, it went well. And I've been having a really good time, which is what it's all about.'

'Cristina, we're looking at footage of yesterday's bout, right?'

'Yes.'

'You're gonna help me a little with the vocabulary, right? "Bout" is the right term, right?'

'Bout, yeah.'

'We're seeing footage from your hometown, in the middle of a fight. You don't, you don't see anything around you, I'm guessing, right?'

'Around?'

'I mean you're, you're, you're focused on your –'

'Yes.'

'– opponent.'

Undaunted, majestic, utterly unfazed by the interviewer's barrage of incoherence: such was the response of the 27-year-old, three-time kickboxing world champion, weighing in at fifty-two kilos and fighting out of the city of Córdoba, with an impressive professional record of forty-seven wins, just seven losses and nine career knockouts – I love you all, O women of mixed martial arts, but I cannot conceal which is my favorite troubler of rules well established, my beloved committer of feminine sins, my dauphine of the Locomotive School – introducing the one, the only: Cristina Moooooooooooooooorales! I sing of thee! Praise be to God and the Ever-Blessed Virgin, to the stars in the heavens above, to destiny, to the indifferent or divine laws of physics, for unto us a fighter was born, unto us a three-time world kickboxing champion is given who shares my name, who hails from my native Andalusia, who walks the earth in my era, who belongs to my generation, and who even studied at my university, which means if we ever meet, we can talk about all the best dives and tapas bars in Granada! I prostrate myself, therefore, with zealous gratitude to existence: amen, namaste, Subhanallah, Sat Sri Akaal.

O Cristina, she of the Long-Range Right Hook, the way that dickbag from Córdoba TV talked to you the day after you defended your title. It's as if a journalist had approached me, a writer, and said:

'Cristina, we're looking at footage of your novel yesterday, right?'

'Yes.'

'You're gonna help me a little with the vocabulary, right? "Novel" is the right term, right?'

'Novel, yeah.'

Don't you agree, Cristina, that he deserves to be ostracized? Expelled from all the social circles to which he belongs? Spat upon wherever he goes? As we have from the beginning, we are going to give first and last names and share the information necessary to locate the reprobates who – through illiteracy, malice, desire for dominance, or wounded macho frustration at their own inability to exert said dominance as intensely as they would like – scorn the fighters whose praises I sing.

In the red corner, introducing: José Antonio Sánchez Baltanar! AKA José House, though on Facebook he uses his full name followed by the quasi-English tagline '(visionary comunicacion)' (again, I'm not bothering with [sic]). A journalist at Córdoba TV and Onda Mezquita, he also manages social media for the Real Academia de Córdoba, a local historical society. Bald, skinny, bespectacled, born in Montilla (Province of Córdoba, Andalusia, Spain), in his upper forties if not older; in his profile picture he's posing in a dark blue blazer and giving a smile that's halfway between dopey and malicious.

Ah, Cristina Morales, tankette patrolling the octagon, instilling terror with a jab rather than a cannon! Moving faster than the speed of sound, at the bell's first reverberation you are already pummeling your opponent with punishing blows! O Cristina Morales of the Long and Deadly Arms, born in a land that not only knows fuck all about combat sports, but openly deplores them and revels in its ignorance as a point of national pride! The first style guide published by *El País*, Spain's most-read newspaper, in 1977: 'The paper does not publish information pertaining to boxing competitions, except reporting on injuries sustained by the pugilists and stories that reflect the sordid world of such activities.' 28 June 1988: The same newspaper, in an editorial, describes boxing as 'organized barbarism extolling man-on-man violence'. 4 October 1991: Another editorial claims that 'the main culprit behind this criminal game and sadistic spectacle' is a 'violent business operation run by international crime syndicates that promise boxers a life of riches, but are indifferent to whether their recruits live or die'.

O Sharp-Kneed Cristina Morales, Twister of the Untwisted, let us laugh together, let our initials cackle together two by two, let us form a twinship against these sexist, racist, elitist windbags who talk about boxing with the inane moral superiority they typically reserve for descriptions of migrants crossing the Mediterranean!

25 May 1997: Journalist Francisco Gor pens an article reviewing all of these claims and adding that boxing is 'an activity rife with man-on-man violence; it is not a sport, but a kind of human cockfight; that is, it poses such a threat to life, bodily integrity and human dignity that the editorial board of *El País* "would not consider it an affront to individual liberties if the government were to prohibit professional boxing", as other countries have done'.

What other countries? Saudi Arabia, where they also ban music? In the blue corner: Francisco Gor! White elephant of the Spanish Transition, eighty-three years old, thirty-eight of which he spent at the PRISA media conglomerate (which, unlike professional boxing, is definitely not a crime syndicate), founder of *El País* (which crime is worse, firebombing a newspaper or founding one?), author of the book *Entre Supremo y 'Supremo'* (La Hoja del Monte, 2012), in which he gets himself off, like the chastened voyeur of our sister-in-arms Joyce Vieira, to the idea that under Franco the courts were unfair and after Franco they became super-duper fair thanks to the wonders of democracy.

Look at him, O Cristina Morales, across your empire stretching from atomweight to flyweight, look upon this old-guard opportunist who toasts to the king, who, when you were just a girl, unwittingly prepared you lukewarm bottles of chastisement for milk, chastisement which now you, with your world titles, with your fighting that is but meditation, with your mere existence, spit back in his face. Farty old Spanish Social Democrats, more boorish than Charles III soundproofing the royal box at the Naples opera house, more philistine than Ferdinand VII banning Carnival, you are bodiless, you flush without looking at the paper, you fuck with the lights off, and that's why you're threatened by a woman in full command of her body and the bodies of others! And you're right to be threatened, Francisco Gor, because watch out, the next body to be commandeered may be your own. The tender caress of twelve-ounce gloves might do you good, might revive your zombie flesh! If male fighters represent a crack in the pillar of modernity that says the State holds the only legitimate monopoly on violence, as they earn a living by exercising violence autonomously, then female fighters, O Revolutionaries, you smash that pillar to smithereens! Cristina, O Cristina Morales, you who cry out with every punch you give, cries that even when heard from the seating area or the other side of the screen make our hair stand on end! We thought this kind of dandruffy sanctimoniousness was a thing of the past, but it turns out that no, twenty-three years later, we've still got to deal with the same status quo shitbags drinking Nespresso instead of rich home-brewed coffee!

'Cristina Morales, three-time world kickboxing champion. Two ISKA belts and one Enfusion championship. Can't believe you've come this far, huh?'

'We've come a long way.'

'A long way, huh?'

'A long way.'

'Let's start at the beginning, because you're a psychologist with a specialization in, you specialized, you have a graduate certificate in, or I mean, you're a psychologist . . .'

'I have a master's in sports psy—'

'In sports psychology,' the interviewer cuts you off.

'Yeah.'

'Uuuuuh . . . you have two kids. You're super young.'

'Yes.'

'Not to mention being world champion in, uh, in kickboxing. What's your secret?'

What do you mean 'not to mention being world champion'? Can't you read? Not that there's anything wrong with not being able to read, but do you even understand the language you use to produce telegarbage? Do you have any fucking clue what 'three-time kickboxing world champion' means? O Cristina, on 14 February 2020 you were stuck being interviewed by this son of an asswipe with his pearly-white smile – surprising given what a massive shiteater he is – on Canal Sur Television. His name is Roberto Leal, forty-one years old, from Alcalá de Guadaíra, and he's performed his two-bit George Clooney of Seville act on several popular shows, most famously *Pasapalabra* on Antena 3. Incidentally, that's the same channel that reported the story of your second world championship win with the headline 'Kickboxing Momma' alongside footage of you breastfeeding your son and which, apparently unconvinced they had sufficiently cast you as a pugilistic Virgin Mary, drove their message home with the riveting tagline 'The Astonishing Story of Cristina Morales: Devoted Mom and World Kickboxing Champion'! But you yourself admit, Roberto Leal, that you didn't learn to read until you went on a diet and started appearing in fat-shaming ads for the fatuous dudebro monthly *Men's Health*: 'I learned how to read the nutrition facts on the back of packages, so really . . . So, really, who needs to go to the library anymore? I just go to the supermarket and spend hours reading.' Of course you do, champ! Pat on the back, high-five with a patent-leather fist mitt and a BDSM gag to dislocate your jaw so you never open your fucking mouth again!

'Let's tell your story, too. So, you're in the middle of studying psychology in Granada and you get pregnant, young. And at that point, I'm sure you're thinking, what do I do? Do I throw in the towel? Do I quit? What went through your head?'

'Right, so . . . I had just won two championships in Spain, and I got pregnant my last year at university, and I thought to myself, what do I do? What's the next move? So, we ended up doing the whole year in a semester, we had to fit eight months of coursework into four, plus the practicum, and the thesis we put off for later . . . The doctors recommended against training, so I used my training time to study.'

'The doctors recommended that you not train. And you did what the doctors said, of course, because . . .'

'For the first pregnancy, yes,' you say, O Cristina, with an expression on your face that says, what else could I do, it was my first time and their fearmongering got to me.

'For the first pregnancy, but then, later, uh, now you have two kids . . .'

'Yes.'

'Huh, and you majored in, I mean you did your master's in sports psychology and, there, uh, your thesis you did, I think it was in, uh, that was what you did it in . . . right?'

'My thesis was on pregnancy and athletic training.'

'To show how you can, how it's maybe even good to train when you're pregnant.'

'Exactly, as long as you're careful, making sure –'

'This footage we're seeing here is very impressive,' he cuts you off again. The next time we'll cut off his tongue. 'Because, what are we looking at, how many months along were you there?'

'Nine. That was in October, and he was born October 23rd, so that was a few days before I gave birth,' you respond, turning to look at the tall screen on set. O Cristina Morales the Unpublished, she who has endowed the audiovisual archives of history with footage of a woman nine months pregnant climbing into the ring, dressed in fighting apparel, of course, and hurling fists and knees at her trainer, who blocks her onslaught with a pair of focus mitts. With your belly already dropped because you're going to give birth within a week, dropped so low that it completely conceals your waistband (the waistband which, when you dress to impress, is emblazoned with CRISTINA in gold embroidery), you cycle through two sets of combos.

'Anyone who didn't know better or who, I mean . . . Oh look, there's your other son behind you,' says Roberto, the paterno-fuckmonger host who can't watch the video of you training because the footage burns his eyes, so instead he turns his attention to the only thing his squelchy infotainment-addled brain can handle: your son.

'Oh yeah, he was there too.'

'. . . but anyone who hasn't studied this like you have might think "Oh my God, what is . . . what is she doing?" But it's not what it looks like.' Earning five figures a month to cover a topic he knows nothing about, this buffoon is blithely unaware that Cristina Morales is performing the following combo: jab, cross, hook, uppercut, liver shot, feint and counterpunch, faster and harder with each repetition.

'It's not. If there's no risk, there's no reason not to train. Just like you don't stop going to work if you get pregnant, why should you stop training? Always being careful, of course, monitoring your temperature, your heart rate, drinking plenty of water, the right clothes, um . . . And, I mean, there's obviously no fighting, but you can still work on technique,' which is exactly what you're doing in your second, shorter combo: hook, knee and hook block, all the while skillfully not kneeing your own eleven-kilo abdomen, even as you drop your hips and further open your pelvic bones, such balance!

'Is it true you breastfed your kids? You'd go to fight or train, climb into the ring, and then, you'd just . . . Really going after that work-life balance, huh?' Roberto Leal, woke as hell, unveiling his total mastery of neoliberal feminist talking points.

'Yeah, for example, with Jesús I was out of the circuit longer, so I stopped training and when I went back my ankles hurt, it was . . . getting back into training again was hard, it took me a year, a year and a half to get back to fighting. But with Alejandro, since I did this program focused on –'

'Training.' Third interruption.

'– pregnancy and training, I was able to fight again three months after having him, so I –'

'You were already fighting after three months?' Fourth.

'Three months, yeah. I didn't train until the first coronavirus lockdown was over, but then –'

'And it's amazing, you were breastfeeding this whole time,' the anthropomorphized speedo interrupts a fifth time, butting in to make sure it's clear that he – a man! – isn't afraid to talk about lactation.

'I was, I was nursing. Actually, it was in December when he, when I weaned him, before the most recent competition.'

'Huh, wow.'

I sing your praises, Cristina Morales, for extracting a tremulous 'huh, wow' from this professional Neanderthal. That was the sound of gnashing teeth transmogrified into political correctness: he's not going to pass up an opportunity to score points for Team Andalusia when one of our own is a world champion, or the opportunity to highlight such a quaint example of the misogycapitalist huck and hustle known as 'work-life balance'. He can't miss this tremendous opportunity to proclaim that as long as you're a mother, they're willing to forgive your audacity at knowing how to dole out black eyes like Halloween candy, a vocation to which your fair sex has not been called. But oof, ugh, bleh, this superlative balancer of work and life, this attractive, enterprising young woman is a little controversial . . . How the fuck do we make the part about a pregnant woman ignoring doctor's orders fit the script? How are we supposed to play the video of her kicking and punching and kneeing her trainer with that nine-month belly of hers? How do we pull it off without mentioning feminism and without fucking up the whole segment? They needed time to plot their depravity, O Morales, Kicking Machine, but they found a solution: by explaining that the trainer is also your partner and the father of your children. That's the ticket! You're not hitting any old stranger, goodness no! This isn't the story of some trigger-happy bitch out for blood, this is a family affair!

'You seem to get along pretty well with your trainer. What's the deal with him?'

'Well, he's my kids' father, my partner, my trainer –'

'Colleague . . .'

'Colleague, hahaha. All that, he's all that.'

'Huh, wow. So you get along pretty well, huh?' You never crack, Cristina! You're friendly and attractive in sickness and in health. You balance work and life with a smile!

'We do, yeah.'

We thought, O Tibia-Breaking Morales, that the insults would stop if we were dealing with combat-sport professionals. We thought, O Intimidator of Opponents Five Centimeters Taller, that the commentators at an event as important as the Enfusion World Title Fight on 26 October 2019 in Wuppertal, Germany, would rightfully honor and praise you and your opponent, another exceptional student of the Locomotive School: Georgina van der Linden, twenty years old, Dutch, fifty-seven kilos, 112 career wins in K-1 and Muay Thai (112 by the age of twenty!), seven by way of knockout.

But no: if there is any empire on which the sun never sets, it is the empire of the sexually repressed, those who know no pleasure but subjugation and schadenfreude, gloating in their own squalid privileges, those crumbs that fly from the table where the heteropatriarchy feasts on its daily banquet, and which they, miserable stewards, gratefully lick up off the floor.

'Lady Killer, Abraham, well . . .' *Noms de guerre* are common in combat sports, and Morales's opponent goes by Lady Killer. Polyana Viana calls herself the Iron Lady; Joyce Vieira calls herself Princess Fiona. Morales doesn't have a *nom de guerre*.

'Lady Killer? Well, Lady Killer won't have it so easy.'

'Twenty years old, 112-6-2.'

'Not too shabby.'

'Her record says it all. But! I mean Cristina's experience is nothing to sneeze at.'

'Definitely, experience is worth its weight in gold. Cristina is a very powerful fighter and, most important of all, she prepares rigorously for every fight.'

'She does, but, Lady Killer, uh, she . . . she still hasn't made her appearance, Abraham . . . Ah, there she is! Gina van der Linden,' the commentator, Borja Rupérez, says her name wrong.

'Still just a girl.' Hello? Is she not twenty years old? Is she not a professional fighter about to compete for the world title?

'Just a little girl. With petroleum jelly rubbed all over her face.' Hi, sorry, say what? Don't literally all fighters (men and women, trans and cis) apply petroleum jelly to their face before a fight? Is it just me or is this an obvious pedophilic stand-in for a girl with semen on her face? 'And, I mean, you know . . . Her cockiness. Disrespectful, right? Being so young isn't doing her any favors. Relishing the moment.' Disrespectful how, exactly? Because she's smiling, waving to the audience? Enjoying her walk to the ring, just like literally every fighter ever? 'And those trendy sandals, oh my God, Abraham! At least she didn't wear them with socks!' Helloooo, are you fucking kidding me? And this piece-of-shit commentator is giving lectures on respect?

'Hahaha!' Hahaha?

'Because, I mean, you know, lately all the kids are wearing socks and sandals! You remember back in the day –'

'It's all the rage, all the rage. We're getting left behind, Borja. We ought to dress that way for the broadcast.'

'I'd rather get left behind.'

'Hahahaha!'

'Oh man, oh man. Anyway, here's Gina van der Linden,' the same commentator gets her name wrong again, 'clearly enjoying her ring walk, it's a ring fight this time . . . Oh Abraham, my brain can't keep up.'

Will someone please find two of those Homer Simpson beer hats with a can of Duff strapped to each side, fit them on these commentators' heads and help them insert the straws in their mouths, if not straight up their nostrils, ears or urethras? Ladies and gentlemen, straight from the sewers of hooliganism with a brief pit stop at Massimo Dutti to buy some shirts and V-neck pullovers, introducing the co-owners of the Titan Channel combat sports production company: Abraham Redondo and Borja Rupérez!

Abraham Redondo: early forties, tall, dark, with the pugilistically classic broken septum, sports director at the channel but also promoter at – exotic enough to be worth highlighting – Arnold Fighters, which Rupérez writes is: 'a huge marcial arts and combat sports project, within the singular and magnificent program of the Arnold Sports Festival created by governer Arnold Schwarzennegar' (withholding [*sic*]). A former fighter in as many combat sports as he can fit on the header of his website, cherokeeoficial.com (Cherokee was his *nom de guerre*), which reads like it was written by a drunken Roman senator because he didn't bother deleting the Latin text from the template. His 'bio' page features a photo of some guy (not him) who looks like a manscaped Incredible Hulk, brandishing his teeth like he's about to chomp down on a rock rather than bite a banana. Is it just me or is all of this absolutely dripping with cryptohomosexuality?

'And so, uh, we'd like to welcome our viewers from all around the world, more or less, because at Titan Channel we're broadcasting this fight throughout the Americas, from Alaska to Argentina, in Georgia, in Armenia, in Azerbaijan, all across the Caucasus and, of course, here in Spain. And so we are, uh, we really are blazing across borders.'

'Blazing across borders, growing and growing, lots of surprises in store.'

'A special welcome to all our fans in Spain, who we're sure are with us today to . . . watching us, listening to us, a huge thanks to all of you, professionals and amateurs, and, uh, I guess, uh, all the . . . I'm sure all of you are supporting the Spanish fighters, because today . . . there's a lot at stake, especially here we're, we're, watching Cristina, who . . . and, Jesús [i.e. her trainer], I don't see him. Have you seen him tonight, Abraham, or . . . ?'

'Yeah, when she came out, he came out with her.'

'Right, so now we're looking at Cristina, she's super focused.

Cristina, who's the mother of two fantastic, beautiful little boys.'

'Imagine that, a mom taking care of her boys, working, and –'

'She's a sports psychologist, too.'

'– training at the championship level, at the highest level.'

'For sure, for sure. I mean the thing I like most about Cristina, Abraham, if you ask me, in the fights we've seen, is how she boxes.'

'She's a great boxer. Great kicker too.'

'She's a very well-rounded fighter. Very well rounded. You know what, I, you know, I was at a match where she wasn't able to fight. She was going to fight in Seville, in Kryssing, but she couldn't because it was the same night, Abraham, the same night she found out she was pregnant.'

'Hahahahaha!'

'Hahahaha! Jesús [i.e. her trainer and, in point of fact, the father of her children], you could've held off a little longer, Jesús!'

Ladies and gentlemen, boys and girls whose parents let them watch and read about combat sports, please welcome the ex-manager of Balearic Public Television's Canal IB3, a self-confessed burglar sentenced to two years in prison for plotting with his wife to ransack her grandmother's house with the assistance of four hired goons, a close personal friend and moneylender to José Ramón Bauzá (former president of the Balearic Islands and card-carrying member of the Partido Popular), the executive director and funding partner at Titan Channel, fifty-something with a gray crew cut that makes him look like a failed drill sergeant, the dumpy, the chumpy: Borjaaaa Ruuuuuuupérez!

'Must've left a bittersweet taste in the mouth. Hahahahaha.'

'Of course, of course.'

'On the one hand, you'd be very, uh, happy at the news, but on the other, you know, after all the training and all . . . hahahaha. What timing.'

'Definitely, definitely. All right, and . . . Here we go, the ref is giving his instructions. Gina van der Linden giving a defiant look,' Rupérez says, getting her name wrong for the third time.

Let's shush here for a second. Let's mute the computer and contemplate the fight in silence, without the nuisance of the commentators and our own interjections. Let's try to mellow the rattling passion in our ribcage, lower our heart rate, let down our guard, allow ourselves to be penetrated from all sides. I'm referring to myself in the plural just like Cristina Morales of the Angelic Yet Troglodytic White-Feather Hot Pants does when she says 'we got our degree in psychology', 'we won the world championship', 'we lost the fight' and even 'we went up two weight classes' and 'we got a little bit of a black eye'. Weren't you and only you the one taking the exams? Weren't you the one pummeling and being pummeled to victory or defeat? Wasn't it your own stomach digesting the meticulously calibrated proteins and carbohydrates, your own bloodstream delivering those nutrients to the rest of your body? Isn't your body yours, and yours alone? When your cheek was struck with punishing impact, did anyone else's swell and bruise? If your injuries aren't exclusively yours, to whom else do they belong? 'I also consider my sport to be a team sport because, even though you compete alone, um, all the training is . . . You train with your team, and your teammates are there to help you, along with your trainer, they're the ones who motivate you, the ones who'll throw you a lifeline if you're having a slumpy day, so, in the end it's, it's also a team sport.'

Cristina Morales, Fire-Breathing Master: I learn from you. With the cabaret coursing through my veins, with the feminist carousing in which I've reveled throughout this literary work – and literature means broken glass and spilled beer, it means pissing between parked cars and pee splashing back onto your ankles – as I ride out this squinting, stumbling bender, massaging my friends on the backs of their necks, may I clumsily summon the courage to say: that 'we' disparages you, my namesake. You snub yourself with the first-person plural, you shoot sexist bullets into your own female foot. There isn't a man alive who describes his success in anything but strictly personal terms, no male boxer who calls his wife and sparring partners 'his team', no male fighter on the face of the planet who poses for post-match photos hugging his small children.

High from so much fighting and high because, win or lose, after a fight I'm gonna get high, I'm not surprised on 26 June 2018, when this happens . . .

'A gold-belt winner worthy of the title. Wow, the belt is heavy as hell. Congratulations, world champ.' José María de la Morena for *El Transistor* on Onda Cero Radio.

'Thank you, thank you.' Joana Pastrana, twenty-nine years old, Spanish, forty-seven kilos, nineteen fights, sixteen wins, five by knockout, three-time world boxing champion.

'It's heavy and, hey, it's got those two little mirrors, I bet you can use those to put on your makeup. You can just put it on your vanity and go: "a little bit over here, a touch-up over there . . ." Perfect, eh?'

'I don't wear makeup much, but it'll be useful for taking a look.'

'No lucky guy around to get dolled up for?'

'There is, yeah, a lucky girl.'

. . . but even though that doesn't surprise me much, I am shocked to my core when this happens the following day:

'José María de la Morena's comments were unfortunate, but I don't believe he made them with ill intent and I don't consider myself offended. He interviewed me several times before I won the championship, when no other journalists were calling, and I'm grateful to him for supporting me and helping create greater visibility for me as a female athlete. His comments were inappropriate, but this whole controversy has been kind of hysterical. I prefer to act natural and respond privately. I'm sure he'll think twice before asking that kind of question again. Unfortunately, this is nothing new for women athletes.' (Some tweets and a statement she made for – surprise, masculosensitives and feminallies! – *El País*.)

O Joana Pastrana, O Cristina Morales, your braids are scourging whips knotted with broken glass and your smiles are grotesque under your mouthguards; your abdominals are jai alai walls, your livers are wrought iron and the smell of your sweat extends to the first rows of the audience. And I, a rubbery play dough churro, dare to lecture you on feminism? Woe unto me, the shame I bring upon myself! And woe unto all of you readers who, in the previous paragraph, felt maligned as hysterical, that obstinate slur deployed against our grievances since time immemorial! Your bricklike delicacy is a humiliation. Shame on all of you who, like me, were more triggered by Pastrana's man-shielding apologetics than by the vile comments from the man himself!

We learn from you, Cristina Invicta, and we speak in the plural because we are legion: stupid, insolent, ignorant women, mediocre readers of four books who have graffitied four paltry walls and taken four dough-armed swings at four chauvinist pricks; we're closer to the closeted rapists you have to endure in your work than we are to you, O Women of Mixed Martial Arts, creatures crafted from the finest material, with your impeccable shifts between martial honor and showboating.

Cristina Morales, Faultless Master of the Knockout, it is you who revises Shakespeare's scene, and I will now read from the corrected version:

'Hath not a female mixed martial artist eyes? Hath not a female mixed martial artist hands, organs, dimensions, senses, affections, passions?'

'She does, but stronger.'

'Is she not fed with the same food?'

'No.'

'Hurt with the same weapons?'

'Definitely not.'

'Subject to the same diseases?'

'Nope.'

'Healed by the same means?'

'Fuck no.'

'Warmed and cooled by the same winter and summer as a female non-fighter is?'

'Not as much.'

'If you prick us, do we not bleed?'

'We bleed less.'

'If you tickle us, do we not laugh?'

'We laugh differently.'

'If you poison us, do we not die?'

'We die slower.'

'And if you wrong us, shall we not revenge? If we are like you in the rest, we will resemble you in that.'

'You aren't like us in anything, stupid Christians, fetishists of sisterhood. We are wronged by nothing but the rift between the human and the divine, and our revenge is beyond your comprehension,' you conclude, O Cristina, swallowing a bacon sandwich.

If only you could access the thrill of watching a woman subsuming another with hooks, elbows, knees and kicks, slamming her to the canvas, suffocating her, and the counter-attacker rising to her feet, freeing herself from the chokehold, sloughing off her opponent, deftly blocking the missiles that are the attacker's joints. If only you cared to marvel at a head bobbling like a bell-clapper after a well-struck blow, recovering and reorienting in less than a second, or else succumbing, because the attacker has seized upon her opponent's momentary blindness. O Splendor of the opening for all-out assault, O Ecstasy of the comeback, of the crossfire in which one can hardly read, for all its abundance, the name of the power. ■

TRANSLATORS

Esther Allen's translation of Antonio Di Benedetto's *Zama* received the 2017 National Translation Award. A professor at City University of New York, she has published essays and translations in the *New York Review of Books*, Poetryfoundation.org, the *Los Angeles Review of Books*, the *Paris Review*, *LitHub*, *Words Without Borders* and elsewhere.

Sarah Booker is a doctoral candidate at UNC-Chapel Hill and translator from Spanish. Recent or forthcoming translations include *The Iliac Crest* and *Grieving: Dispatches from a Wounded Country* by Cristina Rivera Garza and *Jawbone* by Mónica Ojeda.

Nick Caistor is a British translator of more than eighty books from Spanish, French and Portuguese. He is a three-time winner of the Premio Valle-Inclán for translation from Spanish.

Jennifer Croft won the 2020 William Saroyan International Prize for Writing for her memoir *Homesick* and the 2018 Man Booker International Prize for her translation from Polish of Nobel laureate Olga Tokarczuk's *Flights*. She is the author of *Serpientes y escaleras* and *Notes on Postcards* and holds a PhD in Comparative Literary Studies from Northwestern University.

Lizzie Davis is an editor at Coffee House Press and a translator from Spanish. Her recent projects include *Ornamental* by Juan Cárdenas and *The Wonders* by Elena Medel, co-translated with Thomas Bunstead. She has received translation fellowships from the Omi International Arts Center and the Bread Loaf Translators' Conference.

Kevin Gerry Dunn is a Spanish–English translator whose published works include *Easy Reading* by Cristina Morales (forthcoming in 2022), for which he received a PEN/Heim Translation Fund Grant, *Countersexual Manifesto* by Paul B. Preciado, and writing by Daniela Tarazona, Ousman Umar and Cristian Perfumo.

Lucy Greaves is a literary translator and bike mechanic who lives in Bristol, UK. They won the 2013 Harvill Secker Young Translators' Prize and their co-translation of Gabriela Wiener's *Sexographies* is published by Restless Books.

Lindsay Griffiths is a PhD candidate in the Department of English at Princeton University. She is the translator of Mercedes Cebrián's *Burp: Adventures in Eating and Cooking*, and the co-translator, with Adrián Izquierdo, of the forthcoming translation of *Uno nunca sabe por qué grita la gente* by Mario Michelena.

Daniel Hahn is a writer, editor and translator with seventy-something books to his name. His translations (from Portuguese, Spanish and French) have won him the Independent Foreign Fiction Prize and the International Dublin Literary Award and been shortlisted for the Man Booker International Prize, among many others.

Sophie Hughes has translated writers such as Alia Trabucco Zerán, Laia Jufresa, Rodrigo Hasbún, Enrique Vila-Matas and José Revueltas. She has been shortlisted twice for the International Booker Prize, most recently in 2020 for Fernanda Melchor's *Hurricane Season*.

Adrián Izquierdo is an Assistant Professor at Baruch College, City University of New York, where he teaches courses on great works of literature, translation studies and Renaissance literature.

Margaret Jull Costa has worked as a translator for over thirty years, translating the works of many Spanish and Portuguese writers, among them novelists: Javier Marías, Bernardo Atxaga, José Saramago and Eça de Queiroz; and poets: Fernando Pessoa, Sophia de Mello Breyner Andresen, Mário de Sá-Carneiro and Ana Luísa Amaral.

Mara Faye Lethem's recent translations include *Don't Shed Your Tears for Anyone Who Lives on These Streets* by Patricio Pron, *Learning to Talk to Plants* by Marta Orriols and *The Adventures and Misadventures of the Extraordinary and Admirable Joan Orpí, Conquistador and Founder of New Catalonia* by Max Besora. Forthcoming is *When I Sing, Mountains Dance* by Irene Solà.

Megan McDowell is an award-winning Spanish-language translator from Kentucky. She has translated books by Alejandro Zambra, Samanta Schweblin, Mariana Enríquez and Lina Meruane, among others, and her short story translations have appeared in the *New Yorker*, the *Paris Review*, *Harper's* and *Tin House*. She lives in Santiago, Chile.

Christina MacSweeney is an award-winning translator of Latin American literature. She has worked with authors such as Valeria Luiselli, Daniel Saldaña París, Verónica Gerber Bicecci, Julián Herbert and Jazmina Barrera. She has also contributed to anthologies of Latin American literature and published articles and interviews on a wide variety of platforms.

Robin Myers is a Mexico City-based poet and translator. Recent book-length translations include *The Restless Dead* by Cristina Rivera Garza, *Cars on Fire* by Mónica Ramón Ríos and *Animals at the End of the World* by Gloria Susana Esquivel. She writes a monthly column on translation for *Palette Poetry*.

Frances Riddle translates Latin American literature to English. Her most recent book-length translations include *Cockfight* by María Fernanda Ampuero, *Slum Virgin*, by Gabriela Cabezón Cámara and *Theatre of War* by Andrea Jeftanovic. Her translations of *Elena Knows* by Claudia Piñeiro and *Violeta* by Isabel Allende are forthcoming in 2021. She lives in Buenos Aires, Argentina.

Julia Sanches was born in Brazil and grew up in Mexico, the US, Switzerland, Scotland and Catalonia. She translates from Portuguese, Spanish and Catalan into English, and has worked with Geovani Martins, Claudia Hernández, Dolores Reyes and Eva Baltasar, among others.

Samantha Schnee's translation of Carmen Boullosa's *Texas: The Great Theft* was shortlisted for the 2015 PEN America Translation Prize. She won the 2015 Gulf Coast Prize in Translation for her excerpt of Boullosa's *The Conspiracy of the Romantics*, and her translation of Boullosa's novel *The Book of Anna* was published by Coffee House Press in 2020.

Katherine Silver is a writer and an award-winning literary translator. She is the former director of the Banff International Literary Translation Centre and the author of *Echo Under Story*. She does volunteer interpreting for asylum seekers.

Kelsi Vanada's translations include Sergio Espinosa's *Into Muteness* and Berta García Faet's *The Eligible Age*, and she is the author of the poetry chapbook *Rare Earth*. Vanada is the Program Manager of the American Literary Translators Association (ALTA) in Tucson, Arizona.

Will Vanderhyden is a freelance translator of Spanish and Latin American literature. He has received fellowships from the NEA and Lannan foundations. His translation of Rodrigo Fresán's *The Invented Part* won the 2018 Best Translated Book Award for fiction.

Natasha Wimmer is the translator of nine books by Roberto Bolaño, including *The Savage Detectives* and *2666*. Her most recent translations are *Space Invaders* by Nona Fernández and *Sudden Death* by Álvaro Enrigue.

Frank Wynne is an Irish literary translator. In a career spanning twenty years, he has translated numerous French and Hispanic authors, including Michel Houellebecq, Virginie Despentes, Javier Cercas and Emiliano Monge. A number of his translations have won prizes, including the International Dublin Literary Award, the Scott Moncrieff Prize and the Premio Valle-Inclán.